CompTIA Security+™

Review Guide

CompTIA Security+™

Review Guide

James Michael Stewart

WILEY

Wiley Publishing, Inc.

Acquisitions Editor: Jeff Kellum
Development Editor: Kathryn Duggan
Technical Editors: Stephen Rea and Scott Perry
Production Editor: Rachel McConlogue
Copy Editor: Lunaea Hougland
Production Manager: Tim Tate
Vice President and Executive Group Publisher: Richard Swadley
Vice President and Publisher: Neil Edde
Media Project Supervisor: Laura Moss-Hollister
Media Development Specialist: Josh Frank
Media Quality Assurance: Shawn Patrick
Book Designers: Judy Fung and Bill Gibson
Compositor: Craig Johnson, Happenstance Type-O-Rama
Proofreader: Publication Services, Inc.
Indexer: Nancy Guenther
Project Coordinator, Cover: Lynsey Stanford
Cover Designer: Ryan Sneed

Library of Congress Cataloging-in-Publication Data

Stewart, James M.
 CompTIA security+ : review guide / James M. Stewart.
 p. cm.
 ISBN 978-0-470-40484-3 (paper/website)
1. Electronic data processing personnel--Certification. 2. Computer networks--Examinations--Study guides. 3. Computer technicians--Certification--Study guides. I. Title.
 QA76.3.S747 2009
 005.8--dc22
 2008042927

Dear Reader,

Thank you for choosing *CompTIA Security+ Review Guide*. This book is part of a family of premium-quality Sybex books, all of which are written by outstanding authors who combine practical experience with a gift for teaching.

Sybex was founded in 1976. More than thirty years later, we're still committed to producing consistently exceptional books. With each of our titles we're working hard to set a new standard for the industry. From the paper we print on, to the authors we work with, our goal is to bring you the best books available.

I hope you see all that reflected in these pages. I'd be very interested to hear your comments and get your feedback on how we're doing. Feel free to let me know what you think about this or any other Sybex book by sending me an email at nedde@wiley.com, or if you think you've found a technical error in this book, please visit http://sybex.custhelp.com. Customer feedback is critical to our efforts at Sybex.

Best regards,

Neil Edde
Vice President and Publisher
Sybex, an Imprint of Wiley

To Catharine Renee Stewart, I can't believe how amazing it is.

Acknowledgments

Thanks to all those at Sybex that continue to allow me to do what I enjoy most—impart knowledge to others. Thanks to Jeff Kellum, Kathryn Duggan, Rachel McConlogue, and Stephen Charles Rea for professional juggling services adequately rendered. To my parents, Dave and Sue, thanks for your love and consistent support. To my sister Sharon and nephew Wesley, it's great seeing you so often. To Mark, I have been and always shall be your friend. And finally, as always, to Elvis—my son, Xzavier Slayde, spends hours talking to you through refrigerator magnets of your likeness!

About the Author

James Michael Stewart has been working with computers and technology for over 19 years. His work focuses on Windows, certification, and security. Recently, Michael has been teaching job skill and certification courses, such as CISSP, CEH, CHFI, and Security+. Michael has contributed to many Security+ focused materials, including exam preparation guides, practice exams, DVD video instruction, and courseware. In addition, Michael has co-authored numerous books on other security and Microsoft certification and administration topics. He has developed certification courseware and training materials as well as presented these materials in the classroom. Michael holds the following certifications: CISSP, ISSAP, SSCP, MCT, CTT, CEI, CEH, CHFI, TICSA, CIW SA, Security+, MCSE+Security Windows 2000, MCSA Windows Server 2003, MCDST, MCSE NT & W2K, MCP+I, Server+, A+, Network+, and iNet+. Michael graduated in 1992 from the University of Texas at Austin with a bachelor's degree in philosophy. Despite his degree, his computer knowledge is self-acquired, based on seat-of-the-pants, hands-on "street smarts" experience. You can reach Michael by e-mail at michael@impactonline.com.

Contents at a Glance

Contents

Introduction

The Security+ certification program was developed by the Computer Technology Industry Association (CompTIA) to provide an industry-wide means of certifying the competency of computer service technicians in the basics of computer security. The Security+ certification is granted to those who have attained the level of knowledge and security skills that show a basic competency with security needs of both personal and corporate computing environments. CompTIA's exam objectives are periodically updated to keep their exams applicable to the most recent developments. The most recent update occurred in 2008. This book focuses on these newly revised certification objectives.

What Is Security+ Certification?

The Security+ certification was created to offer an introductory step into the complex world of IT security. You only need to pass a single exam to become Security+ certified. However, obtaining this certification doesn't mean you can provide realistic security services to a company. In fact, this is just the first step toward true security knowledge and experience. By obtaining Security+ certification, you should be able to acquire more security experience in order to pursue more complex and in-depth security knowledge and certification.

For the latest pricing on the exam and updates to the registration procedures, please visit www.vue.com or www.prometric.com. If you have further questions about the scope of the exams or related CompTIA programs, refer to the CompTIA website at www.comptia.org.

Is This Book for You?

CompTIA Security+ Review Guide is designed to be a succinct, portable exam review guide that can be used in conjunction with a more complete study guide such as the *CompTIA Security+ Study Guide, 4th Edition* or *CompTIA Security+ Deluxe Study Guide* (Sybex, 2008), CBT courseware, and a classroom/lab environment; or as an exam review for those who don't feel the need for more extensive test preparation. It isn't our goal to give away the answers, but rather to identify those topics on which you can expect to be tested and to provide sufficient coverage of these topics.

Perhaps you've been working with information technologies for years. The thought of paying lots of money for a specialized IT exam-preparation course probably doesn't sound appealing. What can they teach you that you don't already know, right? Be careful, though—many experienced network administrators have walked confidently into the test center only to walk sheepishly out of it after failing an IT exam. After you've finished reading this book, you should have a clear idea of how your understanding of the technologies involved matches up with the expectations of the Security+ test makers.

Or perhaps you're relatively new to the world of IT, drawn to it by the promise of challenging work and higher salaries. You've just waded through an 800-page study guide or taken a week-long class at a local training center. Lots of information to keep track of, isn't it? Well, by organizing this book according to CompTIA's exam objectives, and by breaking up the information into concise, manageable pieces, we've created what we think is the handiest exam review guide available. Throw it in your briefcase and carry it to work with you. As you read the book, you'll be able to quickly identify those areas you know best and those that require a more in-depth review.

How Is This Book Organized?

This book is organized according to the official objectives list prepared by CompTIA for the Security+ exam. The chapters correspond to the six major domains of objective and topic groupings. The exam is weighted across these five domains as follows:

- Domain 1.0—Systems Security (21%)
- Domain 2.0—Network Infrastructure (20%)
- Domain 3.0—Access Control (17%)
- Domain 4.0—Assessments & Audits (15%)
- Domain 5.0—Cryptography (15%)
- Domain 6.0—Organizational Security (12%)

Within each chapter, the top-level exam objectives from each domain are addressed in turn. Each objective's section is further divided into Critical Information, Exam Essentials, and Review Questions:

Critical Information The Critical Information section presents the greatest level of detail about information relevant to the objective. This is the place to start if you're unfamiliar with or uncertain about the technical issues related to the objective.

Exam Essentials Here you're given a short list of topics that you should explore fully before taking the test. Included in the Exam Essentials areas are notations of the key information you should have taken from the Critical Information section of this chapter or the corresponding content from the *CompTIA Security+ Study Guide, 4th Edition* (Sybex, 2008).

 Sybex also publishes the *CompTIA Security+ Deluxe Study Guide.*

Review Questions This section ends every chapter and provides 10 questions to help you gauge your mastery of the chapter.

On the CD

We've included several testing features on the CD-ROM that accompanies this book. These tools will help you retain vital exam content as well as prepare you to sit for the actual exams:

Test engine The CD contains the Sybex Test Engine. Using this custom test engine, you can identify weak areas up front and then develop a solid studying strategy using each of these robust testing features. Our thorough readme file will walk you through the quick, easy installation process.

Electronic flashcards You'll find flashcard questions on the CD for on-the-go review. These are short questions and answers, just like the flashcards you probably used to study in school. You can answer them on your PC or download them onto a Palm device for quick and convenient reviewing.

Glossary of Terms in PDF The CD-ROM contains a very useful Glossary of Terms in PDF (Adobe Acrobat format) so you can easily read it on any computer. If you have to travel and brush up on any key terms, and you have a laptop with a CD-ROM drive, you can do so with this useful resource.

Tips for Taking the Security+ Exams

Here are some general tips for taking your exams successfully:

- Bring two forms of ID with you. One must be a photo ID, such as a driver's license. The other can be a major credit card or a passport. Both forms must include a signature.

- Arrive early at the exam center so you can relax and review your study materials, particularly tables and lists of exam-related information.

- Read the questions carefully. Don't be tempted to jump to an early conclusion. Make sure you know exactly what the question is asking.

- Don't leave any unanswered questions. Unanswered questions are scored against you.

- There will be questions with multiple correct responses. When there is more than one correct answer, a message at the bottom of the screen will prompt you to either "Choose two" or "Choose all that apply." Be sure to read the messages displayed to know how many correct answers you must choose.

- When answering multiple-choice questions you're not sure about, use a process of elimination to get rid of the obviously incorrect answers first. Doing so will improve your odds if you need to make an educated guess.

- On form-based tests (nonadaptive), because the hard questions will eat up the most time, save them for last. You can move forward and backward through the exam.

- For the latest pricing on the exams and updates to the registration procedures, visit CompTIA's website at www.comptia.org.

How to Contact the Publisher

Sybex welcomes feedback on all of its titles. Visit the Sybex website at www.sybex.com for book updates and additional certification information. You'll also find forms you can use to submit comments or suggestions regarding this or any other Sybex title.

The Security+ Exam Objectives

For easy reference and clarification, the following is a complete listing of Security+ objectives.

> Exam objectives are subject to change at any time without prior notice and at CompTIA's sole discretion. Please visit the Security+ Certification page of CompTIA's website (www.comptia.org/certification/security/default.aspx) for the most current listing of exam objectives.

Domain 1.0—Systems Security

1.1 Differentiate among various systems security threats.

- Privilege escalation
- Virus
- Worm
- Trojan
- Spyware
- Spam
- Adware
- Rootkits
- Botnets
- Logic bomb

1.2 Explain the security risks pertaining to system hardware and peripherals.

- BIOS
- USB devices
- Cell phones

- Removable storage
- Network attached storage

1.3 Implement OS hardening practices and procedures to achieve workstation and server security.

- Hotfixes
- Service packs
- Patches
- Patch management
- Group policies
- Security templates
- Configuration baselines

1.4 Carry out the appropriate procedures to establish application security.

- ActiveX
- Java
- Scripting
- Browser
- Buffer overflows
- Cookies
- SMTP open relays
- Instant messaging
- P2P
- Input validation
- Cross-site scripting (XSS)

1.5 Implement security applications.

- HIDS
- Personal software firewalls
- Antivirus
- Anti-spam
- Popup blockers

1.6 Explain the purpose and application of virtualization technology.

Domain 2.0—Network

2.1 Differentiate between the different ports & protocols, their respective threats and mitigation techniques.

- Antiquated protocols
- TCP/IP hijacking
- Null sessions
- Spoofing
- Man-in-the-middle
- Replay
- DOS
- DDOS
- Domain Name Kiting
- DNS poisoning
- ARP poisoning

2.2 Distinguish between network design elements and components.

- DMZ
- VLAN
- NAT
- Network interconnections
- NAC
- Subnetting
- Telephony

2.3 Determine the appropriate use of network security tools to facilitate network security.

- NIDS
- NIPS
- Firewalls
- Proxy servers
- Honeypot
- Internet content filters
- Protocol analyzers

2.4 Apply the appropriate network tools to facilitate network security.

- NIDS
- Firewalls
- Proxy servers
- Internet content filters
- Protocol analyzers

2.5 Explain the vulnerabilities and mitigations associated with network devices.

- Privilege escalation
- Weak passwords
- Back doors
- Default accounts
- DOS

2.6 Explain the vulnerabilities and mitigations associated with various transmission media.

- Vampire taps

2.7 Explain the vulnerabilities and implement mitigations associated with wireless networking.

- 802.11 and 802.11x
- Data emanation
- War driving
- SSID broadcast
- Blue jacking
- Bluesnarfing
- Rogue access points
- Weak encryption

Domain 3.0—Access Control

3.1 Identify and apply industry best practices for access control methods.

- Implicit deny
- Least privilege
- Separation of duties
- Job rotation

3.2 Explain common access control models and the differences between each.

- MAC
- DAC
- Role & Rule based access control

3.3 Organize users and computers into appropriate security groups and roles while distinguishing between appropriate rights and privileges.

3.4 Apply appropriate security controls to file and print resources.

3.5 Compare and implement logical access control methods.

- ACL
- Group policies
- Password policy
- Domain password policy
- User names and passwords
- Time of day restrictions
- Account expiration
- Logical tokens

3.6 Summarize the various authentication models and identify the components of each.

- One, two and three-factor authentication
- Single sign-on

3.7 Deploy various authentication models and identify the components of each.

- Biometric reader
- RADIUS
- RAS
- LDAP
- Remote access policies
- Remote authentication
- VPN
- Kerberos
- CHAP
- PAP

- Mutual
- 802.1x
- TACACS

3.8 Explain the difference between identification and authentication (identity proofing).

3.9 Explain and apply physical access security methods.

- Physical access logs/lists
- Hardware locks
- Physical access control – ID badges
- Door access systems
- Man-trap
- Physical tokens
- Video surveillance – camera types and positioning

Domain 4.0—Assessments & Audits

4.1 Conduct risk assessments and implement risk mitigation.

4.2 Carry out vulnerability assessments using common tools.

- Port scanners
- Vulnerability scanners
- Protocol analyzers
- OVAL
- Password crackers
- Network mappers

4.3 Within the realm of vulnerability assessments, explain the proper use of penetration testing versus vulnerability scanning.

4.4 Use monitoring tools on systems and networks and detect security-related anomalies.

- Performance monitor
- Systems monitor
- Performance baseline
- Protocol analyzers

4.5 Compare and contrast various types of monitoring methodologies.

- Behavior-based
- Signature-based
- Anomaly-based

4.6 Execute proper logging procedures and evaluate the results.

- Security application
- DNS
- System
- Performance
- Access
- Firewall
- Antivirus

4.7 Conduct periodic audits of system security settings.

- User access and rights review
- Storage and retention policies
- Group policies

Domain 5.0—Cryptography

5.1 Explain general cryptography concepts.

- Key management
- Steganography
- Symmetric key
- Asymmetric key
- Confidentiality
- Integrity and availability
- Non-repudiation
- Comparative strength of algorithms
- Digital signatures
- Whole disk encryption
- Trusted Platform Module (TPM)
- Single vs. Dual sided certificates
- Use of proven technologies

5.2 Explain basic hashing concepts and map various algorithms to appropriate applications.

- SHA
- MD5
- LANMAN
- NTLM

5.3 Explain basic encryption concepts and map various algorithms to appropriate applications.

- DES
- 3DES
- RSA
- PGP
- Elliptic curve
- AES
- AES256
- One time pad
- Transmission encryption (WEP, TKIP, etc)

5.4 Explain and implement protocols.

- SSL/TLS
- S/MIME
- PPTP
- HTTP vs. HTTPS vs. SHTTP
- L2TP
- IPSEC
- SSH

5.5 Explain core concepts of public key cryptography.

- Public Key Infrastructure (PKI)
- Recovery agent
- Public key
- Private keys
- Certificate Authority (CA)
- Registration
- Key escrow

- Certificate Revocation List (CRL)
- Trust models

5.6 Implement PKI and certificate management.

- Public Key Infrastructure (PKI)
- Recovery agent
- Public key
- Private keys
- Certificate Authority (CA)
- Registration
- Key escrow
- Certificate Revocation List (CRL)

Domain 6.0—Organizational Security

6.1 Explain redundancy planning and its components.

- Hot site
- Cold site
- Warm site
- Backup generator
- Single point of failure
- RAID
- Spare parts
- Redundant servers
- Redundant ISP
- UPS
- Redundant connections

6.2 Implement disaster recovery procedures.

- Planning
- Disaster recovery exercises
- Backup techniques and practices – storage
- Schemes
- Restoration

6.3 Differentiate between and execute appropriate incident response procedures.

- Forensics
- Chain of custody
- First responders
- Damage and loss control
- Reporting – disclosure of

6.4 Identify and explain applicable legislation and organizational policies.

- Secure disposal of computers
- Acceptable use policies
- Password complexity
- Change management
- Classification of information
- Mandatory vacations
- Personally Identifiable Information (PII)
- Due care
- Due diligence
- Due process
- SLA
- Security-related HR policy
- User education and awareness training

6.5 Explain the importance of environmental controls.

- Fire suppression
- HVAC
- Shielding

6.6 Explain the concept of and how to reduce the risks of social engineering.

- Phishing
- Hoaxes
- Shoulder surfing
- Dumpster diving
- User education and awareness training

CompTIA Security+™

Review Guide

Chapter

1

Systems Security

COMPTIA SECURITY+ EXAM OBJECTIVES COVERED IN THIS CHAPTER INCLUDE THE FOLLOWING:

✓ **1.1 Differentiate among various systems security threats.**

- Privilege escalation
- Virus
- Worm
- Trojan
- Spyware
- Spam
- Adware
- Rootkits
- Botnets
- Logic bomb

✓ **1.2 Explain the security risks pertaining to system hardware and peripherals.**

- BIOS
- USB devices
- Cell phones
- Removable storage
- Network attached storage

✓ **1.3 Implement OS hardening practices and procedures to achieve workstation and server security.**

- Hotfixes
- Service packs
- Patches
- Patch management

- Group policies
- Security templates
- Configuration baselines

✓ **1.4 Carry out the appropriate procedures to establish application security.**

- ActiveX
- Java
- Scripting
- Browser
- Buffer overflows
- Cookies
- SMTP open relays
- Instant messaging
- P2P
- Input validation
- Cross-site scripting (XSS)

✓ **1.5 Implement security applications.**

- HIDS
- Personal software firewalls
- Antivirus
- Anti-spam
- Popup blockers

✓ **1.6 Explain the purpose and application of virtualization technology.**

The Security+ exam will test your basic IT security skills—those skills needed to effectively secure stand-alone and networked systems in a corporate environment. To pass the test and be effective in implementing security, you need to understand the basic concepts and terminology related to systems security as detailed in this chapter.

1.1 Differentiate among various systems security threats.

Knowing how to recognize and respond to a wide variety of security threats is an essential skill in today's networking environments. Security is not just about locking down the environment against threats, but also about detecting breaches and being prepared to respond to incidents. This section discusses several common threats that all environments must be prepared to face.

For more information on this topic, refer to Chapter 1 of the *CompTIA Security+ Study Guide, 4th Edition* (Sybex, November 2008).

Privilege escalation

Privilege escalation is the malicious event when a user is able to obtain privileges or capabilities beyond what they were assigned or which they are authorized to have or use. Privilege escalation can be performed by a normal user, an administrator, or an outside attacker.

Privilege escalation can be performed by exploiting administrative oversights or misconfiguration of the environment. It could also be performed by clever manipulation of the systems or even through hacks. Some hacks, such as GetAdmin, temporarily grant the current user account full administrative privileges, while other hacks, such as X.exe, create a new user account in the Administrators group with a known password. Privilege escalation hacks can also be performed by stealing the credentials of another user account (such as through password guessing, password cracking, or authentication packet sniffing).

The best defenses against privilege escalation include clearly defined job descriptions with privileges that are enforced and restricted on a detailed basis, strong password policies, and detailed auditing of the environment.

Virus

Viruses are just one example of malicious code, malicious software, or malware. *Malicious code* is any element of software that performs an unwanted or undesired function from the perspective of the legitimate user or owner of a computer system. Malicious code includes viruses, worms, Trojan horses, spyware, adware, rootkits, botnets, logic bombs, and sometimes even spam.

Viruses get their name from their biological counterparts. They are programs designed to spread from one system to another through self-replication and to perform any of a wide range of malicious activities. The malicious activities performed by viruses include data deletion, corruption, alteration, and theft. Some viruses replicate and spread so rapidly that they consume system and network resources, thus performing a type of denial-of-service (DoS) attack.

Most viruses need a host to latch onto. The host can be a file (as in the case of *common viruses*) or a sector of a hard drive. Viruses that attach themselves to the boot sector of a hard drive and thus are loaded in memory when the drive is activated are known as *boot sector viruses*. *Polymorphic viruses* have the ability to alter their own code in order to avoid detection by antivirus scanners. *Macro viruses* live within documents or e-mails and exploit the scripting capabilities of productivity software. *Stealth viruses* attempt to avoid detection by masking or hiding their activities. *Armored viruses* are designed to be difficult to detect and remove. *Retroviruses* specifically target antivirus systems to render them useless. *Phage viruses* modify or infect many aspects of a system so they can regenerate themselves from any remaining unremoved parts. A *companion virus* borrows the root filename of a common executable, and then gives itself the .com extension in an attempt to get itself launched rather than the intended application. *Multipart or multipartite viruses* perform multiple tasks and may infect a system in numerous ways.

The best countermeasure to viruses is an antivirus scanner that is updated regularly and which monitors all local storage devices, memory, and communication pathways for viral activities. Other countermeasures include avoiding downloading software from the Internet, not opening e-mail attachments, and avoiding the use of removable media from other environments.

Worm

Worms are self-contained applications that do not require a host to infect. Worms typically are focused on replication and distribution, rather than on direct damage and destruction. However, due to the expanding capabilities (although malicious) of viruses, worms are no longer an easily identifiable, distinct category of malicious code. Worms are designed to exploit a vulnerability in a system (operating system, protocol, service, or application) and then use that flaw to spread themselves to other systems with the same flaw. Worms may

be used to deposit viruses, Trojan horses, logic bombs, zombies/agents/bots for botnets, or they may perform direct virus-like maelstrom activities on their own.

Countermeasures for worms are the same as for viruses, with the addition of keeping systems patched.

Trojan

A *Trojan horse* is a form of malicious software that is disguised as something useful or legitimate. The most common forms of Trojan horses are games and screensavers, but any software can be made into a Trojan horse. The goal of a Trojan horse is to trick a user into installing it on their computer. This allows the malicious code portion of the Trojan horse to gain access to the otherwise secured environment. Some of the most common Trojan horses are tools that install DDoS zombies or remote control agents onto systems (see Chapter 2 for more information on denial-of-service).

Countermeasures for Trojan horses are the same as for viruses.

Spyware

Spyware is any form of malicious code or even business or commercial code that collects information about users without their direct knowledge or permission. Spyware can be fully malicious when it seeks to gain information to perform identity theft or credential hijacking. However, many advertising companies use less-malicious forms of spyware to gather demographics about potential customers. In either case, the user is often unaware that the spyware tool is present or that it is gathering information that is periodically transmitted back to some outside entity. Spyware can be deposited by viruses, worms, or Trojan horses, or it can be installed as extra elements from commercial, freeware, or shareware applications.

Countermeasures for spyware are the same as for viruses, with the addition of specific spyware-scanning tools.

Spam

Spam is any type of e-mail that is undesired and/or unsolicited. Think of spam as the digital equivalent of junk mail and door-to-door solicitations.

 Some studies have shown that more than half of all e-mail now consists of spam.

Spam is a problem for numerous reasons:

- Some spam carries malicious code such as viruses, logic bombs, or Trojan horses.
- Some spam carries a social-engineering attack (also known as hoax e-mail).

- Unwanted e-mail wastes your time while you sort through it looking for legitimate messages.

- Spam wastes Internet resources: storage capacity, computing cycles, and throughput.

The primary countermeasure against spam is an e-mail filter. An e-mail filter is a list of e-mail addresses, domain names, or IP addresses where spam is known to originate. If a message is received from one of the listed spam sources, the e-mail filter blocks or discards it. Some e-mail filters are becoming as sophisticated as antivirus scanners. These e-mail filters can examine the header, subject, and contents of a message to look for keywords or phrases that identify it as a known type of spam, and then take the appropriate actions to discard, quarantine, or block the message. In addition to client application or client-side spam filters, there are also enterprise spam tools. Some enterprise tools are actually stand-alone devices themselves, often called anti-spam appliances, while others are software additions to internal enterprise e-mail servers. The benefits of enterprise spam filtering is to reduce spam distribution internally by blocking and discarding unwanted messages before they waste storage space on e-mail servers or make their way to clients.

However, e-mail spam filters are problematic. Just because a message includes keywords that are typically found in spam doesn't mean that every message with those words is spam. Some legitimate, if not outright essential, messages include spam words. One method of addressing this issue is for the spam-filtering tool to place all suspected spam messages into a quarantine folder. Users can peruse this folder for misidentified messages and retrieve them.

Another important issue to address when managing spam is spoofed e-mail. A *spoofed* e-mail is a message that has a fake or falsified source address. When an e-mail server receives an e-mail message, it should perform a reverse lookup on the source address of the message. If the source address is fake or nonexistent, the message should be discarded.

Hoaxes

A *hoax* is an e-mail message that includes incorrect or misleading information. This is a written or static form of a social-engineering attack. Hoaxes are common and widespread because they expertly prey on human nature. If e-mail recipients aren't prepared for hoaxes, they can be easily caught up in them or persuaded by them. Hoaxes may inform you of intended court cases or legislation and encourage you to support one side or the other with a donation. They may warn you of a quickly spreading virus and provide details on how to sanitize your computer, such as deleting certain files or editing the Registry. Hoaxes also include chain letters that promise good fortune, bypassing of bad luck, or accumulation of wealth by passing the message on to others.

Although a hoax isn't the same as a virus in that it does not cause any direct damage, it often ends up causing nearly as much damage as a virus would. When ignorant users follow the instructions of a hoax—especially those that instruct readers to delete files or alter their system configuration via the Registry—the users usually end up damaging their operating system so severely as to require a reinstall or restoration from backup. Even if the damage isn't immediately or obviously severe, sometimes the instructions in a hoax

open up vulnerabilities so that real viruses, remote-control hacker tools, or other forms of malicious code can gain access.

Your primary weapon against hoaxes is education and awareness. E-mail users should be on the lookout for any message that promises the unlikely, seems too good to be true, or has dire warnings that require immediate action.

One method for improving the security of your organization when it comes to dealing with e-mail hoaxes as well as spam and other unwanted messages is to develop a response policy. A spam response policy should define the steps users should follow when they receive a message that might be a hoax, whether intentional or not. Some recommended response steps include the following:

1. Notify your network administrator that you have received a suspected hoax.

2. Check with your antivirus vendor for confirmation of malicious code–related issues.

3. Check with your antivirus vendor for e-mail hoax–related issues (most maintain a database of hoaxes).

4. Find at least three other reliable, public, trusted sources to corroborate any message, especially if it involves legal or monetary issues.

5. Don't forward any message to others if the message specifically directs you to do so. If there is a legitimate security issue spreading across the Internet, the security watchdogs will respond and inform the public appropriately.

6. Never follow the directions in an e-mail from an unknown or untrusted source. Always validate procedures from a trusted, reliable source (such as Microsoft, a software vendor, an antivirus vendor, or your ISP).

If you discover a hoax, especially one that isn't already cataloged in your antivirus vendor's hoax database, send the vendor a copy so it can inform others. Be sure to contact the vendor and ask how to submit examples of hoaxes; don't just forward the message.

E-mail

E-mail allows for fast, efficient communications across the Internet. There are more e-mail addresses than there are actual Internet users, because many people have multiple e-mail addresses, whether by chance or by choice. E-mail offers individuals and companies alike a means to communicate without paying any type of per-message fee (such as postage fees associated with snail mail) and allows messages to be delivered in seconds rather than days. However, these abilities of e-mail also make it ripe for exploitation by those with malicious or at least nonbenevolent intentions, such as spam or hoaxes.

E-mail relaying is another important issue. That topic is discussed in the "SMTP open relays" section later in this chapter.

Because e-mail is so widely used, it has become the most prevalent delivery vehicle for malicious code such as viruses, logic bombs, and Trojan horses. To combat this threat, you should deploy an antivirus scanner to scan e-mail content and attachments. You should even consider stripping or blocking e-mail attachments (especially those with known extensions of scripts or executables) as they enter your network (on an e-mail gateway, firewall, and so on). It is always the more secure option to scan, check, and if necessary, strip e-mail on SMTP servers before it reaches an end user's client system.

E-mail servers should also check for invalid, corrupted, or malformed messages. An e-mail message with a corrupted *MIME header* can cause an unprepared e-mail server to crash or freeze. Thus, attackers can use invalid e-mail formats as a method of waging a DoS attack against your e-mail systems. By keeping e-mail servers properly updated and deploying antivirus scanners and e-mail filters, you can avoid most of the problems and attacks associated with e-mail.

Adware

Adware is a variation on the idea of spyware (discussed earlier). Adware displays pop-up advertisements to users based on their activities, URLs visited, applications accessed, etc. Adware is used to target advertisements to prospective customers. Unfortunately, most adware products arrive on client systems without the knowledge or consent of the user. Thus, legitimate commercial products are often seen as intrusive and abusive adware.

Countermeasures for adware are the same as for spyware and viruses, with the addition of specific spyware/adware-scanning tools.

Rootkits

A *rootkit* is a special type of hacker tool that embeds itself deep within an operating system. The rootkit positions itself at the heart of an operating system (OS) where it can manipulate information seen by the OS. Often, a rootkit replaces the OS kernel or shims itself under the kernel, so that whatever information it feeds or hides from the OS, the OS thinks is normal and acceptable. This allows a rootkit to hide itself from detection, prevent its files from being viewed by file management tools, and prevent its active processes from being viewed by task management or process management tools. Thus, a rootkit is a type of invisibility shield. A rootkit can be used to hide other malicious tools and/or perform other functions. A rootkit or other tools hidden by a rootkit could capture keystrokes, steal credentials, watch URLs, take screen captures, record sounds via the microphone, track application use, or grant a remote hacker back door access or remote control over the compromised target system.

After a rootkit has infected a system, that system can no longer be trusted or considered secure. There are rootkits that are still undetectable and/or cannot be effectively removed. Thus, any rootkit-compromised system can never be trusted again. To use a silly analogy: If you are fighting an invisible army, how can you be sure that you have defeated all of them?

There are several rootkit detection tools, some of which are able to remove some rootkits. However, once you know a rootkit is on a system, the only truly secure response is

reconstitution. Reconstitution is the action of performing a low-level formatting operation on all storage devices on that system, reinstalling the OS and all applications from trusted original sources, and then restoring files from trusted rootkit-free backups. Obviously, the best protection against rootkits is defense rather than response.

Botnets

The term *botnet* is a shortened form of the phrase *robot network*. It is used to describe a massive deployment of malicious code onto numerous compromised systems that are all controlled by a hacker. A botnet is the culmination of traditional DoS attacks into a concept known as a distributed denial-of-service (DDoS) attack. A DDoS attack occurs when a hacker has deposited remote-controlled agents, zombies, or bots onto numerous secondary victims, and then uses the deployed bots as a single entity to attack a primary target.

Botnets are either directly or indirectly controlled by a hacker. Sometimes the hacker is labeled as a bot herder, a master, or even a handler. Direct control of a botnet occurs when the bot herder sends commands to each bot. Therefore, bots have a listening service on an open port waiting for the communication from the bot herder. Indirect control of a botnet can occur through any intermediary communication system, including IRC, IM, FTP, e-mail, Web, blogging, Twitter, and so on. When indirect control is used, the bots listen on an intermediate communication service for messages from the master hacker.

Botnets are possible because most computers around the world are accessible over the Internet, and many of those computers are not fully secure. A botnet creator writes his botnet code to exploit a common vulnerability in order to spread the botnet agent far and wide—often using the same techniques used by viruses, worms, and Trojan horses. Botnets are typically comprised of thousands (if not hundreds of thousands) of compromised secondary victims. The secondary victims are the hosts of the botnet agent itself and are not affected or damaged beyond the initial intrusion and planting of the botnet agent. The hackers want the secondary victims fully functional so when they launch their botnet attack against the primary victim, they can use all the resources of the secondary victims against the primary target.

A botnet can be used to perform any type of malicious activity. Although they are most often used to perform DoS flooding attacks, botnets can also be used to transmit spam; perform massively distributed parallel processing to crack passwords or encryption keys; perform phishing attacks; capture network packets; or perform any other conceivable activity.

The best defense against a botnet is to keep your systems hardened and to not become the host of a botnet agent (in other words, don't become a secondary victim). Also, most antivirus software and anti-spyware/adware tools include well-known botnet agents in their detection databases.

If you are the primary victim of a botnet attack, there is little you can do to stop the attack. Your responses are often limited to disconnecting from the Internet, contacting your ISP, and reporting the incident to law enforcement.

Logic bomb

A *logic bomb* is a form of malicious code that remains dormant until a triggering event occurs. The triggering event can be a specific time and date, the launching of a specific program, or the accessing of a specific URL (such as your online banking logon page). Logic bombs can perform any malicious function the programmer wishes, from causing system crashes to deleting data to altering configurations to stealing authentication credentials.

Countermeasures for logic bombs are the same as for viruses.

Exam Essentials

Privilege escalation Privilege escalation is the theft of privileges or access to resources that a user is not authorized to possess.

Viruses Viruses are programs that are designed to spread from one system to another through self-replication and to perform any of a wide range of malicious activities.

Worms Worms are designed to exploit a single flaw in a system (operating system, protocol, service, or application) and then use that hole to replicate itself to other systems with the same flaw.

Trojan horses A Trojan horse is a form of malicious software that is disguised as something useful or legitimate.

Spyware and adware Spyware gathers information about users and may employ that information to target advertisements or steal identities. Adware gathers information about users and uses it to direct advertisements to the user. Both spyware and adware are usually unwanted software that gathers information without authorization.

Spam Spam is undesired or unsolicited e-mail. It's a problem for numerous reasons. First, spam can be the carrier for malicious code such as viruses, logic bombs, and Trojan horses. Second, spam can be the carrier of a social-engineering attack (hoax e-mail). Third, unwanted e-mail wastes your time while you're sorting through it looking for legitimate messages. Fourth, spam wastes Internet resources such as storage capacity, computing cycles, and throughput.

E-mail filters An e-mail filter is a list of e-mail addresses, domain names, or IP addresses where spam is known to originate.

Spoofed e-mail A spoofed e-mail is a message that has a fake or falsified source address. When an e-mail server receives an e-mail message, it should perform a reverse lookup on the source address of the message.

Hoaxes A hoax is an e-mail message that includes incorrect or misleading information. This is a written or static form of a social-engineering attack. Your primary weapons against hoaxes are education and awareness. Notify your network administrator when you receive a suspected hoax.

Rootkit A rootkit is a type of malicious code that fools the OS into thinking that active processes and files don't exist. Rootkits render a compromised system completely untrustworthy.

Botnet A botnet is a network of robots or malicious software agents controlled by a hacker in order to launch massive attacks against targets.

Logic bombs A logic bomb is a form of malicious code that remains dormant until a triggering event occurs. The triggering event can be a specific time and date, the launching of a specific program, or the accessing of a specific URL (such as your online banking logon page).

Malicious code countermeasures The best countermeasure to viruses and other malicious code is an antivirus scanner that is updated regularly and which monitors all local storage devices, memory, and communication pathways for viral activities. Other countermeasures include avoiding downloading software from the Internet, not opening e-mail attachments, and avoiding the use of removable media from other environments.

1.2 Explain the security risks pertaining to system hardware and peripherals.

System hardware and peripherals require physical access controls and protections in order to maintain the logical security imposed by software. Without access control over the facility and physical environment, otherwise secured systems can be quickly compromised. Physical protections are used to protect against physical attacks, whereas logical protections protect only against logical attacks. Without adequate layers of protection, security is nonexistent. This section discusses several issues that often lead to security compromise because they are overlooked or deemed nonserious threats.

For more information on this topic, refer to Chapter 1 of the *CompTIA Security+ Study Guide, 4th Edition* (Sybex, November 2008).

BIOS

BIOS (basic input/output system) is the basic low-end firmware or software embedded onto the hardware's EEPROM (electrically erasable programmable read-only memory). BIOS identifies and initiates the basic system hardware components, such as the hard drive, optical drive, video card, and so on, so that the bootstrapping process of loading an OS can begin. This essential system function is a target of hackers and other intruders because it may provide an avenue of attack that is not secured or monitored.

BIOS attacks, as well as CMOS and device firmware attacks, are becoming a common target of physical hackers as well as of malicious code. If hackers or malware can alter the BIOS, CMOS, or firmware of a system, they may be able to bypass security features or initiate otherwise prohibited activities.

Protection against BIOS attacks requires physical access control to all hardware of a sensitive or valuable nature. Additionally, strong malware protection such as current antivirus software is important.

USB devices

USB devices are ubiquitous these days. Nearly every worker who uses a computer possesses a USB storage device, and most portable devices (such as phones, music players, and still or video cameras) connect via USB. However, this convenience comes at a cost to security. There are at least two main issues. First, just about any USB device can be used to either bring malicious code into or leak sensitive, confidential, and/or proprietary data out of an otherwise secure environment. Second, most computers built within the last three to five years have the ability to boot off USB. This could allow a user to boot a computer to an alternate OS (such as a live Linux distribution), which fully bypasses any security the native OS would have imposed.

To protect against USB threats, the only real option is to fully disallow use of all USB devices and lock down all USB ports. Otherwise, allowing the use of USB typically leaves your organization's system vulnerable to these threats.

Cell phones

Cell phones are an ever increasing security risk as they become more and more capable of interacting with the Internet as well as corporate networks. Cell phones often support memory cards, thus they could be used to smuggle malicious code in or confidential data out of organizations. Cell phones often contain sensitive data such as contacts, text messages, e-mail, and possibly notes and documents. The loss or theft of a cell phone could mean the compromise of personal and/or corporate secrets.

As cell phones become PDAs or even ultra-portable personal computing devices (miniature computers that are almost desktop replacements), they are becoming the target of hackers and malicious code. It is important to keep nonessential information off of portable devices, run a firewall and antivirus product (if available), and keep the system locked and/or encrypted (if possible).

Many cell phones also support USB connection to perform synchronization of communications and contacts with desktop and/or notebook computers as well as the transfer of files, documents, music, video, and so on. As discussed in the previous section, USB devices pose risks to malicious code and data theft.

Additionally, cell phones are not immune to eavesdropping. With the right type of sophisticated equipment, most cell phone conversations can be tapped into—not to mention the fact that anyone within 15 feet can hear you talking. Be careful what you discuss over a cell phone, especially when you are in a public place.

 Please see Chapter 2, where additional cell phone issues of blue jacking and bluesnarfing are discussed.

Removable storage

Removable media drives, and removable storage in general, are considered both a convenience and a security vulnerability. The ability to add and remove storage media to a computer system makes it more versatile. However, it also makes it vulnerable to data theft and malicious code planting.

Removable media include the electronic, logical, or digital storage mechanisms listed in the following sections as well as printed materials. Any time media is no longer needed, it should be properly destroyed to prevent disclosure of sensitive and confidential information to unauthorized entities. For example, failing to destroy printouts or burned CDs may provide dumpster-diving attackers with treasures.

Tape is a form of removable media commonly used for backup purposes. It's a form of sequential storage, so data elements are written and read in sequential order rather than semi-randomly as with hard drives. Tape media often support larger storage capacities than most removable media, excluding hard drives. This makes them suited for backup operations.

The topic of CD-Rs (recordable compact disks) includes the wide range of optical media that can be written to. This includes CDR, CD-RW, DVD-R, and DVD-RW (plus numerous other variants). Writable CDs and DVDs are often inappropriate for network backups due to their size (a maximum of 650MB for CD-R/RW and 4GB or more for DVD-R/RW), but they're useful for personal (home) or client-level backups. However, the data on a CD isn't protected and thus is vulnerable to unauthorized access if you don't maintain physical control over the media.

Hard drives are usually thought of as the permanent internal storage devices of a computer. This is true, but hard drives are also available in removable formats. These include hard drives that are plugged into the case or attached by SCSI, eSATA, USB, or IEEE 1394 (FireWire) connections with their own external power-supply connections.

Diskettes, or floppies, are removable media that can store only a small amount of data (about 1.4MB). However, even though they're small, they represent a significant security threat to a protected environment if they get into the wrong hands.

A *flashcard*, or memory card, is a form of storage that uses EEPROM or NVRAM memory chips in a small form-factor case. Flashcards often use USB connectors or are themselves inserted into devices such as MP3 players and digital cameras. Some flashcards are almost as small as a quarter and are therefore easy to conceal.

Smartcards can be used for a wide variety of purposes. They can be used as an authentication factor (specifically, it is an example of a Type 2 authentication factor commonly known as "something you have"). When used as such, the smartcard hosts a memory chip that stores a password, PIN, certificate, private key, or digital signature. The authentication system uses this stored data item to verify a user's identity. Smartcards are used as an authentication mechanism by networks, portable computers, PDAs, satellite phones, PKI devices, and more. A smartcard can even function as a credit card (like the American Express Blue card).

A smartcard can also be used as a storage device. Most smartcards have a very limited amount of storage, but sometimes being able to move a few kilobytes of data is all someone needs to steal something of great value. Account numbers, credit card numbers, or a user's private key are all small items that can be very valuable.

Network attached storage

Network attached storage (NAS) is a storage system connected directly to a LAN in order to provide network file storage without the need for a dedicated file server. A NAS device is basically a hard drive storage bay that has just enough intelligence to share the drive with the network. NAS is used to quickly and easily expand the storage capacity of an organization without significant overhead expense of additional server hardware. However, NAS is not necessarily a secure option. Not all NAS solutions offer strong security such as user authentication or authorization.

If a rogue user gains access to a NAS, they may be able to access any or all of the organization's confidential, private, and proprietary information. Additionally, such access may allow the rogue user to corrupt the data or plant malicious code.

Exam Essentials

BIOS BIOS (basic input/output system) is the basic low-end firmware or software embedded onto the hardware's EEPROM used to initialize bootstrapping.

USB devices A USB device is any device that connects to a system via USB. USB devices may pose a security risk via information leakage, planting of malicious code, or allowing booting to alternate operating systems.

Removable media or storage Removable media include the electronic, logical, or digital storage mechanisms listed here as well as printed materials. Any time media is no longer needed, it should be properly destroyed to prevent disclosure of sensitive and confidential information to unauthorized entities.

1.3 Implement OS hardening practices and procedures to achieve workstation and server security.

It's important to realize that a key element in securing a system is to reduce its attack surface. The *attack surface* is the area that is exposed to untrusted networks or entities and that is vulnerable to attack. If a system is hosting numerous services and protocols, its attack surface is larger than that of a system running only essential services and protocols.

 For more information on this topic, refer to Chapter 1 of the *CompTIA Security+ Study Guide, 4th Edition* (Sybex, November 2008).

It's tempting to install every service, component, application, and protocol available to you on every computer system you deploy. However, this temptation is in direct violation of a security best practice stating that you should have each system host only those services and protocols that are absolutely essential to its mission-critical operations.

The real issue is that software isn't trusted. Software (services, applications, components, and protocols) is written by people and therefore, in all likelihood, it isn't perfect. But even if software were without bugs, errors, oversights, mistakes, and so on, it would still represent a security risk. Software that is working as expected can often still be exploited by a malicious entity. Therefore, every instance of software deployed onto a computer system represents a collection of additional vulnerability points that may be exposed to external, untrusted, and possibly malicious entities.

From this perspective, you should understand that all nonessential software elements should be removed from a system before it's deployed on a network, especially if that network has Internet connectivity. But how do you know what is essential and what isn't? Here is a basic methodology:

1. Plan the purpose of the system.

2. Identify the services, applications, and protocols needed to support that purpose. Make sure these are installed on the system.

3. Identify the services, applications, and protocols that are already present on the system. Remove all that aren't needed.

Often, you won't know if a specific service that appears on a system by default is needed. Thus, a trial-and-error test is required. If software elements aren't clearly essential, disable them one by one and test the capabilities of the system. If the system performs as you expect, the software probably isn't needed. If the system doesn't perform as expected, then the software will need to be reenabled. This process is known as application and system hardening.

You may discover that some services and protocols offer features and capabilities that aren't necessary to the essential functions of your system. If so, find means to disable or restrict those characteristics. This may include restricting ports or reconfiguring services through a management console.

The essential services on a system are usually easy to identify—they generally have recognizable names that correspond to the function of the server. However, you must determine which services are essential on your specific system. Services that are essential on a web server may not be essential on a file server or an e-mail server. Some examples of possible essential services include the following:

- File sharing
- E-mail
- Web
- File Transfer Protocol (FTP)
- Telnet
- Remote access
- Network News Transfer Protocol (NNTP)
- Domain Name Service (DNS)
- Dynamic Host Configuration Protocol (DHCP)

Nonessential services are more difficult to identify. Just because a service doesn't have the same name as an essential function of your server doesn't mean that it isn't used by the underlying operating system or as a support service. It's extremely important to test and verify whether any service is being depended on by an essential service. However, several services are common candidates for nonessential services that you may want to locate and disable first (assuming you follow the testing method described earlier). These may include the following:

- NetBIOS
- Unix RPC
- Network File System (NFS)
- X services
- R services
- Trivial File Transfer Protocol (TFTP)
- NetMeeting
- Instant messaging
- Remote-control software
- Simple Network Management Protocol (SNMP)

Operating system hardening is the process of reducing vulnerabilities, managing risk, and improving the security provided by or for an operating system. This is usually accomplished by taking advantage of an operating system's native security features and supplementing them with add-on applications, such as firewalls, antivirus software, and malicious-code scanners.

Hardening an operating system includes protecting the system from both intentional directed attacks and unintentional or accidental damage. This can include implementing security countermeasures as well as fault-tolerant solutions for both hardware and software. Some of the actions that are often included in a system hardening procedure include the following:

- Deploy the latest version of the operating system.

- Apply any service packs or updates to the operating system.

- Update the versions of all device drivers.

- Verify that all remote-management or remote-connectivity solutions that are active are secure. Avoid FTP, Telnet, and other clear text or weak authentication protocols.

- Disable all unnecessary services, protocols, and applications.

- Remove or securely configure SNMP.

- Synchronize time zones and clocks across the network with an Internet time server.

- Configure event viewer log settings to maximize capture and storage of audit events.

- Rename default accounts.

- Enforce strong passwords on all accounts.

- Force password changes on a periodic basis.

- Restrict access to administrative groups and accounts.

- Hide the last-logged-on user's account name.

- Enforce account lockout.

- Configure a legal warning message that's displayed at logon.

- If file sharing is used, force the use of secure sharing protocols or use virtual private networks (VPNs).

- Use a security and vulnerability scanner against the system.

- Scan for open ports.

- Disable *Internet Control Message Protocol* (ICMP) functionality on publicly accessible systems.

- Consider disabling NetBIOS.

- Configure auditing.

- Configure backups.

The file system in use on a system greatly affects the security offered by that system. A file system that incorporates security, such as access control and auditing, is a more secure choice than a file system without incorporated security. One great example of a secured file system is the Microsoft New Technology File System (NTFS). NTFS was first deployed under Windows NT, but it's now found in Windows 2000, Windows XP, Windows Server 2003, and Windows Vista. It offers file- and folder-level access permissions and auditing capabilities. Examples of file systems that do *not* include security are FAT (file allocation table) and FAT32.

Workstations are the computer systems that people use to interact with a network. Workstations are also called *clients*, *terminals*, or *end-user computers*. Access to workstations should be restricted to authorized personnel. One method to accomplish this is to use strong authentication, such as two-factor authentication with a smartcard and a password or PIN.

Servers are the computer systems on a network that support and maintain the network. Servers provide services or share resources with the network. They require greater physical and logical security protections than workstations because they represent a concentration of assets, value, and capabilities. End users should be restricted from physically accessing servers, and they should have no reason to log on directly to a server—they should interact with servers over a network through their workstations.

Hotfixes

A *hotfix* is often a single-issue update (however, there are some multi-issue hotfixes) that corrects a single problem. Hotfixes aren't as thoroughly tested as other updates—they're quickly designed and released to deal with immediate issues and problems. You should install them if you're experiencing the problem they're designed to correct or you're threatened by the vulnerability they're designed to address.

Service packs

Service packs are collections of hotfixes and other previously unreleased updates and features as a single entity. They're thoroughly tested and generally should be applied to all systems once they're made available. Service packs are cumulative, so you only need to apply the most recent service pack to keep your systems current.

Patches

A *patch* is an update that corrects programming flaws that cause security vulnerabilities. Patches are single-issue utilities that are more thoroughly tested than hotfixes.

Patch management

Security is always a moving target. A system that is secure today may be vulnerable tomorrow. New methods of attacks, new attack tools, new viruses, new weaknesses, accidents in your environment, and much more can cause new risks, threats, and vulnerabilities at any time. Staying vigilant against new security issues is essential in today's business environment. One method to stay as secure as possible is to install updates from vendors.

Vendor *updates* to operating systems, applications, services, protocols, device drivers, and any other software are the absolute best way to protect your environment from known attacks and vulnerabilities. Not all vendor updates are security related, but any error, bug, or flaw that can be exploited to result in damaged data, disclosure of information, or obstructed access to resources should be addressed.

The best procedure to keep your systems updated is through a good patch management system that includes the following steps:

1. Watch vendor websites for information about updates.

2. Sign up for newsletters, discussion groups, or notifications.

3. Download all updates as they're made available.

4. Test all updates on nonproduction systems.

5. Document changes to your test systems and plan the implementation on production systems.

6. Back up production systems before implementing updates.

7. Implement updates on production systems.

8. Evaluate the effect of the updates on the production systems.

9. If negative effects are discovered, roll back the update.

Patch management can be implemented via a manual process, or an intelligent software tool can be used to automate this essential activity. Although security is not just patch management, security management requires that patches and updates are properly installed.

Group policies

A group policy is a mechanism of Microsoft Active Directory domain networks that is used to distribute and apply configuration settings to servers and clients. Group policies, commonly known as group policy objects or GPOs, are a collection of configuration settings that are applied to systems upon bootup and/or upon user login. There are settings for function, environment, network, performance, auditing, and security. There are settings for the computer and operating system as well as settings only for specific user accounts.

GPOs are a common mechanism used to manage and maintain the configuration and security of a large Windows-based network environment. New security requirements can be easily distributed throughout the network using GPO.

Security templates

A security template is a set of security settings that can be mechanically applied to a computer to establish a specific configuration. Security templates can be used to establish baselines or bring a system up to compliance with a security policy. Security template can be custom designed for workstations and server function/task/purpose. Security templates are a generic concept; however, there are specific security templates that can be applied via Windows's group policy system.

Security templates can be built by hand or by extracting settings from a preconfigured master. Once a security template exists, it can be used to configure a new or existing machine (by applying the template to the target either manually or through a GPO), or it can be used to compare the current configuration to the desired configuration. This latter process is known as *security template analysis* and often results in a report detailing the gaps in compliance.

Configuration baselines

One mechanism often used to help maintain a hardened system is to use a security baseline. A *security baseline* is a standardized minimal level of security that all systems in an organization must comply with. This lowest common denominator establishes a firm and reliable security structure on which to build trust and assurance. The security baseline is defined by the organization's security policy. It may include requirements of specific hardware components, operating system versions, service packs, patches/upgrades, configuration settings, add-on applications, service settings, and more.

The basic procedure for establishing a security baseline or hardening a system is as follows:

1. Remove unneeded components, such as protocols, applications, services, and hardware (including device drivers).
2. Update and patch the operating system and all installed applications, services, and protocols.
3. Configure all installed software as securely as possible.
4. Impose restrictions on information distribution for the system, its active services, and its hosted resources.

Documentation is an important aspect of establishing a security baseline and implementing security in an environment. Every aspect of a system, from design to implementation, tuning, and securing, should be documented. Failing to have sufficient documentation is often the primary cause of difficulty in locking down or securing a server. Without proper documentation, all the details about the operating system, hardware configuration, applications, services, updates, patches, configuration, and so on must be discovered before security improvements can be implemented. With proper documentation, a security professional can quickly add to the existing security without having to reexamine the entire environment.

Creating or defining a baseline requires that you examine three key areas of an environment: the operating system, the network, and the applications. The following sections examine issues related to security baseline establishment for these areas.

Exam Essentials

Hotfixes, service packs, patches, and updates Hotfixes, service packs, patches, and updates are improvements to distributed products produced by vendors to improve or fix issues. To maintain security, all hardware and software should be kept current with vendor-released patches.

Security risks of nonessential software Nonessential software increases the attack surface of your systems. Removing every element of software that isn't required will improve the security of a system.

Security baselines A security baseline is a standardized minimal level of security that all systems in an organization must comply with. This lowest common denominator establishes a firm and reliable security structure upon which to build trust and assurance. The security baseline is defined by the organization's security policy.

Documentation Documentation is an important aspect of establishing a security baseline and implementing security in an environment. Every aspect of a system, from design through implementation, tuning, and securing, should be documented. Failing to have sufficient documentation is often the primary cause of difficulty in locking down or securing a server.

Operating system hardening Operating system hardening is the process of reducing vulnerabilities, managing risk, and improving the security provided by or for an operating system. This is usually accomplished by taking advantage of the native security features of an operating system and supplementing them with add-on applications, such as firewalls, antivirus software, and malicious-code scanners.

File system security The file system in use on a system greatly affects the security offered by that system. A file system that incorporates security, such as access control and auditing, is a more secure choice than a file system without incorporated security.

1.4 Carry out the appropriate procedures to establish application security.

Application hardening is the task of imposing security on required applications and services. This usually involves tuning and configuring the native security features of the installed software and installing supportive security applications as needed. When you're developing new applications in house, it's also important to include security design, implementation, and integration throughout the development process.

For more information on this topic, refer to Chapter 1 of the *CompTIA Security+ Study Guide, 4th Edition* (Sybex, November 2008).

Application hardening is often seen as a subelement of operating system hardening. In fact, many of the same steps and procedures used to lock down an operating system are used to harden an application or service. In addition to the general notion of disabling any unneeded protocols and services, you should also disable any unneeded features, functions, or capabilities of a service or protocol based on the server's role and the capabilities your organization needs.

ActiveX

ActiveX is a mobile code technology developed by Microsoft. ActiveX controls or components are stand-alone programs that can be attached to or embedded in web documents to perform a wide range of functions. ActiveX components are executed with the same security privileges as the current user. However, the ActiveX component is saved to the hard drive and can be accessed at a later time, even after you've left the website where it was obtained. Thus, ActiveX can be a significant security issue. It's recommended that ActiveX components not be downloaded or executed except from websites you're sure you can trust. In many cases, web browsers can be configured to always allow, always block, or prompt the user each time an ActiveX component is presented by a website.

One method that helps reduce the number of malicious elements of mobile code downloaded and executed on a system is a mechanism known as applet signing. A *signed applet* is a piece of mobile code that has been digitally signed using the creator's or owner's certificate. A signed applet clearly indicates to the user the source of the applet. Web browsers can be configured to accept only signed applets or to prompt whenever any applet is offered by a website. It's important to understand that a signed applet only proves the applet's identity or source; it provides no guarantee as to the reliability or quality of the applet. Just because you know where an applet comes from doesn't mean that the applet isn't malicious code or that it won't cause a problem with your computer system.

Java

Java is a programming language created by Sun Microsystems specifically to operate in the distributed environment of the Internet. Java is a write-once, run-anywhere solution that allows a programmer to write an applet once and have it run on any platform. There is a requirement that a Java Virtual Machine (JVM) be installed on every system, but since there is a JVM for every commercial/public OS, this is usually not an issue.

Java is designed to operate within a restricted memory space and execution container known as a sandbox. This limits the functions of Java, which makes it harder to craft malicious code in Java. Java applets are not saved to the hard drive and do not fully take on the access privileges of the user. Thus, Java is designed as a more secure mobile code system. However, there are malicious Java applets and many of them perform social-engineering-based attacks rather than direct code-based attacks.

Java should only be allowed to execute if it is from a known trusted source.

Scripting

Scripting is a type of programming where the lines of the program or script remain in their original human readable form and which does not need to be precompiled to execute. Instead, the OS or a scripting interpreter (such as Perl) will perform JIT (just in time) compiling as needed. Scripting is a powerful and flexible tool used by a wide number of tech-savvy administrators. However, scripting can also be employed for malicious purposes, so it is always a good idea to inspect and/or scan all scripts for malicious code before use.

JavaScript is a scripting programming language that can be embedded directly into the HTML of a web page. It's executed by the web browser and can be used to perform a wide range of functions, both benign and malicious. Unlike its namesake Java, JavaScript doesn't run in a restricted security zone; rather, it has nearly unrestricted access to all system resources. Due to its power and unpredictability, it's generally recommended that you disable the download and execution of JavaScript except from websites you're sure you can trust.

Common Gateway Interface (CGI) is a mechanism developed early in the life of the Web to allow a web browser to submit information from a user back to a web server for processing by a server-side script or application. Although CGI scripting isn't used as widely as JavaScript or ActiveX today, it's still a default-enabled feature of both web servers and web browsers.

CGI has numerous vulnerabilities, the most prevalent of which is the ability of a user to submit data that results in the script's failure, a buffer overflow attack, or the performance of an unauthorized or unwanted activity (at least from the perspective of the web server owner).

Another issue with CGI is that all directories on the web server that host CGI scripts must be configured to allow web visitors to execute files. If the web server's folder hierarchy isn't properly protected, this could enable a user to upload their own scripts and then execute them.

To protect against CGI vulnerabilities, either don't use it or properly lock down the web folders appropriately. Also, thoroughly inspect all CGI scripts for malicious code before use. When possible, write your own scripts rather than use someone else's.

Browser

A browser (or web browser) is the client software used to interact with the Web. Browsers are usually graphical in nature, but there are several popular text-only or command-line browsers. Browsers grant users access to the vast repositories of information and resources distributed around the globe via the Internet's World Wide Web. Unfortunately, browsers bring security risks to their host computers.

A browser can be used to access malicious websites, which can result in information leakage, identity theft, or downloading of malicious code. It is important to practice safe surfing habits by being cautious and not downloading content from sources you don't fully trust.

Browsers should be kept current with patches and updates from the vendor. The OS should be hardened, and both a firewall and antivirus software should be running and kept updated. Block access to all known risky or malicious sites. Only accept downloadable code from known trusted and signed sources.

Buffer overflows

Software exploitation attacks are directed toward known flaws, bugs, errors, oversights, or normal functions of the operating system, protocols, services, or installed applications. One of the most common forms of software exploitation is a buffer overflow attack.

A buffer overflow attack occurs when an attacker submits data to a process that is larger than the input variable is able to contain. Unless the program is properly coded to handle excess input, the extra data is dropped into the system's execution stack and may execute as a fully privileged operation. Buffer overflow attacks can result in system crashes, corrupted data, user privilege escalation, or just about anything a hacker can think of. The only countermeasures to buffer overflow attacks are to patch the software when issues are discovered and to properly code software to perform input validation checks before accepting input for processing.

Once a weakness is discovered in software, a hacker often writes an exploit or attack tool. These tools are easily accessible on the Internet. They allow anyone to grab the tool and point it at a victim to perform the attack, even when the attacker has no knowledge of how to perform the attack.

A *buffer overflow* occurs when a program receives input that is larger that it was designed to accept or process. The extra data received by the program is shunted over onto the CPU without any security restrictions; it's then allowed to execute (assuming it's a valid command, script, system call, and so on) with system-level privileges. There are many possible results of a buffer overflow, including a program crash, a system freeze or crash, opening a port, disabling a service, creating a user account, elevating the privileges of an existing user account, accessing a website, or executing a utility. Clever attackers can do just about anything they wish if they can execute a command or script unrestricted access to a system.

Sometimes a buffer overflow attack can be labeled as a form of DoS attack, since a buffer overflow occurs when a system receives more data than it can handle (a bit like a flooding attack). This is especially true when the buffer overflow event results in a system no longer being able to process legitimate data or requests.

Poor programming quality controls and not including input validation checks in software lead to buffer overflow attacks. Unfortunately, there is little commercial software that isn't vulnerable to buffer overflow attacks; web server software is attacked most frequently. Fortunately, buffer overflow vulnerabilities are often easily patched with vendor updates.

Cookies

A *cookie* is a tracking mechanism developed for web servers to monitor and respond to a user's serial viewing of multiple web pages. A cookie is often used to maintain an

e-commerce shopping cart, focus product placement, or track your visiting habits. However, the benign purposes of cookies have been subverted by malevolent entities. Now cookies are a common means of violating your privacy by gathering information about your identity, logon credentials, surfing habits, work habits, and much more. A cookie can be easily exploited against a web browser to gather sufficient information about a user to allow the attacker to impersonate the victim online. It's generally recommended that you block third-party cookies from everyone and first-party cookies from all but the most trusted sites. Trusted sites are usually those entities that protect your identity by not including such details in a cookie. Instead, these sites only place a session ID in the cookie and thus keep all of your personal information in a backside database. Without allowing trusted first-party cookies (a.k.a. session cookies), functions such as e-commerce shopping carts, online banking, and even posting to discussion forums would be disabled.

SMTP open relays

E-mail is the most widely used communication vehicle on the Internet. However, it has also become one of the primary delivery mechanisms for malicious code and social-engineering attacks. Understanding e-mail security issues is essential to the Security+ exam.

Internet-based e-mail relies primarily on a single protocol: *Simple Mail Transport Protocol (SMTP)*. As you can see in Figure 1.1, SMTP has proven itself over more than 20 years as a reliable e-mail delivery system. However, it has one significant flaw: its nearly complete lack of security. SMTP doesn't offer encryption for transmitted messages. Thus, any and all e-mail can be snooped and examined. As e-mail becomes the basis for business communications, cleartext communication is no longer a viable option. Fortunately, SMTP supports add-on capabilities that bring encryption and other security services to e-mail. SMTP operates over TCP port 25.

Other protocols are involved with a complete e-mail solution. *Post Office Protocol (POP3)* and *Internet Message Access Protocol (IMAP)* are used to pull e-mail from an e-mail server down to a client, but they aren't involved in moving e-mail across the Internet. POP3 operates over TCP port 110, and IMAP operates over TCP port 143. Because e-mail is natively insecure, several encryption options have been developed to add security to e-mail used over the Internet. Two of the most common solutions are Secure Multipurpose Internet Mail Extensions (S/MIME) and Pretty Good Privacy (PGP).

S/MIME is an Internet standard for encrypting and digitally signing e-mail. It uses RSA (an asymmetric encryption scheme) to encrypt and protect e-mail.

PGP is used to encrypt and digitally sign e-mail messages. It uses RSA or Diffie-Hellman asymmetric cryptography solutions.

SMTP relay is the feature or function of an SMTP or e-mail server when it receives an e-mail from a client or other SMTP server and then forwards it on to another SMTP server. The forwarding action is similar to normal network packet routing, in that the purpose is to transmit the e-mail message to its destination. E-mail relaying is an essential part of the success of Internet e-mail, but it can be abused.

FIGURE 1.1 E-mail connections between clients and a server

E-mail relaying abuse often leads to DoS attacks or spam. Spam (specifically, spoofed spam) is often sent by rogue solicitors who find e-mail servers on the Internet that aren't properly configured to authenticate clients and servers before accepting e-mail. When an SMTP server fails to authenticate clients and servers before accepting e-mail, it's known as an *open relay*.

When you're deploying and securing an SMTP server, it's important to disable the open relay feature. However, even after an SMTP server has been secured, a clever attacker may be able to reenable relaying using a Trojan horse, buffer overflow, or remote access attack against the system. Thus, it's important to regularly check the performance logs and configuration settings of e-mail servers. One important item to look for is the presence of a universal acceptance configuration that would allow for the unrestricted and unverified relaying of e-mail. For example, on Unix systems, the e-mail server will have a list of domains that are authorized to submit e-mail. If this file includes a universal include coding statement, which is usually represented by a dot and an asterisk (.*), delete that entry and reboot the system to force the change to take effect.

Instant messaging

Instant messaging (IM) is a mechanism that allows for real-time text-based chat between two users located anywhere on the Internet. Some IM utilities allow for file transfer, multimedia, voice and video conferencing, and more. However, unlike many Internet information services, such as the Web, FTP, and e-mail, IM is a peer-to-peer service. There is no need for a centralized controlling server. This makes IM easy for end users to deploy and use, but it's difficult to manage from a corporate perspective. IM is insecure. It has numerous vulnerabilities, such as susceptibility to packet sniffing, it lacks true native security capabilities, and it provides no protection for privacy.

Instant messaging offers little in the way of security or privacy. Many IM clients are susceptible to malicious code deposit or infection through their file transfer capabilities. Also, IM users are often subject to numerous forms of social-engineering attacks, such as impersonation or convincing a victim to reveal information that should remain confidential (such as passwords).

Most IM clients don't use encryption when transmitting messages. Thus, most communications are subject to *packet sniffing* and *eavesdropping* attacks.

IM clients do not provide any direct protection for user privacy. The fact that IM clients perform communications in the clear and do not offer encryption or security services makes all private and confidential transmissions subject to packet sniffing and eavesdropping attacks.

P2P

P2P (peer to peer) is a file-sharing system that allows for the decentralized distribution of files over the Internet. P2P can be used to distribute legitimate free, open-source, or public content. However, P2P is often used to distribute illegal content such as pirated music, software, and movies. There are many varieties of P2P mechanisms; one of the more prevalent systems is known as BitTorrent.

Because P2P is a file distribution system, common precautions should be taken. First, try not to download files from untrusted sources. Second, scan every file with an antivirus scanner before use. Third, don't access or distribute content that is not free and legal to distribute. Even with these precautions, P2P can be a bandwidth hog and there is always the possibility that the P2P software can involve your system in distributing illegal content even without your direct permission. Because of these issues, organizations often ban P2P as a standard policy.

Input validation

Input validation is an aspect of defensive programming intended to ward off a wide range of input-focused attacks, such as buffer overflows and fuzzying. A fuzzying attack occurs when an attacker sends a variety of types and sizes of content to input points to see if they can trigger an abnormal response. Input validation checks each and every input received before it is allowed to be processed. The check could be a length, character type, language type, domain, or even timing check to prevent unknown, unwanted, or unexpected content to make it to the core program.

Cross-site scripting (XSS)

Cross-site scripting (XSS) is a form of malicious code injection attack where an attacker is able to compromise a web server and inject their own malicious code into the content sent to other visitors. Hackers have discovered numerous and ingenious methods to inject their own malicious code into websites via CGI scripts, web server software vulnerabilities, SQL

injection attacks, frame exploitation, DNS redirects, cookie hijacks, and many other forms of attack. A successful XSS attack could result in identity theft, credential theft, data theft, financial losses, or planting of remote control software on visiting clients.

Defenses against XSS include maintaining a patched web server, using firewalls, and auditing for suspicious activity. As a web user, you can defend against XSS by keeping your system patched, running antivirus software, and avoiding nonmainstream websites.

Exam Essentials

ActiveX ActiveX is a mobile code framework from Microsoft. ActiveX controls take on the privileges of the user. Only allow signed applets from sites you trust.

Java Java is a mobile code language from Sun Microsystems. Java was designed as a secure solution for the distributed Internet. Java runs in a sandbox.

JavaScript JavaScript is a scripting programming language that can be imbedded directly into the HTML of a web page. JavaScript, unlike its namesake Java, doesn't run in a restricted security zone; rather, it has nearly unrestricted access to all system resources. Due to its power and unpredictability, it's generally recommended that you disable the download and execution of JavaScript except from those websites you're sure you can trust.

Signed applets A signed applet is a piece of mobile code that has been digitally signed using the creator's or owner's certificate. A signed applet clearly indicates to the user the source of the applet.

Buffer overflows Buffer overflows occur due to a lack of secure defensive programming. The exploitation of a buffer overflow can result in a system crash or arbitrary code execution. A buffer overflow occurs when a program receives input that is larger that it was designed to accept or process. The extra data received by the program is shunted over onto the CPU without any security restrictions; it's then allowed to execute. Results of buffer overflows can include a program crash, a system freeze or crash, opening a port, disabling a service, creating a user account, elevating the privileges of an existing user account, accessing a website, or executing a utility.

Cookies A cookie is a tracking mechanism developed for web servers to monitor and respond to a user's serial viewing of multiple web pages. A cookie may allow identity theft.

SMTP open relay An SMTP open relay can be abused to send spam, hoaxes, or malicious attachments.

SMTP Simple Mail Transport Protocol (SMTP) moves e-mail messages across the Internet from sender to recipient. It doesn't include native encryption. It operates over TCP port 25.

POP3 and IMAP Post Office Protocol (POP3) and Internet Mail Access Protocol (IMAP) are used to pull e-mail from an e-mail server down to a client. POP3 operates over TCP port 110. IMAP operates over TCP port 143.

XSS Cross-site scripting (XSS) is a form of malicious code injection attack where an attacker is able to compromise a web server and inject their own malicious code into the content sent to other visitors.

Application hardening Application hardening is the task of imposing security on required applications and services. This usually involves tuning and configuring the native security features of the installed software and installing supportive security applications as needed. When you're developing new applications in house, it's also important to include security design, implementation, and integration throughout the development process.

1.5 Implement security applications.

Imposing security is often a long and complex process. One important part of this process is the installation or implementation of security applications. A security application is software designed specifically to perform a set of security functions. The following sections discuss some common security applications.

 For more information on this topic, refer to Chapter 1 of the *CompTIA Security+ Study Guide, 4th Edition* (Sybex, November 2008).

HIDS

A host-based intrusion detection system (HIDS) is a security application designed to monitor or watch the local computer system for malicious or anomalous activity. (IDS is discussed in detail in Chapter 2.) HIDS is different from a network-based IDS in that it is only able to monitor or oversee the activities within a single computer, rather than monitoring the activity across an entire network. An HIDS can be installed on a client or a server system. Because it is an active process, an HIDS does consume some system resources. An HIDS is dependent upon the auditing and logging systems of the host OS. It is effective at detecting known attacks against the local system.

Common examples of HIDS are antivirus software, anti-spyware scanners, and security anomaly detectors.

Personal software firewalls

A personal software firewall is a security application that is installed on client systems. A client firewall is used to provide protection for the client system from the activities of the user and from communications from the network or Internet. A personal firewall must

be kept current with patches and updates. It is often able to limit communications to only approved applications and protocols and usually can prevent external initiations of communications.

Antivirus

Antivirus software is an essential security application. Antivirus software is one example of a host IDS. It monitors the local system for evidence of malware in memory, in active processes, and in storage. Most antivirus products can remove detected malicious code and repair any damage caused by such malicious code. In order for antivirus software to be effective, it must be kept current with daily signature database updates. It is also important to use the most recent engine as new methods of detection and removal are only found in the most current versions of antivirus software.

Anti-spam

Anti-spam is a variation on the theme of antivirus software. Anti-spam specifically monitors e-mail communications for spam and other forms of unwanted e-mail in order to stop hoaxes, identity theft, waste of resources, and possible distribution of malicious software. Some antivirus software products include an anti-spam component.

Popup blockers

Popup blockers are used to prevent websites from opening additional web browser windows without your consent. Often these popup windows are used for advertisements or possibly to distribute malicious code or interact with questionable content. Popup blockers simply prevent active web browser processes or code from websites from launching or initiating new windows. There is usually an easy bypass for those times when you want to allow popups. One common bypass is to hold down the Ctrl key while the popup opens. Popup blockers are common components of modern web browsers, but they may also be part of antivirus software or stand-alone third-party applications.

Exam Essentials

HIDS A host-based IDS is used to protect the local client, user, and network from various malicious events.

1.6 Explain the purpose and application of virtualization technology.

Virtualization technology is used to host one or more operating systems within the memory of a single host computer. This mechanism allows virtually any OS to operate on any hardware. It also allows multiple operating systems to work simultaneously on the same hardware. Common examples include VMWare, Microsoft's Virtual PC, Microsoft Virtual Server 2005, Hyper-V with Windows Server 2008, and Apple's Bootcamp.

For more information on this topic, refer to Chapter 1 of the *CompTIA Security+ Study Guide, 4th Edition* (Sybex, November 2008).

Virtualization has several benefits, such as being able to launch individual instances of servers or services as needed, real-time scalability, and being able to run the exact needed OS version for the needed application. Virtualized servers and services are indistinguishable from traditional servers and services from a user's perspective. Additionally, recovery from damaged, crashed, or corrupted virtual systems is often quick: Simply replace the virtual system's main hard drive file with a clean backup version, and then relaunch it.

Exam Essentials

Virtualization technology Virtualization technology is used to host one or more operating systems within the memory of a single host computer.

Review Questions

1. Which of the following is commonly found to be a nonessential service on a web server?

 A. Server service

 B. DNS service

 C. FTP service

 D. Print spooler service

2. Which is the best countermeasure against malicious code?

 A. Manage user behavior

 B. Prevent reuse of external removable media

 C. Use antivirus software

 D. Disable mobile code on web browsers

3. What TCP port does IMAP function over?

 A. 143

 B. 25

 C. 110

 D. 443

4. What is the first action you should take when you receive an e-mail that describes a removal process to clean your system from a rapidly spreading high-risk virus?

 A. Follow the instructions immediately

 B. Forward the message to everyone you know

 C. Open any attachment enclosed with the message

 D. Report the message to your network administrator

5. Which of the following threats is eliminated when only signed applets are allowed to download through a web browser?

 A. CGI

 B. ActiveX

 C. Cookies

 D. Instant messaging

6. Which of the following actions in operating system hardening should come earliest in the process?

 A. Enable secure remote administration

 B. Remove unneeded services and protocols

 C. Enable logging and auditing

 D. Connect the system to the network/Internet

7. Illegal or unauthorized zone transfers are a significant and direct threat to what type of network server?

 A. Web

 B. DHCP

 C. DNS

 D. Database

8. What type of virus is able to regenerate itself if a single element of its infection is not removed from a compromised system?

 A. Polymorphic

 B. Armored

 C. Retro

 D. Phage

9. A rootkit has been discovered on your mission-critical database server. What is the best step to take to return this system to production?

 A. Reconstitution

 B. Run an antivirus tool

 C. Install an HIDS

 D. Apply vendor patches

10. A security template can be used to perform all but which of the following tasks?

 A. Capture the security configuration of a master system

 B. Apply security settings to a target system

 C. Return a target system to its precompromised state

 D. Evaluate compliance with security of a target system

Answers to Review Questions

1. D. A nonessential service is any element that isn't needed by the primary function of the server. In most cases, a web server doesn't use the print spooler service, but it often uses the server, DNS, and FTP services.

2. C. The most reliable countermeasure against malicious code is an antivirus scanner. User-behavior modification, managing media, and disabling mobile code are all countermeasures against malicious code, but they aren't as reliable and effective as antivirus scanners.

3. A. IMAP functions over TCP port 143. SMTP functions over TCP port 25. POP3 functions over TCP port 110. SSL and TLS function over TCP port 443.

4. D. This e-mail is likely a hoax. When you receive an e-mail hoax, the first step is to inform your network administrator. Don't follow its directions, forward it to others, or open any attachments.

5. B. If only signed applets are allowed to download through a web browser, you gain protection from unknown sourced ActiveX components. Applet signing doesn't affect CGI, cookies, or IM.

6. B. Removing unneeded services and protocols is an operating system hardening step that should come before any of the other three.

7. C. Illegal or unauthorized zone transfers are a significant and direct threat to DNS servers.

8. D. A phage virus is able to regenerate itself from any of its remaining parts.

9. A. The only real option to return a system to a secure state after a rootkit is reconstitution.

10. C. A security template alone cannot return a system to its precomprised state.

Chapter 2

Network Infrastructure

COMPTIA SECURITY+ EXAM OBJECTIVES COVERED IN THIS CHAPTER INCLUDE THE FOLLOWING:

✓ **2.1 Differentiate between the different ports & protocols, their respective threats and mitigation techniques.**

- Antiquated protocols
- TCP/IP hijacking
- Null sessions
- Spoofing
- Man-in-the-middle
- Replay
- DOS
- DDOS
- Domain Name Kiting
- DNS poisoning
- ARP poisoning

✓ **2.2 Distinguish between network design elements and components.**

- DMZ
- VLAN
- NAT
- Network interconnections
- NAC
- Subnetting
- Telephony

✓ **2.3 Determine the appropriate use of network security tools to facilitate network security.**

- NIDS
- NIPS

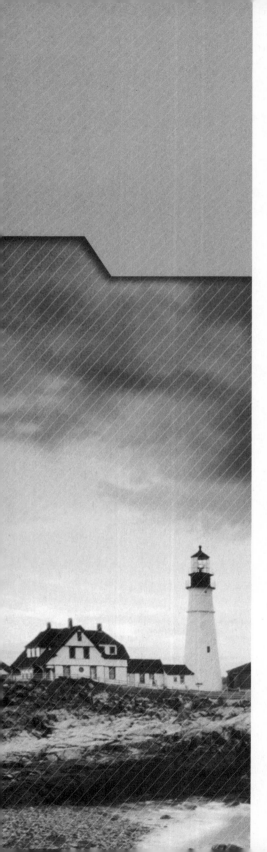

- Firewalls
- Proxy servers
- Honeypot
- Internet content filters
- Protocol analyzers

✓ **2.4 Apply the appropriate network tools to facilitate network security.**

- NIDS
- Firewalls
- Proxy servers
- Internet content filters
- Protocol analyzers

✓ **2.5 Explain the vulnerabilities and mitigations associated with network devices.**

- Privilege escalation
- Weak passwords
- Back doors
- Default accounts
- DOS

✓ **2.6 Explain the vulnerabilities and mitigations associated with various transmission media.**

- Vampire taps

✓ **2.7 Explain the vulnerabilities and implement mitigations associated with wireless networking.**

- 802.11 and 802.11x
- Data emanation
- War driving
- SSID broadcast
- Blue jacking
- Bluesnarfing
- Rogue access points
- Weak encryption

The Security+ exam will test your basic IT security skills—those skills needed to effectively secure stand-alone and networked systems in a corporate environment. To pass the test and be effective in implementing security, you need to understand the basic concepts and terminology related to network infrastructure security as detailed in this chapter.

2.1 Differentiate between the different ports & protocols, their respective threats and mitigation techniques.

Any computer system connected to any type of network is subject to various methods of attack. The rate at which networked systems are attacked is increasing at an alarming rate. Systems that aren't even connected to the Internet, but just to a private network, may come under attack. There are myriad ways to attack a computer system. Your familiarity with a modest collection of these attacks and how to respond to them is an essential skill for the Security+ exam. The following section discusses common attack methods.

For more information on topics in this section, refer to Chapter 2 of the *CompTIA Security+ Study Guide, 4th Edition* (Sybex, November 2008).

Antiquated protocols

Antiquated protocols are protocols that were not specifically designed with security as a primary focus. Many of the protocols commonly used over the Internet or within a private network are of this ilk. Many protocols that computer users rely on daily—such as for e-mail, the Web, and FTP—were developed over 30 years ago and have little to no security built into them. Unfortunately, these antiquated protocols often cannot be replaced with secure alternatives, due to lack of interoperability or backwards compatibility of the secure protocols with legacy services and clients. Therefore, you must be aware of the limitations of antiquated protocols and take precautions against potential security breaches.

The antiquated protocols of e-mail—SMTP, POP3, and IMAP4—are discussed in the "SMTP open relays" section of Chapter 1. The antiquated protocol of web communications— HTTP—is discussed the "HTTP vs. HTTPS vs. SHTTP" section of Chapter 5.

The antiquated protocol of file transfer or exchange is *File Transfer Protocol* (*FTP*). This protocol is often used to move files between one system and another either over the Internet or within private networks. Understanding the basics of FTP and the secured alternative file transfer solutions is important for the Security+ exam.

FTP is an in-the-clear file exchange protocol. It is supported by any computer system that uses the TCP/IP protocol. An FTP server system is configured to allow authenticated or anonymous FTP clients to log on in order to upload or download files. FTP employs TCP ports 20 and 21 to establish and maintain client-to-server communications, and it then often uses a randomly selected higher port (above 1023) for file transfers.

The exchange of files is a common practice on the Internet, intranets, and extranets. FTP is platform independent and thus makes file exchanges between different operating systems simple. It's one of the common services deployed in a demilitarized zone (DMZ)—an extension of a private network where Internet users can access services such as the Web and e-mail—in order to provide controlled public access to company resources while still allowing internal clients to access the services.

Secure File Transfer Protocol (S/FTP)

Secure FTP (*S/FTP*) is a secured alternative to standard FTP. Standard FTP sends all data, including authentication traffic, in the clear. Thus, there is no confidentiality protection. S/FTP encrypts both authentication and data traffic between the client and server by employing SSH (Secure Shell) to provide secure FTP communications. Thus, S/FTP provides protection for both the authentication traffic as well as the data transfer occurring between a client and server.

 Other alternatives to standard FTP are to use FTP over an SSL connection, S/FTP, or FTP across a secured SSL or VPN link. Any of these options effectively provides protection for all FTP traffic.

No matter what secure FTP solution is employed, both the server and the client must have the same solution. The client and the server must have compatible or interoperable FTP tools in order to establish a connection and support the exchange of files. Otherwise, FTP session establishment and subsequent file transfer communications won't be possible.

Anonymous and blind FTP

Anonymous FTP is a form of nameless logon to an FTP server. Usually, visitors to an FTP site who wish to log on anonymously use the word *anonymous* as the logon name. They are then prompted to provide their e-mail address as the password, but any text string suffices.

Site administrators should carefully configure FTP servers that allow anonymous access. Anonymous users should not be able to download (or, in many cases, view) any files

uploaded by anonymous users. Anonymous upload and download should be enabled only if absolutely necessary. When possible, don't allow both authenticated and anonymous FTP logons on the same FTP site. Most FTP servers have anonymous FTP enabled by default, so usually it must be specifically disabled in order to limit access to authenticated users.

If FTP upload is allowed—especially when anonymous FTP uploading is allowed— ensure that it isn't possible to access upload folders from a web URL. If you don't take this precaution, web visitors may be able to download files from the FTP site through HTTP, or they may be able to execute uploaded files. Both of these tactics are commonly used by hackers in a wide number of intrusion attacks.

Blind FTP is a configuration of anonymous FTP or authenticated FTP where uploaded files are unseen and unreadable by visitors. Thus, users can upload files but not see the resulting uploads. Additionally, even if a user knows the exact pathname and filename of a file deposited onto your blind FTP site, the deposited files are write-only and thus reading or downloading is not possible. This ensures that your FTP site isn't overrun by file swappers using your system as a file exchange point. File swappers often exchange illegal (unlicensed) copies of software, music, and movies through unsecured FTP servers. Uploaded files on a blind FTP server become accessible only after the administrator has either changed the files' permissions or moved them into a folder configured to allow downloads.

Packet sniffing

Because all FTP traffic is transmitted in the clear, all FTP traffic is vulnerable to packet sniffing and other forms of eavesdropping. It's important not to use the same user account and password on FTP that is used in a secure environment. Otherwise, if an attacker captures your FTP logon traffic, they also obtain the logon credentials needed to log in to your secured network. Always use a separate and distinct user account for FTP logons. Sniffers and protocol analyzers are discussed in the "Protocol analyzers" section later in this chapter.

8.3 naming conventions

Not all operating systems or file systems support long filenames. If an FTP server's host operating system and file systems support only the 8.3 naming convention, then uploaded files with longer filenames will be automatically truncated to comply with 8.3 restrictions. Likewise, if an FTP client's host operating system and file systems support only the 8.3 naming convention, then downloaded files with longer filenames will be automatically truncated to comply with 8.3 restrictions. In either case, this can result in files that are hard to locate or will cause filename conflicts.

TCP/IP hijacking

TCP/IP hijacking is a form of attack where the attacker takes over an existing communication session. The attacker can take over the role of the client or the server, depending on the purpose of the attack. TCP/IP hijacking (a.k.a. session hijacking) is a simpler one-sided form of man-in-the-middle attack. Many of the same tools and techniques are used in

both forms of attack. With a session hijacking, the other partner in the communication is disconnected—they're aware that they are no longer communicating and that their session was interrupted. However, they may not immediately realize that they were the collateral damage in a session hijacking attack.

Figure 2.1 shows a TCP/IP hijacking attack.

FIGURE 2.1 TCP/IP hijacking attack

Countermeasures to TCP/IP hijacking attacks include using encrypted protocols and performing reauthentication during a session. Additionally, modern or secured protocols are often designed with preventive features that make session hijacking very difficult or impossible. These features include complex nonlinear sequencing rules as well as time-stamps with short time-out values.

Null sessions

A null session is a connection made to a system where no credentials are supplied by the client and thus no authentication process is performed by the server. The target of a null session need not be a network server, but can be any system supporting a version of Windows. The *null* in the name of this connection refers to the user account—it indicates that no user account credentials are used; thus the user is unknown. Another way of stating this is that a null session establishes a communication link anonymously.

Null sessions are vulnerabilities that exist in any version of Windows that supports NetBIOS. Earlier versions of Windows, such as Windows 2000 and earlier, would allow null session connections by default. Newer versions of Windows, such as Windows XP and later, have null sessions and other forms of anonymous access disabled by default. However, even newer versions of Windows can be vulnerable to null sessions if the security feature preventing them is disabled.

Establishing a null session is quite simple. In fact, it takes only the following single command line:

```
net use * \\<servername>\IPC$ "" /u:""
```

After a null session is established, the attacker is able to extract any data from the target system that is accessible via NetBIOS communications. This includes usernames, computer name, workgroup or domain names, ACLs, Registry settings, account policies, and much more. In fact, nearly anything that is accessible to the Everyone group is accessible via null sessions. There are numerous command-line and GUI tools that can exploit null sessions to extract data and enumerate targets.

Stopping null sessions is quite simple with a setting found in the Security Options section of the Group Policy Object for Windows 2000, XP, 2003, and Vista.

Spoofing

Spoofing is the act of falsifying data. Usually the falsification involves changing the source address of network packets. As a result of the changed source address, victims are unable to locate the true attackers or initiators of a communication. Also, by spoofing the source address, the attacker redirects packet responses, replies, and echoes to some other system (as in the case of smurf, fraggle, and land DoS attacks).

Spoofing is also a common activity for unsolicited e-mail, commonly known as spam. Spoofed e-mail means that you're unable to reply to the e-mail or determine where it originally came from.

There are innumerable forms of spoofing attacks. Spoofing can be used to redirect packets, bypass traffic filters, steal data, perform social engineering attacks, and even falsify websites.

Countermeasures against spoofing attacks include the following:

- Use e-mail spam and spoofing filters.

- Drop all inbound packets received by border systems that have a source destination from inside your private network (this indicates spoofing).

- Drop all outbound packets received by border systems that have a source destination from outside your private network (this also indicates spoofing).

Man-in-the-middle

A *man-in-the-middle attack* is a communications eavesdropping attack. Attackers position themselves in the communication stream between a client and server (or any two communicating entities). The client and server believe that they are communicating directly with each other—they may even have secured or encrypted communication links. However, the attacker can access and potentially modify the communications.

Waging a man-in-the-middle attack is complex. It involves altering network traffic and possibly poisoning name resolution systems (such as DNS or WINS) in order to fool the client into perceiving the attacker as the server and to fool the server into perceiving the attacker as the client. When that charade is successful, the client will submit their logon credentials to the fake server (the masked attacker), which in turn sends the credentials to the actual server while masquerading as the actual client. As a result, the client establishes a communication link (maybe even an encrypted link) with the attacker, and the attacker

establishes a communication link with the server. As data is transmitted in either direction between the true client and server systems, the attacker can read and access all the data and can choose to modify the traffic to further the subterfuge.

Figure 2.2 shows a man-in-the-middle attack.

FIGURE 2.2 A man-in-the-middle attack occurring between a client and a web server

| Client | Man in the Middle | Server |

Such attacks are usually most successful when routing and name resolution systems are first compromised in order to position the attacker before the client-to-server communication is initiated. However, man-in-the-middle attacks can be conducted against existing client/ server communication links (usually assuming they aren't encrypted). This second form of attack is much more difficult due to existing routing, name resolution, TCP sequencing, and the speed of the communication. However, several tools exist that perform the necessary operations against both sides of the communication connection in order to implement a man-in-the-middle injection. Some of these tools include Juggernaut, T-Sight, and Hunt.

Countermeasures to man-in-the-middle attacks include strong encryption protocols, such as IPSec, and the use of strong authentication, such as Kerberos, certificates, multi-factor authentication, Server Message Block (SMB) signing, and mutual authentication.

Replay

A *replay attack* is just what it sounds like: An attacker captures network traffic and then replays the captured traffic in an attempt to gain unauthorized access to a system. Most commonly, the attacker focuses on network traffic that is the exchange between a client and server performing authentication. If an attacker can capture the authentication traffic— especially the packets containing the logon credentials, even if they are more than just username and password (such as certificates, token responses, or biometric values)—then a replay attack may grant the attacker the ability to log on to a system by retransmitting the captured packets.

Figure 2.3 shows a replay attack.

If a replay attack succeeds, the attacker gains the same level of access as the user that originally submitted the authentication information. Fortunately, most modern operating systems, networks, protocols, services, and applications use various replay protection mechanisms to directly prevent such attacks. Two of the most common countermeasures are packet sequencing and timestamps. Packet sequencing ensures that any packet received that isn't in the proper order (or within a reasonable margin) is dropped and ignored. Packet timestamps ensure that any packet received outside of a specific time window is dropped and ignored. A great example of this is Kerberos, which is not vulnerable to replay attacks due to its use of timestamps.

FIGURE 2.3 A replay attack occurring

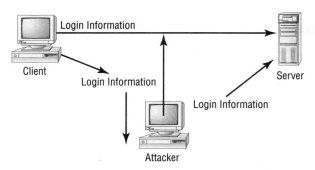

DOS

Denial-of-service (DoS) is a form of attack that has the primary goal of preventing the victimized system from performing legitimate activity or responding to legitimate traffic. There are two basic types of DoS attack. The first form exploits a weakness, error, or standard feature of software to cause a system to hang, freeze, consume all system resources, and so on. The end result is that the victimized computer is unable to process any legitimate tasks. The second form floods the victim's communication pipeline with garbage network traffic. The end result is that the victimized computer is unable to send or receive legitimate network communications. In either case, the victim has been denied the ability to perform normal operations (services).

DoS isn't a single attack but rather an entire class of attacks. Some attacks exploit flaws in operating system software, whereas others focus on installed applications, services, or protocols. Some attacks exploit specific protocols, including Internet Protocol (IP), *Transmission Control Protocol (TCP), Internet Control Message Protocol (ICMP),* and *User Datagram Protocol (UDP).*

DoS attacks typically occur between one attacker and one victim. However, they don't have to be waged in that simple a manner. Most DoS attacks employ some form of intermediary system (usually an unwilling and unknowing participant) in order to hide the attacker from the victim. For example, if an attacker sends attack packets directly to a victim, it's possible for the victim to discover who the attacker is. This is made more difficult, although not impossible, through the use of spoofing (discussed earlier in this chapter).

Many DoS attack are waged by first compromising or infiltrating one or more intermediary systems that serve as launch points or attack platforms. These intermediary systems are commonly referred to as secondary victims. The attacker installs remote-control tools, often called *bots*, *zombies*, or *agents*, onto these systems. Then, at an appointed time or in response to a launch command from the attacker, the DoS attack is conducted against the victim. In this manner, the victim may be able to discover the one or many zombied systems that are causing the DoS attack but probably won't be able to track down the actual attacker. This form of attack involving zombied systems is known as distributed denial-of-service

(DDoS), as shown in Figure 2.4. Recently, such deployments of numerous bots or zombies across numerous unsuspecting secondary victims are known as *botnets*.

FIGURE 2.4 DDoS attack

There is a third level of DoS known as distributed reflective denial-of-service (DRDoS). This form of attack employs an *amplification* or *bounce* network that is an unwilling and unknowing participant but that has unfortunately left on its ability to receive broadcast messages and create message responses, echoes, or bounces. In effect, the attacker sends spoofed message packets to the amplification network's broadcast address. This causes each single inbound received packet to be distributed to all the hosts inside that network (which could be in the 10,000 or 100,000 range). Each host then responds to each packet, but since the source of the original packet was falsified, the response goes to the victim instead of the true sender (the attacker). So, what originated from the attacker as a single packet is transformed into numerous packets exiting the amplification network and ultimately flooding the victim's communication link.

There are numerous specific DoS, DDoS, and DRDoS attack tools and methods. Here are a few that you should be able to recognize:

Smurf This form of DRDoS uses Internet Control Message Protocol (ICMP) echo reply packets (ping packets). See Figure 2.5 for an example.

Fraggle This form of DRDoS uses User Datagram Protocol (UDP) packets commonly directed to port 7 (echo port) or 19 (chargen [character generator] port).

FIGURE 2.5 A smurf attack underway against a network

SYN flood This type of attack is an exploitation of a TCP three-way handshake. Every TCP session starts with the client sending a SYN (synchronize) packet to a server, the server responding with a SYN/ACK (synchronize/acknowledgment) packet, and the client sending a final ACK packet. The attack consists of the attacker serving as a client and sending numerous SYN packets but never any final ACK packets. This causes the server to consume all system resources opening incomplete communication sessions. Figure 2.6 shows an example of a TCP SYN flood attack.

FIGURE 2.6 TCP SYN flood attack

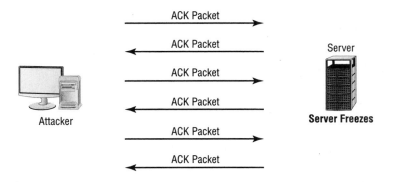

Teardrop Numerous partial IP packets are sent to a victim with overlapping sequencing and offset values. The victim attempts to assemble complete IP packets from the received partials, but the fragments overwrite each other and may produce a packet of an invalid size. This causes the victim to freeze or crash.

Land attack Numerous SYN packets are sent to the victim with source and destination addresses spoofed as the victim's address. The victim is confused because it's unable to respond to a packet it sent to itself that it has no record of sending. This often results in a freeze or crash.

Ping flood The attacker sends numerous ping echo requests to a victim. The victim responds with the echo. If enough inbound and outbound packets are transmitted, no legitimate traffic will be able to use the communication link.

Ping of death The attacker sends oversized ping packets to the victim; the victim doesn't know how to handle invalid packets, and it freezes or crashes.

Bonk The attacker sends a corrupt UDP packet to DNS port 53. This type of attack may cause Windows systems to crash.

Boink The same as Bonk, but the corrupt UDP packets are sent to numerous ports. The result may cause a Windows system to crash.

SYN flood, teardrop, land attack, ping flood, ping of death, bonk, and boink are typically labeled DoS attacks, but they can be waged as a DDoS if the attacker compromises several intermediary systems and uses those as launching points to attack the victim. Fortunately, most of the basic DoS attacks that exploit error-handling procedures (such as ping of death, land attack, teardrop, bonk, boink, and so on) are now automatically handled by improved versions of the protocols installed in the operating system. However, many of the current DDoS and DRDoS attacks aren't as easy to safeguard against.

Some countermeasures and safeguards against these attacks include the following:

- Adding firewalls, routers, and intrusion detection systems (IDSs) that detect DoS traffic and automatically block the port or filter out packets based on the source or destination address

- Disabling echo replies on external systems

- Disabling broadcast features on border systems

- Blocking spoofed packets from entering or leaving your network

- Keeping all systems patched with the most current security updates from vendors

DDOS

DDoS (distributed denial-of-service) attacks are discussed in the preceding "DOS" section.

Domain Name Kiting

Domain name kiting is a scheme or scam used to discover which new domain names drive the most profitable traffic and then keep those domain names indefinitely without having to pay the registration fees. The scheme or scam is based on the ability to obtain a full refund within a five-day waiting period for a domain name registration. Scammers register hundreds or thousands of domain names, and then post simple websites with advertisements or

e-commerce shops on them. Often, the scammers grab domains that expired but which still have lots of traffic driven to them by search engines. Over the next five days, they watch to see which domains generate the most profit. Those that are not generating much money are deleted and they obtain a full refund of their registration fee. On those are profitable, the scammer might elect to actually pay for the registration of the profitable domains (this is known as domain tasting), or they could delete it and then immediately re-register it to obtain another free five-day period. If the scammer can repeat this latter action, they may be able to keep a domain name for free indefinitely. Domain name tasting allows profiteers to try out a domain name to test its profitability before being locked into the registration fee. If a domain shows profitability, high traffic, or is likely to be a popular domain to resell to a third party, the taster will keep the domain and try to use it as a money maker.

This type of scheme is not just performed by scammers. There have also been incidents where a few domain registrars have been accused of domain name front running. Front running is a related scheme to domain name kiting where registrars abuse the five-day grace period to control registrations or drive up prices. The accusation is that the registrars automatically register any domain that a visitor searches for but does not actually register. This effectively locks up that domain for five days at that specific registrar. If the visitor returns within those five days to actually obtain the domain they previously searched for, they will discover that either it is no longer available or it is being offered to them at a much higher registration price. This practice also prevents a user from searching for a domain on one registrar's site then actually registering the domain on another.

In any case, the practice of domain name kiting, tasting, or front running is occurring at an alarming rate. In 2007, GoDaddy.com claimed that in one year only 3.6 million registrations were actually paid for while over 51 million were deleted before their five-day grace period expired. In January 2008, ICANN proposed changes that should help reduce most of the abuse of the five-day grace period. There is a $0.20 registration fee paid to ICANN by the registrars for every purchased registration. This fee is not applied to any domain that is deleted before its five-day grace period is over. The proposal, which is said to start applying in 2009, is that if any single user deletes 10 percent of their net new registrations or 50 domains (whichever is greater) within the five-day grace period over the space of one year, they will be charged the $0.20 per domain fee.

DNS poisoning

DNS poisoning is the act of falsifying the DNS information used by a client to reach a desired system. DNS poisoning can take place in many ways. Whenever a client needs to resolve a DNS name into an IP address, it may go through the following four-step process:

1. Check local cache.
2. Check local HOSTS file.
3. Send DNS query to known DNS server.
4. Send broadcast query to any possible local subnet DNS server. (This step is not widely supported.)

If the client does not obtain a DNS-to-IP resolution from any of these steps, the resolution fails and the communication cannot be sent. DNS poisoning can take place at any of these steps, but easiest is to corrupt the HOSTS file or the DNS server query.

One method is to deploy a rogue DNS server. A rogue DNS server can listen in on network traffic looking for either any DNS query or just specific DNS queries related to a target site. Then the rogue DNS server sends a DNS response to the client with false IP information. This attack requires that the rogue DNS server get its response back to the client before the real DNS server's response. Once the client receives the response from the rogue DNS server, the client closes the DNS query session, which causes the response from the real DNS server to be dropped and ignored as an out of session packet. A second method for DNS poisoning is to attack the real DNS server and place incorrect information into its zone file. This causes the real DNS server to send back false data to clients. A third method is to alter the HOSTS file on the client and place false DNS data into it. A fourth method is to corrupt the TCP/IP configuration either directly on the client or on the network's DHCP server to pass out false DNS server information. A fifth method, which only works against web communications, is to plant false web proxy data into a client's browser, then host a rogue proxy server. A rogue proxy server can modify the HTTP traffic packets to reroute requests to whatever site the hacker wishes.

Although there are many DNS poisoning methods, here are some basic security measures you can take that can greatly reduce their threat:

- Limit the ability of zone transfers from internal DNS servers to external DNS servers.
- Limit the external DNS servers that internal DNS servers pull zone transfers from to only trusted servers.
- Deploy a NIDS to watch for abnormal DNS traffic.
- Properly harden all DNS, server, and client systems within your private network.

ARP poisoning

Address Resolution Protocol (ARP) poisoning is the act of falsifying the IP-to-MAC address resolution system employed by the TCP/IP protocol. ARP operates at Layer 2, the Data Link layer of the OSI model. ARP is responsible for resolving IP addresses into MAC addresses. This allows Layer 2 to physically address transmissions before sending them to the Physical layer (Layer 1). Similar to DNS, ARP resolution is a multistep process, but it only has two steps instead of four: (1) check local ARP cache, then, if that fails, (2) transmit ARP broadcast. The ARP broadcast is a transmission to all possible recipients within the local subnet asking all hosts if they own the IP address in question. If the owner of the IP address is present, it responds with a direct replay back to the source system with its MAC address.

MAC addresses are essential for TCP/IP communications as transmissions occur from host to host and router to router not based solely on IP address but based primarily on MAC addresses. When a host sends data to another host, if that host is in the same subnet, it transmits the signal from its MAC addressed NIC to the target's MAC addressed NIC. If the target is in a different subnet, it sends the message to the MAC addressed NIC of the

default gateway (which is the router interface in that subnet). Then, that router takes over and tries to find the target host either with a subnet directly off of one of its ports or sends the message to another router that may have a greater chance of being connected to the target host's subnet. Without proper ARP activity, this process is not possible.

ARP poisoning can take place in many ways. The most common are to either poison the local ARP cache or to transmit poisoned ARP replies or announcements. In either case, if a host obtains a false MAC address for an IP address, then its transmission is likely to go to the wrong location. This tactic is most effective within a single subnet, but does have an effect across multiple subnets. ARP poisoning is commonly used in active sniffing attacks where false ARP announcements are used to overload the MAC mapping cache of a switch in order to force it into a fault tolerant mode of transmitting all data out all ports.

The best defense against ARP poisoning is to use a NIDS to monitor network traffic for ARP abuse and abnormalities.

Exam Essentials

FTP File Transport Protocol (FTP) is an in-the-clear file exchange solution. An FTP server system is configured to allow authenticated or anonymous FTP clients to log on in order to upload or download files. FTP employs TCP ports 20 and 21.

S/FTP Secure FTP (S/FTP) is a secured alternative to standard or basic FTP that encrypts both authentication and data traffic between the client and server. S/FTP employs SSH to provide secure FTP communications.

Anonymous FTP Anonymous FTP is a form of nameless logon to an FTP server. Site administrators should carefully configure FTP servers that allow anonymous access.

Blind FTP Blind FTP is a configuration of anonymous FTP or authenticated FTP where uploaded files are unseen and unreadable by visitors. Thus, users can upload files but not see the resulting uploads.

FTP vulnerabilities Because all FTP traffic is transmitted in the clear, all FTP traffic is vulnerable to packet sniffing and other forms of eavesdropping. Not all operating systems or file systems support long filenames. If an FTP server's host operating system and file systems support only the 8.3 naming convention, then uploaded files with longer filenames will be automatically truncated to comply with 8.3 restrictions.

TCP/IP hijacking attacks TCP/IP hijacking is a form of attack where the attacker takes over an existing communication session.

Null session A null session is a connection made to a system where no credentials are supplied by the client and thus no authentication process is performed by the server.

Spoofing Spoofing is the act of falsifying data. Usually the falsification involves changing the source address of network packets. Because the source address is changed, victims are unable to locate the true attackers or initiators of a communication. Also, by spoofing the source address, attackers redirect responses, replies, and echoes to packets to some other system.

Man-in-the-middle attack A man-in-the-middle attack is a form of communications eavesdropping attack. Attackers position themselves in the communication stream between a client and server (or any two communicating entities). The client and server believe they are communicating directly with each other.

Replay attack An attacker captures network traffic and then replays the captured traffic in an attempt to gain unauthorized access to a system.

DoS Denial-of-service (DoS) is a form of attack that has the primary goal of preventing the victimized system from performing legitimate activity or responding to legitimate traffic. One form exploits a weakness, error, or standard feature of software to cause a system to hang, freeze, consume all system resources, and so on. The end result is that the victimized computer is unable to process any legitimate tasks. Another form floods the victim's communication pipeline with garbage network traffic. The end result is that the victimized computer is unable to send or receive legitimate network communications.

Domain name kiting Domain name kiting is a scheme or scam used to discover which new domain names drive the most profitable traffic and then keep those domains names indefinitely without having to pay the registration fees. Related schemes include domain name tasting and front running.

DNS poisoning DNS poisoning is the act of falsifying the DNS information used by a client to reach a desired system.

ARP poisoning ARP poisoning is the act of falsifying the IP-to-MAC address resolution system employed by the TCP/IP protocol.

2.2 Distinguish between network design elements and components.

Networks are becoming ever more complex structures. Small home or SOHO networks might consist of a handful of computers, a central file and print server, a router or switch, and an Internet link. Enterprise networks can be comprised of tens or hundreds of thousands of computers and thousands of servers with a seemingly endless string of cables, routers, switches, and other network devices. Enterprise networks often employ hundreds of subnets, require proxies and NAT servers, use VLANs, support VPNs, host virtualized servers, connect to DMZs and extranets, and more. Obviously, the larger and more complex a network is, the more there is to know about its components, elements, and security needs. This section takes a look at a few common network elements and components that are addressed on the Security+ exam.

For more information on topics in this section, refer to Chapter 2 of the *CompTIA Security+ Study Guide, 4th Edition* (Sybex, November 2008).

DMZ

A DMZ is a special purpose subnet. However, we need to discuss a few foundational ideas before we can properly address the topic of DMZ. First, a network comprises networking components (such as cables and switches) and hosts (such as clients and servers). Often, large networks are logically and physically subdivided into smaller interconnected networks. These smaller networks are known as subnets. Subnets are similar to the zip code areas in large cities—there is still just one city, but there are different logical divisions within that city. Subnets are usually fairly generic, but some have special uses and/or configurations.

A second important topic is security zones. *Security zones* are logical and/or physical divisions or segments of a LAN that allow for supplementary layers of security and control (see Figure 2.7). Each security zone is an area of a network that has a single defined level of security. That security may focus on authorized access, preventing access, protecting confidentiality and integrity, or limiting traffic flow. Different security zones usually host different types of resources with different levels of sensitivity.

FIGURE 2.7 A typical LAN connection to the Internet

By combining the ideas of subnets and security zones, several new types of network elements emerge. The Security+ exam focuses on three of these emergent network elements: DMZ, intranet, and extranet.

A *demilitarized zone (DMZ)* is an area of a network that is designed specifically for public users to access (see Figure 2.8). Access to a DMZ is usually controlled or restricted by a firewall and router system. The DMZ acts as a buffer network between the public untrusted Internet and the private trusted LAN. If the DMZ (as a whole or as individual systems within the DMZ) is compromised, the private LAN is unaffected and uncompromised.

FIGURE 2.8 A typical DMZ

A DMZ gives an organization the ability to offer information services, such as web browsing, FTP, and e-mail, to both the public and internal clients without compromising the security of the private LAN. Often a DMZ is deployed through the use of a multihomed firewall. Such a firewall has three interfaces: one to the Internet, one to the private LAN, and one to the DMZ.

Intranet

An *intranet* (see Figure 2.9) is any private LAN that uses the same protocol and information services as the Internet. Thus, any private network that uses TCP/IP and offers services such as web browsing, FTP, e-mail, and so on is an intranet. The use of the term *intranet* has faded as most LANs are intranets and have been for over a decade.

Extranet

An *extranet* (see Figure 2.10) is an intranet that functions as a DMZ for business-to-business transactions. It allows an organization to offer specialized services to business partners, suppliers, distributors, or customers. Extranets are based on TCP/IP and often use the common Internet information services, such as web browsing, FTP, and e-mail. Extranets aren't accessible to the general public. Extranets often require that outside entities connect using a VPN. This restricts unauthorized access and ensures that all communications with the extranet are secured. Another important security concern with extranets is that companies that are partners today may be competitors tomorrow. Thus, never place data into an extranet that you are unwilling to have a future competitor have access to.

FIGURE 2.9 An intranet network

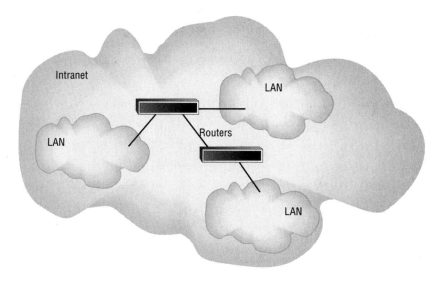

FIGURE 2.10 A typical extranet between two organizations

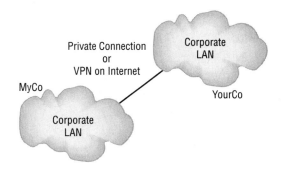

VLAN

A *virtual local area network (VLAN)* consists of subnets that are logically created out
of a single physical network. They're often created using switches (see Figure 2.11). Basi-
cally, the ports on a switch are numbered; each port is assigned the designation VLAN1 by
default. By assigning ports other designations, such as VLAN2 or VLAN3, you can create
additional virtual networks.

FIGURE 2.11 A typical segmented VLAN

VLANs function in much the same way as traditional subnets. In order for communications to travel from one VLAN to another, the switch operates as a router to control and filter traffic between its VLANs.

VLANs are used to logically segment a network without altering its physical topology. They're easy to implement, have little administrative overhead, and are a hardware-based solution.

VLANs let you control and restrict broadcast traffic and reduce a network's vulnerability to sniffers. This is due to the fact that a switch treats each VLAN as a separate subnet. In order to communicate between subnets, the switch must provide a routing function. It is the routing function that blocks broadcasts between subnets and VLANs, because a router (or devices performing Layer 3 routing functions) does not forward broadcasts. This feature of a switch blocking broadcasts between VLANs helps protect against broadcast storms. A broadcast storm is a flood of unwanted broadcast network traffic.

Tunneling is when a special protocol (such as a VPN protocol) is used to create a communication pathway (known as a *tunnel*) across an intermediary (often untrusted) network. The concept of tunneling is the basis of VPNs.

NAT

In order for systems to communicate across the Internet, they must have an Internet-capable TCP/IP address. Unfortunately, leasing a sufficient number of public IP addresses to assign one to every system on a network is expensive. Plus, assigning public IP addresses to every system on the network means those systems can be accessed (or at least addressed) directly by external benign and malicious entities. One method around this issue is to use *network address translation (NAT)* (see Figure 2.12).

FIGURE 2.12 A typical Internet connection to a local network

NAT converts the private IP addresses of internal systems found in the header of network packets into public IP addresses. It performs this operation on a one-to-one basis: Thus a single leased public IP address can allow a single internal system to access the Internet. Since Internet communications aren't usually permanent or dedicated connections, a single public IP address could effectively support three or four internal systems if they never needed Internet access simultaneously. So, when NAT is used, a larger network only needs to lease a small number of public IP addresses.

NAT provides the following benefits:

- It hides the IP addressing scheme and structure from external entities.

- It serves as a basic firewall by only allowing incoming traffic that is in response to an internal system's request.

- It reduces expense by requiring fewer leased public IP addresses.

- It allows the use of *private IP addresses* (RFC 1918).

RFC 1918

RFC 1918 defines the ranges of private IP addresses that aren't routable across the Internet. These ranges of addresses were specifically reserved for use by private networks. Anyone can use them at no expense; however, a NAT gateway must be deployed in order for systems using RFC 1918 addresses to communicate with the Internet. The ranges of IP addresses reserved for this purpose by RFC 1918 are as follows:

- 10.0.0.0–10.255.255.255 (10.0.0.0 /8 subnet): 1 Class A range

- 172.16.0.0–172.31.255.255 (172.16.0.0 /12 subnet): 16 Class B ranges

- 192.168.0.0–192.168.255.255 (192.168.0.0 /16 subnet): 255 Class C ranges

Closely related to NAT is *port address translation (PAT)*, which allows a single public IP address to host up to 65,536 simultaneous communications from internal clients (a theoretical maximum; in practice you should limit the number to 10 or less in most cases). Instead of mapping IP addresses on a one-to-one basis, PAT also uses the TCP port numbers to host multiple simultaneous communications across each public IP address.

The use of the term *NAT* in the IT industry has come to include the concept of PAT. Thus, when you hear or read about NAT, you can assume that the material is referring to PAT. This is true for most Microsoft Windows operating systems and services; it's also true of the Security+ exam.

Another issue to be familiar with is that of NAT Traversal (NAT-T). Traditional NAT does not support IPSec VPNs due to the requirements of the IPSec protocol and the changes NAT makes to packet headers. However, NAT-T was designed specifically to support IPSec and other tunneling VPN protocols, such as L2TP, so organizations can benefit from both NAT and VPNs across the same border device/interface.

Network interconnections

Network interconnections are the links between subnets and/or other networks that ultimately make up small networks, enterprise networks, and the Internet. Most network interconnections are created using either routers or switches.

A *router* (see Figure 2.13) is used to connect several network segments. Routers enable traffic from one network segment to traverse into another network segment (see Figure 2.14). However, the traffic must pass through the router's filters in order to make the transition. A common router is basically a packet filtering firewall. Routers direct traffic based on a routing table and grant or deny access using access control lists (ACLs), such as rules or filters. The routing table informs the router which direction to transmit a received packet based on the best-known pathway (route).

FIGURE 2.13 Router connecting a LAN to a WAN

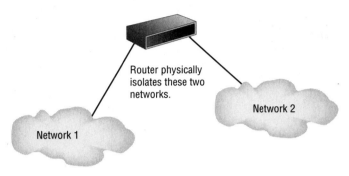

FIGURE 2.14 A corporate network implementing routers for segmentation and security

Routers can manage traffic for both inbound and outbound communications. An *ingress filter* is a traffic filter on packets coming into a secured area from outside (inbound communications). They're the best defense against IP spoofing attacks. An ingress filter should drop any packet received from an outside source that claims to have originated from an inside source.

A *switch* (see Figure 2.15) is like an intelligent multiport bridge. It receives signals in one port and transmits them out the port where the intended recipient is connected. Switches accomplish this traffic control task by maintaining a table of the MAC addresses of devices located off of each switch port. The switch examines the source MAC address of each packet it receives, and records the MAC and the related port in its MAC table. Thus the MAC table is dynamic and is constantly being updated. The switch analyzes the header of each packet it receives to determine the destination MAC address, and then transmits each packet only

out the port where that MAC address is known to reside. If a MAC address is encountered that is not known (it's not in the MAC table), the unknown destination packet is transmitted out all ports.

 VLANs are discussed in more detail in the "VLAN" section earlier in this chapter.

FIGURE 2.15 Switching between two systems

Switches are good defenses against *sniffing attacks* from random clients within a network. A switch transmits messages only on those specific network links between the source and destination systems. A sniffer could only intercept traffic that happened to be transmitted on the segment it was connect to. Thus, using switches instead of hubs is a great defense against sniffing. However, there are logical and physical attacks to overcome this protection. If a hacker can gain physical access, they can connect to the audit/monitor/mirror port or reconfigure the switch to obtain full access to all data it sees. If a hacker has only logical (network) access to the switch, then a MAC flooding attack can overload a switch's MAC table to push out valid MAC addresses and populate them with invalid MAC addresses. When this attack is successful, the switch often reverts to a hub-like fault-tolerance mode transmitting data out all ports instead of only a single port. This type of attack is often called *active sniffing*, because the hacker has to attack the switch (or sometimes hosts on the network with ARP flooding attacks) in order to obtain access to all network traffic. There are advanced switches that have native IDS-like detection and defense features to prevent MAC flooding attacks from being successful.

NAC

Network Access Control (NAC) is a concept of controlling access to an environment through strict adherence to and implementation of security policy. The goals of NAC are to prevent/reduce zero-day attacks, enforce security policy throughout the network, and use identities to perform access control. The goals of NAC can be achieved through the use of strong detailed security policies that define all aspects of security control, filtering, prevention, detection, and response for every device from client to server and for every internal or external communication. NAC is to be an automated detection and response system that is able to react in real time to stop threats as they occur and before they cause damage or

a breach. Originally, 802.1x was thought to embody NAC, but most supporters feel that 802.1x is only a simple form of NAC or just one component in a complete NAC solution.

NAC can be implemented with a pre-admission philosophy or a post-admission philosophy. The pre-admission philosophy is where a system must meet all current security requirements (such as patch application and antivirus updates) before it is allowed to communicate with the network. The post-admission philosophy is when allow/deny decisions are made based on user activity, which is based on a predefined authorization matrix. NAC can also be deployed with aspects of both of these philosophies.

Other issues around NAC include: client/system agent versus overall network monitoring (agentless); out-of-band versus inband monitoring; and resolving any remediation, quarantine, or captive portal strategies.

Many organizations have released products with the NAC concept in mind (often in the title of their offering), such as Cisco, McAfee, Symantec, and so on. There are many open-source solutions as well.

Subnetting

Subnetting is a divisioning process used on networks to divide larger groups of hosts into smaller collections. The act of subnetting may be mandated by maximum size of a subnet based on desired IP class restrictions, physical limitations, differentiation of business function, or other concerns. Subnetting is mainly a logical activity, but it can be used to direct or guide physical divisioning. In fact, many large organizations mimic their logical subnetting infrastructure in their physical deployment for easier troubleshooting and maintenance.

Subnet size is no longer strictly limited to the IP class range restrictions, such as only 254 hosts per Class C networks if CIDR subnetting is used. This topic not directly relevant to Security+, so please search on the term **CIDR** on the Internet for more information.

Ultimately, within the TCP/IP v4 protocol, subnetting is defined by the assigned host IP address and its related subnet mask. The subnet mask is a 32-bit binary number that indicates which portions of a host IP address (also a 32-bit binary number, at least for TCP/IP v4) define the network ID (or subnet ID) and which portions define the host ID. Network or subnet IDs are unique within each organization's private network or across the public Internet. Host IDs are only unique within the local subnet. In much the same way that an area code defines the general area where a phone number resides, a network ID defines where a subnet resides. Within one area code and another, there are duplicate 7-digit phone numbers, as within multiple subnets there are duplicate host IDs. However, unlike phone numbers, IP addresses are always presented with their entire complement of numbers, and when necessary or important their related subnet mask.

IP address 193.25.172.56 with a subnet mask of 255.255.0.0 can be converted from this dotted decimal notation to binary as follows:

IP address: 11000001000110011010110000111000

Subnet mask: 11111111111111110000000000000000

By reading only the portions of the IP address marked or masked by the 1s from the subnet mask, the network ID is revealed: 11000001000110010000000000000000 or 193.25.0.0.

By reading only the portions of the IP address marked or masked by the 0s from the subnet mask, the host ID is revealed: 0.0.172.56.

A host within a subnet is able to communicate directly with any other host in that same subnet. However, to communicate with hosts in other subnets, traffic must be directed out of the subnet toward the destination host's subnet. This is done by sending the data stream to the default gateway of the local subnet. The default gateway is just the interface of a router in your local subnet. The router then reads the destination IP address and directs the traffic toward its destination subnet.

Subnetting can be used to control communications, block access, divide security zones, and much more. This is only a general and generic overview of the idea of subnetting. If you are not already familiar with how to subnet TCP/IP, please consult Network+ study materials or search for this content online.

Telephony

Telephony is the collection of methods by which telephone services are provided to an organization or the mechanisms by which an organization uses telephone services for either voice and/or data communications. Traditionally, telephony included POTS or PSTN services combined with modems. However, this has expanded to include PBX, VoIP, and VPN.

A *private branch exchange (PBX)* (also known as telecom), shown in Figure 2.16, is a computer- or network-controlled telephone system. PBXs are deployed in large organizations; they offer a wide range of telephone services, features, and capabilities, including conference calls, call forwarding, paging, call logging, voicemail, call routing, and remote calling.

Remote calling is the ability to dial in to a PBX system from outside and then access a dial tone in order to place a call. The second call can be long distance, and all toll charges are accumulated on the PBX system, not on the user's telephone. This is a commonly attacked feature of PBX systems.

Methods to secure PBX systems include the following:

- Disabling maintenance features
- Changing all default passwords, accounts, and access codes
- Enabling logging
- Restricting long-distance calling
- User awareness and training

FIGURE 2.16 A modern digital PBX system integrating voice and data onto a single network connection

VoIP (voice over IP) is a tunneling mechanism used to transport voice and/or data over a TCP/IP network. VoIP has the potential to replace or supplant PSTN as it often is less expensive and offers a wider variety of options and features. VoIP can be used as a direct telephone replacement on computer networks as well as mobile devices. However, VoIP is able to support video and data transmission to allow video conferencing and even remote collaboration on projects. VoIP is available in both commercial and open source options. Some VoIP solutions require specialized hardware to either replace traditional telephone handsets/base stations or to allow these to connect to and function over the VoIP system. Some VoIP solutions are software only, such as Skype, and allow the user's existing speakers, microphone, or headset to replace the traditional telephone handset. Others are more hardware-based, such as MagicJack, which allows the use of existing PSTN phone devices plugged into a USB adapter to take advantage of VoIP over the Internet. Often, VoIP-to-VoIP calls are free (assuming the same or compatible VoIP technology) while VoIP-to-land-line calls are often at a per-minute fee.

VPN (virtual private networks) are discussed in the "VPN" section in Chapter 3.

Exam Essentials

Security zones A security zone is an area of a network that has a single defined level of security. That security may focus on authorized access, preventing access, protecting confidentiality and integrity, or limiting traffic flow. Different security zones usually host different types of resources with different levels of sensitivity.

DMZs A demilitarized zone (DMZ) is an area of a network that is designed specifically for public users to access. The DMZ is a buffer network between the public untrusted Internet and the private trusted LAN. Often a DMZ is deployed through the use of a multi-homed firewall.

Intranets An intranet is any private LAN that uses the same protocol and information services as the Internet.

Extranets An extranet is an intranet that functions as a DMZ for business-to-business transactions. Extranets let organizations offer specialized services to business partners, suppliers, distributors, or customers.

VLANs Switches are often used to create virtual LANs (VLANs)—a logical creation of subnets out of a single physical network. VLANs are used to logically segment a network without altering its physical topology. They're easy to implement, have little administrative overhead, and are a hardware-based solution.

NAT NAT converts the IP addresses of internal systems found in the header of network packets into public IP addresses. It hides the IP addressing scheme and structure from external entities. NAT serves as a basic firewall by only allowing incoming traffic that is in response to an internal system's request. It reduces expense by requiring fewer leased public IP addresses, and it allows the use of the private IP addresses (RFC 1918).

RFC 1918 RFC 1918 defines the ranges of private IP addresses that aren't routable across the Internet: 10.0.0.0–10.255.255.255 (10.0.0.0 /8 subnet), 1 Class A range; 172.16.0.0–172.31.255.255 (172.16.0.0 /12 subnet), 16 Class B ranges; and 192.168.0.0–192.168.255.255 (192.168.0.0 /16 subnet), 255 Class C ranges.

Routers Routers enable traffic from one network segment to traverse into another network segment. However, the traffic must pass through the router's filters in order to make the transition.

Switches A switch is like an intelligent multiport bridge. It receives signals in one port and transmits them out the port where the intended recipient is connected. Switches are often used to create VLANs.

Subnetting Subnetting is a divisioning process used on networks to divide larger groups of hosts into smaller collections.

PBX A private branch exchange (PBX, also known as telecom) is a computer- or network-controlled telephone system. Protections for PBX include disabling maintenance features, changing defaults, logging, and restricting long-distance calling.

VoIP VoIP (voice over IP) is a tunneling mechanism used to transport voice and/or data over a TCP/IP network. VoIP has the potential to replace or supplant PSTN as it often is less expensive and offers a wider variety of options and features.

Modems A modem is a device that creates a network communication link between two computers (or networks) over a telephone line.

2.3 Determine the appropriate use of network security tools to facilitate network security.

Networks are becoming ever more complex structures. The larger and more complex a network is, the more there is to know about its components, elements, and security needs. This section takes a look at several common network security elements and components that are addressed on the Security+ exam.

 For more information on topics in this section, refer to Chapter 2 of the *CompTIA Security+ Study Guide, 4th Edition* (Sybex, November 2008).

NIDS

Intrusion detection is an important security capability. *Intrusion detection systems (IDS)* are considered complementary security solutions to firewalls (see Figure 2.17). There are two primary types of IDS, namely network IDS (NIDS) and host IDS (HIDS). A NIDS can detect malicious activity that occurs within the network (it doesn't cross the firewall) and activity that is able to pass through the firewall. A HIDS can detect malicious activity that occurs on a single host.

FIGURE 2.17 An IDS and a firewall working together to secure a network

The most common problem with an IDS, excluding misconfiguration, is the occurrence of false positives. A *false positive* occurs when legitimate traffic or user activity is mistaken for intruder activity.

A *network-based IDS* watches network traffic in real time (see Figure 2.18). It monitors network traffic patterns, scans packet header information, and may examine the contents of packets to detect security violations or attacks. A network-based IDS is reliable for detecting network-focused attacks, such as bandwidth-based denial-of-service (DoS) attacks.

FIGURE 2.18 A network-based IDS placement in a network determines what data will be analyzed.

A *host-based IDS* watches the audit trails and log files of a host system (see Figure 2.19). This type of IDS is limited to the auditing and logging capabilities of the host system (which includes the operating system and installed applications and services). A host-based IDS can detect problems only if sufficient information is captured by the host's auditing capabilities. It's reliable for detecting attacks directed against a host, whether they originate from an external source or are perpetrated by a user locally logged in to the host.

There are two common forms of IDS detection mechanisms: *signature detection* and *anomaly detection*. Signature detection (see Figure 2.20) compares event patterns against known attack patterns (signatures) stored in the IDS database. Anomaly detection watches the ongoing activity of the environment and looks for abnormal occurrences (see Figure 2.21). In other words, anomaly-detection IDS is trained on normal activity—it looks for anything that isn't normal.

FIGURE 2.19 A host-based IDS interacting with the operating system

FIGURE 2.20 A signature-detection IDS in action

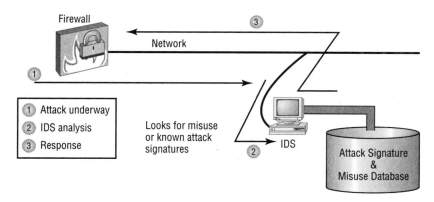

FIGURE 2.21 An anomaly-detection IDS using expert system technology to evaluate risks

An IDS with active detection and response is designed to take the quickest action to reduce the potential damage caused by an intruder (see Figure 2.22). This response may include shutting down the server or just the affected service or disconnecting suspicious connections (see Figures 2.23 and 2.24).

FIGURE 2.22 The components of an IDS working together to provide network monitoring

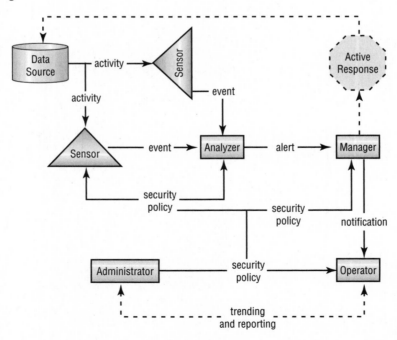

FIGURE 2.23 IDS instructing TCP to reset all connections

1. Attack detected
2. IDS analysis/response
3. TCP reset command

FIGURE 2.24 IDS instructing the firewall to close port 80 for 60 seconds to thwart an IIS attack

1. Attack occurs
2. IDS analysis/response
3. Port 80 closed

An IDS with passive detection and response will take no direct action against the intruder; instead it may increase the amount of data being audited and recorded and notify the administrators about the intrusion. IDS is good at detecting DoS attacks; exploitation of bugs, flaws, or hidden features; and port scanning. It isn't reliable for detecting spoofed e-mail. Passive IDS response is usually unseen by the intruder and does not directly affect the violating activity, whereas active IDS response is seen by the intruder as it directly interrupts and interferes with the violating activity.

NIPS

A network intrusion prevention system (NIPS) is a derivation or refinement of NIDS. However, where a NIDS seems to focus on detecting the security breach after it happens, a NIPS is focused on preventing the security breach before it occurs. Although this distinction may seem mostly semantic, it is worth discussing as a security philosophy and because of its presence on the Security+ exam.

NIPS is usually placed out of band rather than inline on the connections they are monitoring. NIPS, like NIDS, rarely is assigned an IP address and its NICs are usually without MAC addresses—thus making them invisible to the network and any attempts to probe for security barriers. A NIPS monitors network traffic looking for any abnormal or malicious content. Based upon what it detects and how it is configured, it can react in real time to interfere with any attack or intrusion attempts before they are successful against the network or any internal targets. Most commonly the response of a NIPS to malicious packets is to just drop them, thus rendering their payloads ineffective. However, NIPS can also be configured to disconnect sessions, reconfigure firewalls, as well as initiate alerts, expand monitoring, and even quarantine intruders in honeypots or padded cells.

Firewalls

A *firewall* is a hardware or software component designed to protect one network from another (see Figure 2.25). Often, firewalls are deployed between a private trusted network and a public untrusted network (such as the Internet) or between two networks that belong to the same organization but are from different departments. Firewalls provide protection by controlling traffic entering and leaving a network.

Firewalls manage traffic using *filters*. A filter is just a rule. If a packet meets the identification criteria of a rule, then the action of that rule is applied. If a packet doesn't meet the criteria of a rule, then no action from that rule is applied, and the next rule is checked.

Firewalls usually have lots of filters, which are defined in a priority order. The first rule to match criteria with a packet defines the action to take against that packet; no other subsequent rules are checked. Thus, the first rule to apply to a packet is the only rule applied to a packet.

Filter lists are created with the most specific and detailed rules first, followed by successively more general rules, until a final default universal rule is reached, which specifies denial. Therefore, if a packet fails to meet the criteria of any earlier rule, the last denial rule will always be used. This way, only packets meeting the custom-defined filters or rules are allowed to cross the security barrier.

FIGURE 2.25 A proxy firewall blocking network access from external networks

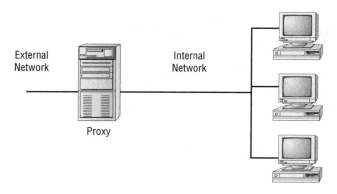

There are three basic types of firewalls, plus an additional form (stateful inspection) that combines the features of the first three:

Packet filter A *packet filter firewall* filters traffic based on basic identification items found in a network packet's header. This includes source and destination address, port numbers, and protocols used. Packet-filtering firewalls operate at the Network layer (Layer 3) of the OSI model. They can also be called *common routers*.

Circuit-level gateway A *circuit-level gateway firewall* filters traffic by monitoring the activity within a session between an internal trusted host and an external untrusted host. This monitoring occurs at the Session layer (Layer 5) of the OSI model. This type of firewall ensures that the packets involved in establishing and maintaining the circuit (a virtual circuit or session) are valid and used in the proper manner.

Application-level gateway An *application-level gateway firewall* filters traffic based on user access, group membership, the application or service used, or even the type of resources being transmitted. This type of firewall operates at the Application layer (Layer 7) of the OSI model. Such a firewall can be called a *proxy*.

Stateful inspection firewall A *stateful inspection firewall* combines features of the three basic firewall types and includes the ability to understand the context of communications across multiple packets and across multiple layers. Thus a stateful inspection firewall can make more intelligent and complex filtering decisions based on higher-order information. One of the key functions of this type of firewall is to ensure that each packet is part of an established TCP communication session. All rogue, or unassociated, packets are blocked.

The first step in effectively designing, deploying, and implementing a firewall is to design or develop a *firewall policy:* a security policy that focuses on the purposes, uses, functions, and security of the firewalls in an organization. This policy clearly defines how the firewall should filter traffic and the types of traffic that should be blocked or allowed.

Most firewalls are deployed with at least two network interfaces. Such firewalls are called *dual-homed* (see Figure 2.26) or *multihomed* (for two or more NICs). Dual- or multihomed firewalls provide a clear security distinction between one network and another; thus

packets must successfully pass the filters of a firewall in order to move from one network to another. In this manner, firewalls provide strong and reliable security.

FIGURE 2.26 A dual-homed firewall segregating two networks from each other

Some firewalls with three or more network interfaces can manage access to multiple networks simultaneously. One common deployment uses one of these additional network interfaces to connect to a demilitarized zone (DMZ). The DMZ hosts publicly accessible servers, such as Web or FTP. The firewall provides secured but public access to the DMZ, but it prevents unauthorized access to the private network. If such a multihomed firewall is compromised, only the systems in the DMZ are directly threatened or exposed.

When a port is opened in a firewall to allow a virtual private network (VPN) connection to take place, keep in mind that all encrypted data will pass through the firewall without being inspected or filtered. A firewall, unless it's the intended communication partner, is unable to view and inspect the contents of encrypted data.

Proxy servers

A proxy server is a variation of an application firewall or circuit level firewall. A proxy server is used as a proxy or middleman between clients and servers. Often a proxy serves as a barrier against external threats to internal clients. This is usually performed by hiding the IP configuration of internal clients and substituting the IP configuration of the proxy server's own public external NIC in outbound requests. This effectively prevents external hosts from learning the internal configuration of the network. A proxy server typically has the default setting to ignore all external queries and only manage communications that are responses from previous queries. Additionally proxy servers can support NAT features, provide caching, and site or content filtering.

Honeypot

A *honeypot* is a fictitious environment designed to fool and lure attackers and intruders away from the private secured network (see Figure 2.27). A honeypot is often deployed as a buffer network between an untrusted network, such as the Internet, business partners, or a DMZ, and the private network.

FIGURE 2.27 A network honeypot deceives an attacker and gathers intelligence

The honeypot looks and acts like a real system or network, but it doesn't contain any valuable or legitimate data or resources. Intruders may be fooled into wasting their time attacking and infiltrating a honeypot instead of your actual network. All the activity in the honeypot is monitored and recorded.

The purpose of deploying a honeypot is to provide an extra layer of protection for your private network and to gather sufficient evidence for prosecution against malicious intruders and attackers. A honeypot can often gather sufficient information to determine the identity of the intruder; the type of data, resource, or system being attacked or focused on; and the methods and tools of attack.

Honeypots are effective if they are easier for a hacker or intruder to find than the real private LAN being protected. Honeypots should be modestly secured so they seem like a real network, but not overly secured. The goal of a honeypot is to distract and lure attackers away from your intranet so you can learn about new attacks and potentially be able to track down criminals for prosecution. If a honeypot seems too easy or does not react and act like a real production network, experienced hackers and intruders will not be fooled and may be provoked to find and attack your actual production network.

Another form of honeypot is known as a padded cell. While a honeypot is usually a distracting network that is always on, a padded cell is a containment area that is only activated when an intrusion is detected.

Internet content filters

Internet content filters are tools used to limit access to resources that are deemed insecure or inappropriate. Filters can be configured to apply to inbound and/or outbound traffic. An outbound filter (a.k.a. egress filters) stops all outbound requests that match a filtered destination or content. Thus, the requests or traffic never make it out. An inbound filter (a.k.a. ingress filters) stop all inbound traffic that matches a filtered source or content. Thus, inbound traffic is stopped before it can cause harm, abuse, or other unwanted occurrences.

Filters often focus on blocking access to known security risky locations or sites with content that is inappropriate for the organization. This can be done via domain or URL matching or via content pattern matching. While hand-crafting filters for blocking Internet traffic is possible, there are many services that provide blacklists of known problematic locations that can be employed instead.

Internet content filters can be used by proxy servers as well as firewalls and even IDS/IPS systems.

Protocol analyzers

A protocol analyzer is a tool used to examine the contents of network traffic. Commonly known as a sniffer, a protocol analyzer can be a dedicated hardware device or software installed onto a typical host system. A protocol analyzer usually places the NIC into promiscuous mode in order to see and capture all packets on the local network segment rather than just those with the destination MAC address of its local NIC. In promiscuous mode, the NIC ignores the destination MAC address of packets and collects each one it sees.

Once a network packet is collected, it is either saved to the hard drive in a log file or retained in memory in a buffer. The protocol analyzer can examine individual packets down to the binary level. Most analyzers or sniffers automatically parse out the contents of the header into an expandable outline form. Any configuration or setting can be easily seen in the header details. The payload of packets is often displayed in both hexadecimal and ASCII.

Sniffers typically offer both capture filters and display filters. A capture filter is a set of rules to govern which packets are saved into the capture file or buffer and which are just discarded. Capture filters are used to collect only packets of interest and keep the number of retained packets to a minimum. A display filter is used to show only those packets from the packet file or buffer that match your requirements. Display filters act like search queries to locate packets of interest.

Protocol analyzers vary from simple raw packet capturing tools to fully automated analysis engines. There are both open source (such as Wireshark) and commercial (such as NetWitness and Network General) options.

Exam Essentials

IDS An intrusion detection system (IDS) is an automated system that either watches activity in real time or reviews the contents of audit logs in order to detect intrusions or security policy violations. The two types of IDS are network-based and host-based.

NIDS A network-based IDS (NIDS) watches network traffic in real time. It's reliable for detecting network-focused attacks, such as bandwidth-based DoS attacks.

HIDS A host-based IDS (HIDS) watches the audit trails and log files of a host system. It's reliable for detecting attacks directed against a host, whether they originate from an external source or are being perpetrated by a user locally logged in to the host.

Detection mechanisms Signature detection compares event patterns against known attack patterns (signatures) stored in the IDS database. Anomaly detection watches the ongoing activity of the environment and looks for abnormal occurrences.

Response methods An IDS with active detection and response is designed to take the quickest action to reduce potential damage caused by an intruder. This response may include shutting down the server or the affected service or disconnecting suspicious connections. An IDS with passive detection and response takes no direct action against the intruder; instead it may increase the amount of data being audited and recorded and notify the administrators about the intrusion.

Firewalls Firewalls provide protection by controlling traffic entering and leaving a network. They manage traffic using filters or rules.

Types of firewalls The three basic types of firewalls are packet filtering, circuit-level gateway, and application-level gateway. A fourth type combines features from these three and is called a stateful inspection firewall.

Honeypots A honeypot is a fictitious environment designed to fool and lure attackers and intruders away from the private secured network. The purpose of deploying a honeypot is to provide an extra layer of protection for your private network and to gather sufficient evidence for prosecution against malicious intruders and attackers.

Protocol analyzer A protocol analyzer is a tool used to examine the contents of network traffic.

2.4 Apply the appropriate network tools to facilitate network security.

Knowledge of the elements or tools of network security is not sufficient to protect against security breaches. One must actually apply the tools and technique to an organization's infrastructure to obtain the benefits of security. This process is known as network hardening.

Network hardening takes the concept of operating system hardening and applies it to the network. In this instance, the network includes those components on each system that support network communications: the NIC, device drivers, and protocols, as well as the network media (cables or wireless) and network devices (routers, switches, hubs, and so on). Every aspect of a network should be as secure as possible to minimize the potential entry points for an intruder or malicious code. By improving the security of the network, you gain security for each individual system.

Network hardening includes the activities of applying firmware updates and managing configuration issues.

The issue of updates for network hardening includes all the information discussed earlier for operating system hardening. You must also consider the issue of updating firmware. *Firmware* is the software code stored on memory chips in network devices (such as NIC, routers, and switches). This software code is similar to an operating system but is specifically for network devices. Keeping the firmware updated on all devices is an important part of maintaining a network's security.

 For more information on topics in this section, refer to Chapter 2 of the *CompTIA Security+ Study Guide, 4th Edition* (Sybex, November 2008).

Proper configuration of systems connected to the network directly affects the security of the overall network. A weak system serves as the weak link in an environment. If one system is compromised, it could lead to the compromise of other systems on the network. It's important to impose strong security on every computer system and device connected to a network. This includes securing systems using the aspects of operating system hardening and application hardening.

In addition to operating system hardening and application hardening, network hardening procedures should include or address the following:

- Disable all unneeded network services, applications, and protocols.

- Limit access to network devices to administrators.

- Password-protect or account-lock all configuration consoles on network devices.

- Restrict and monitor access to logical and physical console access to network devices.

- Use secure remote network devices administration tools, such as Secure Shell (SSH), instead of Telnet.

- Disable all unneeded interfaces or connections.

- Close all unused ports.

- Use a firewall to monitor and control use of ports at network borders.

- Use access control lists on all network border devices to manage access and limit network traffic.

- Use the most current version of a routing protocol or switch to a more secure routing protocol.
- Log network activity, especially on network border devices.
- Keep all network devices time synchronized.
- Securely configure or remove SNMP.

NIDS

NIDS is discussed in the previous section, specifically in the "NIDS" subsection.

Firewalls

Firewalls are discussed in the previous section, specifically in section 2.3 under the "Firewalls" subhead.

Proxy servers

Proxy servers are discussed in the previous section, specifically in section 2.3 under the "Proxy servers" subsection.

Internet content filters

Internet content filters are discussed in the previous section, specifically in section 2.3 under the "Internet content filters" subsection.

Protocol analyzers

Protocol analyzers are discussed in the previous section, specifically in section 2.3 under the "Protocol analyzers" subsection.

Exam Essentials

Network hardening Network hardening takes the concept of operating system hardening and applies it to the network. In this instance, the network consists of those components on each system that support network communications, which includes the NIC, device drivers, and protocols, as well as the network media (cables or wireless) and network devices (such as routers, switches, hubs, and so on).

Network configuration security Proper configuration of systems connected to the network directly affects the security of the overall network. A weak system serves as the weak link in an environment. If one system is compromised, it could lead to the compromise of other systems on the network.

2.5 Explain the vulnerabilities and mitigations associated with network devices.

Network devices are hosts, routers, switches, firewalls, and anything else connected to a network with some sort of cable or wireless connection. Every device used on a network throughout an organization needs to be examined in light of its unique vulnerabilities. Each device needs to be hardened according to its issues and uses. The following sections discuss issues that are common on network devices.

 For more information on topics in this section, refer to Chapter 2 of the *CompTIA Security+ Study Guide, 4th Edition* (Sybex, November 2008).

Privilege escalation

Privilege escalation is the occurrence of a user being able to obtain greater permissions, access, or privileges than what they are assigned by the organization. Privilege escalation can occur accidentally or due to administration oversight, but usually this term refers to the specific and intentional abuse of a system to steal access.

Privilege escalation can take place via weaknesses in the operating system. Often a hacker tool is used to exploit a programming flaw or buffer overflow that may allow the attacking user to obtain permanent or temporary access to the administrators group. In other cases, privilege escalation occurs through identity theft or credential compromise, such as keystroke capturing or password cracking.

Privilege escalation is a violation of security. Specifically, it is a breach of authorization restrictions and may be a breach of authentication. In order to prevent or stop privilege escalation, all operating systems should be kept current with patches from the vendor. Additionally, auditing and monitoring should be configured to watch for privilege escalation symptoms. These include repeated attempts to perform user account management by non-administrators as well as repeated attempts to access resources beyond a user's assigned authorization level.

Weak passwords

Weak passwords are short or otherwise easy to guess. Weak passwords often allow hackers or unscrupulous employees to obtain access to another person's logon credentials. Compromising weak passwords is possible through a wide variety of attacks, including password guessing or cracking.

Password guessing is an attack aimed at discovering the passwords employed by user accounts. Password guessing is often called password *cracking*. There are several forms of password-guessing attack tools: Some attempt to guess passwords by attacking a logon prompt, others try to extract passwords directly from an accounts database, and others attempt to capture authentication traffic and extract passwords out of the network packet. In most cases, the latter two options employ birthday attack (reverse hash matching) methods to discover the password used by a user account.

Hashing is a one-way function that creates a fixed-length output (known as the hash, hashing value, fingerprint, message digest, and so on) from an input of any length. A hash serves as an ID code to detect when the original data source has been altered, since no two data sources produce the same hash. Passwords are usually stored in a hashed format due to the security provided by its one-way-ness. However, even though it is not possible to reverse the hash process directly, it is possible to reverse-engineer a hash. Reverse-engineering a hash (a.k.a. reverse hash matching), is the idea of taking a potential data set, hashing it, then comparing it to the hash you wish to crack. Repeating that process until success or exhaustion with different potential data sets (i.e., possible passwords) can lead to the revealing (i.e., cracking) of passwords.

There are innumerable password-guessing tools on the Internet. No matter what tool is used to discover passwords, the most important countermeasure against password crackers is to use long, complex passwords and change them on a regular basis.

Brute force

A *brute-force* attack is designed to try every possible valid combination of characters to construct possible passwords in the attempt to discover the specific passwords used by user accounts. Brute-force attacks rarely begin at 0000001 or 000000a but rather take a statistical probability approach to the selection of possible passwords. Most noncomplex passwords under 8 characters long can be discovered in less than 30 minutes.

Longer and more complex passwords make brute-force attacks less successful. However, given enough time, a brute-force attack will always succeed. Thus, regularly changing a password will thwart the use of any discovered old passwords.

Dictionary

A *dictionary attack* performs password guessing by using a preexisting list of possible passwords. Password lists can include millions of possible passwords. Often password lists or dictionaries are constructed around topics. Thus, if an attacker knows basic information about you as a person, they can attempt to exploit human nature's propensity to select passwords using words common or familiar to you. For example, if an attacker knows that you

work in the medical industry, you have cats, and you enjoy sailing, they can select password dictionaries that include words, acronyms, and phrases common to those subjects.

Dictionary attacks are surprisingly effective against users who have not been trained in the methods and skills of creating complex passwords.

Birthday attack

A *birthday attack* is used against a specific form of cryptography called hashing. The birthday attack gets its name from a bar bet that exploits the mathematical probability of shared birthdays: It takes only 23 people in a room for there to be a greater than 50 percent probability that any two of those people share the same birthday. (The bar bet is that you'll drink for free if two people in the bar share a birthday; otherwise you'll buy the house a round of drinks.)

The birthday attack exploits a mathematical property that states that if the same mathematical function is performed on two values and the result for each is the same, then the original values are the same. This concept is often represented with the following syntax:

```
f(M)=f(M') therefore M=M'
```

Birthday attacks can be waged against any use of hashing. However, they're most commonly employed during password-guessing attacks (discussed in the following section). In a password-guessing attack, a program compares possible passwords with passwords stored in an accounts database. But passwords stored in an accounts database are secured because only their hash values are stored there. Thus, the password-cracking program first performs the same hashing function used by the secured system on each possible password before scanning the accounts database for a match. If a match is found, then the password-guessing tool has discovered a password based on the f(M)=f(M') property. This is more specifically known as *reverse hash matching*.

Back doors

The term *back door* can refer to two types of problems or attacks on a system. The first and oldest meaning of back door was a developer-installed access method that bypassed all security restrictions. The back door was a special hard-coded user account, password, or command sequence that allowed anyone with knowledge of the access hook (sometimes called a *maintenance hook*) to enter the environment and make any changes. This sounds great from a developer's perspective, especially during the coding and debugging process. Unfortunately, such programming shortcuts are often forgotten about when the product nears completion; thus, they end up in the final product. Fortunately, once a back door is discovered in a released product, the vendor usually releases a patch to remove the back door code from the installed product. The possible presence of back doors is another good reason to stay current with vendor-released updates and patches.

The second meaning of *back door* is a hacker-installed remote access client. These small, maliciously purposed tools can be easily deposited on a computer through a Trojan horse, a virus, or a website mobile code download, or even as part of an intrusion activity. Once

active on a system, they open up access ports and wait for an inbound connection. Thus, a back door serves as an access portal for a hacker so they can bypass any security restrictions and gain (or regain) access to a system. Some common back door tools include Back Orifice, NetBus, and Sub7 (all of which function on Windows). These and other common back door tools are detected and removed by virus scanners and spyware scanning tools.

Figure 2.28 shows a back door attack in progress.

FIGURE 2.28 A back door attack in progress

Preemptive measures against back doors include the following:

- Restricting mobile code from being automatically downloaded to your systems
- Using software policies to prevent unauthorized software from being installed
- Requiring software and driver signing

Default accounts

Default accounts (a.k.a. well-known accounts) are any accounts that are predefined by the vendor. Default accounts exist in operating systems, application software, and even hardware devices. These accounts can range from administrative accounts to guest user accounts. In any case, it is the responsibility of the user (or whoever deploys the product) to define a strong password for each default account and consider renaming or possibly even disabling the default accounts.

The problem with default accounts is that everyone knows they exist. If you only use passwords for authentication, an attacker only needs to figure out the password for a default account in order to gain access. This is even more problematic if you leave the default passwords on default accounts. There are many websites that maintain a current list of default accounts, passwords, and so on for commercial products that anyone can access. Check this out for yourself by searching with the keywords **default passwords**. You must be aware of the defaults of the products you deploy and change them whenever possible.

DOS

Denial-of-service attacks are discussed in an earlier section, specifically in section 2.1 under the "DOS" subhead.

Exam Essentials

Privilege escalation Privilege escalation occurs when a user account is able to obtain unauthorized access to higher levels of privileges, such as a normal user account that can perform administrative functions.

Password guessing Password guessing is an attack aimed at discovering the passwords employed by user accounts. It's often called password cracking. There are two primary categories of password-guessing tools, based on the method used to select possible passwords for a direct logon prompt or birthday attack procedure: brute force and dictionary.

Birthday attacks The birthday attack exploits a mathematical property that states that if the same mathematical function is performed on two values and the result is the same, then the original values are the same. This concept is often represented with the syntax f(M)=f(M') therefore M=M'.

Back door attacks The term *back door* can refer to two types of problems or attacks on a system: a developer-installed access method that bypasses any and all security restrictions, or a hacker-installed remote access client.

Default accounts Default accounts are any accounts that are predefined by the vendor. These are common targets of attackers.

2.6 Explain the vulnerabilities and mitigations associated with various transmission media.

Transmission media is any cable or radio transmission that is used to carry signals between a sender and a receiver. Unfortunately, outsiders, unauthorized users, or even hackers may want to intercept and eavesdrop on your communications. Depending upon the transmission media itself, this may be a difficult or easy task. The following sections discuss issues related to copper- and fiber optic–based media. For information on wireless media, please see section 2.7 later in this chapter.

For more information on topics in this section, refer to Chapter 2 of the *CompTIA Security+ Study Guide, 4th Edition* (Sybex, November 2008).

Coaxial cable, commonly known as *coax*, is a type of cable that uses a center copper conductor surrounded by an insulation sheath, which is surrounded by a metal braid that serves as the second conductor (see Figure 2.29). This conductor, in turn, is surrounded by a final insulation covering. Coax cable used in networking is similar to that used by cable television.

FIGURE 2.29 Coaxial cable construction

Networking coax cable comes in two forms: *10Base2* and *10Base5*. 10Base2, also known as *ThinNet*, supports communications of 10Mbps, is a *baseband* form of connection, and has a maximum usage length of 185 meters (hence the 2, which is 1.85 hectometers rounded up). 10Base5, also known as *ThickNet*, supports communications of 10Mbps, is a baseband form of connection, and has a maximum use length of 500 meters. ThinNet uses BNC connectors (see Figure 2.30) to connect directly to a NIC or networking device. ThickNet uses vampire taps (see Figure 2.31) to connect to an external attachment unit interface (AUI), which is connected to a NIC or networking device. A vampire tap uses sharp pins to penetrate the insulation and connect to the internal copper conductors.

FIGURE 2.30 Common BNC connectors

BNC male connector

BNC inline connector

BNC female connector

BNC T-connector

FIGURE 2.31 A vampire tap and a T-connector on a coax

Vampire Tap

The screw fang
pierces the shielding
and connects with the core.

BNC
Connector

Coax

Coax

BNC
Connector

T-Connector

Common problems with coax cable include bending it past its minimum arc radius, which breaks the center conductor; deploying it past its maximum use length, which causes *attenuation* (loss of signal strength due to excess cable length); and failing to properly terminate the cable (see Figure 2.32), which results in an inability to support communications. If ThickNet is used and vampire taps are employed, it is possible for the vampire taps to damage or sever the cable. Plus, when the vampire tap is removed, evidence of its use remains.

FIGURE 2.32 Network termination in a coax network

Twisted pair is the most common form of networking cable. It looks similar to a telephone cable, but twisted pair cabling has more wires, and its RJ-45 connector is slightly larger than the RJ-11 or RJ-14 connectors used by telephone cables. Twisted pair cabling is known as *10BaseT*. It supports 10Mbps of throughput, is a baseband form of connection (see Figure 2.33), and has a maximum use length of 100 meters. The *T* in the name indicates that the cable conductors are twisted rather than the maximum use length as was the case for 10Base2 and 10Base5.

FIGURE 2.33 Baseband versus broadband signaling

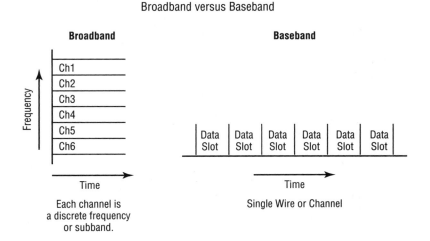

There are two forms of 10BaseT wiring: *unshielded twisted pair (UTP)* and *shielded twisted pair (STP)* (see Figure 2.34). The only difference between the two is that STP has a metal foil insulator wrapped around it just under its exterior plastic sleeve. This provides STP with a slightly greater resistance to electromagnetic interference (EMI) and reduces the effect of EMI on other cables.

FIGURE 2.34 UTP and STP cable construction

Higher throughput forms of twisted pair include 100BaseT and 1,000BaseT, which are 100Mbps (megabit Ethernet) and 1Gbps (gigabit Ethernet), respectively.

UTP and STP are commonly categorized according to their ability to support various speeds of throughput (bandwidth) for communications. Table 2.1 shows the common UTP/STP cable specifications.

Generally, twisted pair wiring is more susceptible to EMI than coax, with UTP the more vulnerable of the two. Twisted pair wiring is also vulnerable to excess cable length, which causes attenuation.

TABLE 2.1 Common UTP/STP Cable Specifications

Category	Speed	Usage
Category 1	Voice-grade cable	Used strictly for telephone and modems.
Category 2	4Mbps speed	Used extensively in older mainframe systems.
Category 3	10Mbps Ethernet	Used in 10BaseT networks.
Category 4	16Mbps	Used extensively in Token Ring networks.

TABLE 2.1 Common UTP/STP Cable Specifications *(continued)*

Category	Speed	Usage
Category 5, 5e	100Mbps, 1,000Mbps	Used in 10-, 100-, and 1,000BaseT (5e) and similar networks. The most common wiring in newer networks.
Category 6	1,000Mbps	Used in high-speed network installations. Not yet common.
Category 7	10Gbps	Used in very-high-speed network installations. Not available—a proposed standard.

Fiber optic cable (see Figure 2.35) uses pulses of light instead of electric pulses to transmit data. Thus, fiber optic cable isn't susceptible to EMI. It's also considered invulnerable to most eavesdropping and interception attacks. Although it is technically possible to eavesdrop on fiber optic cables, it is an expensive and complicated task and is usually detectible at the receiving end of the light signal.

FIGURE 2.35 Commonly used fiber connectors

Fiber optic cabling offers throughputs in excess of 1Gbps and has maximum deployment lengths of 2km to 26km. The drawbacks of fiber optic cabling include its expense, the difficulty of installing it, and its susceptibility to breakage due to cable stress, stretching, and bending.

Shielding is used to restrict or control interference from electromagnetic or radio frequency disturbances (see Figure 2.36). This can include using shielded cabling, such as *shielded twisted pair* (STP), or cabling that is resistant to interference, such as fiber optic. It can include running networking cables and electrical power source cables through shielding conduit throughout the facility. Shielding can also refer to the use of metal walls, reflective wall coatings, or TEMPEST-level emanation shielding techniques (such as Faraday cages).

FIGURE 2.36 Electromagnetic interference (EMI) pickup in a data cable

Vampire taps

While vampire taps are primarily for coax cables, there are similar devices for tapping into twisted pair and even fiber optic cables. The use of vampire taps on these other cable types is usually done for unauthorized eavesdropping purposes and often damages the cable beyond use, especially as the vampire taps are removed.

Exam Essentials

Vampire taps A vampire tap uses sharp pins to penetrate the insulation and connect to the internal copper conductors. Vampire taps were often used on ThickNet coax, but there are vampire taps for other types of media. The use of vampire taps often damages the cable.

2.7 Explain the vulnerabilities and implement mitigations associated with wireless networking.

Wireless networking has become common on both corporate and home networks. Properly managing wireless networking for reliable access as well as security isn't always an easy or straightforward proposition. This section examines various wireless security issues.

Wireless cells are the areas within a physical environment where a wireless device can connect to a wireless access point. Wireless cells can leak outside the secured environment and allow intruders easy access to the wireless network. You should adjust the strength of the wireless access point to maximize authorized user access and minimize intruder access.

Doing so may require unique placement of wireless access points, shielding, and noise transmission.

 For more information on topics in this section, refer to Chapter 2 of the *CompTIA Security+ Study Guide, 4th Edition* (Sybex, November 2008).

802.11 is the IEEE standard for wireless network communications. Various versions (technically called amendments) of the standard have been implemented in wireless networking hardware, including 802.11a, 802.11b, 802.11g, and 802.11n. 802.11x is sometimes used to collectively refer to all of these specific implementations as a group, however 802.11 is preferred as 802.11x is easily confused with 802.1x, which is an authentication technology independent of wireless. But you may see these two terms used interchangeably when discussing standard wireless issues. Each version or amendment to the 802.11 standard offered slightly better throughput: 2MB, 11MB, 54MB, and 100MB+, respectively. The 802.11 standard also defines Wired Equivalent Privacy (WEP), which provides eavesdropping protection for wireless communications.

Wired Equivalent Privacy (WEP) is defined by the IEEE 802.11 standard. It was designed to provide the same level of security and encryption on wireless networks as is found on wired or cabled networks. WEP provides protection from packet sniffing and eavesdropping against wireless transmissions.

A secondary benefit of WEP is that it can be configured to prevent unauthorized access to the wireless network. WEP uses a predefined shared secret key; however, rather than being a typical dynamic symmetric cryptography solution, the shared key is static and shared among all wireless access points and device interfaces. This key is used to encrypt packets before they are transmitted over the wireless link, thus providing confidentiality protection. A hash value is used to verify that received packets weren't modified or corrupted while in transit; thus WEP also provides integrity protection. Knowledge or possession of the key not only allows encrypted communication, but it also serves as a rudimentary form of authentication because, without it, access to the wireless network is prohibited.

WEP was cracked almost as soon as it was released. Today, it is possible to crack WEP in minutes, thus rendering it a worthless security precaution. Fortunately, there are alternatives to WEP, namely WPA and WPA-2. WPA or WiFi Protected Access is an improvement over WEP in that it does not use the same static key to encrypt all communications. Instead, it negotiates a unique key set with each host. However, a single passphrase is used to authorized the association with the base station (i.e., allow a new client to set up a connection). If the passphrase is not long enough, it could be guessed. Usually 14 characters or more for the passphrase is recommended.

WPA was not designed as the replacement for WEP; it was a temporary fix until the new 802.11i amendment was completed. The process of crafting the new amendment took years, and thus WPA established a foothold in the marketplace and is still widely used today. Additionally, WPA can be used on most devices, whereas the features of 802.11i exclude some lower-end hardware.

802.11i is the amendment that defines a cryptographic solution to replace WEP. When finalized, the WPA solution was already widely used, so they could not use the WPA name as originally planned, thus it was branded WPA-2. But this does not indicate that 802.11i is the second version of WPA. In fact, they are two completely different sets of technologies. 802.11i or WPA-2 implements concepts similar to IPSec to bring the best-to-date encryption and security to wireless communications.

Wireless networking has made networking more versatile than ever before. Workstations and portable systems are no longer tied to a cable, but can roam freely around an office or environment—anywhere within the signal range of the deployed wireless access points. However, this freedom comes at the cost of additional vulnerabilities. Wireless networks are subject to the same vulnerabilities, threats, and risks as any cabled network, plus there are the additional issues of distance eavesdropping and packet sniffing as well as new forms of DoS and intrusion.

When you're deploying wireless networks, you should deploy wireless access points configured to use *infrastructure mode* rather than *ad hoc mode*. Ad hoc mode means that any two wireless networking devices, including two wireless network interface cards (NICs), can communicate without a centralized control authority. Infrastructure mode means that a wireless access point is required, wireless NICs on systems can't interact directly, and the restrictions of the wireless access point for wireless network access are enforced.

One method used to discover areas of a physical environment where unwanted wireless access might be possible is to perform a site survey. A *site survey* is the process of investigating the presence, strength, and reach of wireless access points deployed in an environment. This task usually involves walking around with a portable wireless device, taking note of the wireless signal strength, and mapping this on a plot or schematic of the building. Site surveys should be conducted to ensure that sufficient signal strength is available at all locations that are likely locations for wireless device usage, while at the same time minimizing or eliminating the wireless signal from locations where wireless access shouldn't be permitted (public areas, across floors, into other rooms, or outside the building). A site survey is useful for evaluating existing wireless network deployments, planning expansion of current deployments, and planning for future deployments.

Data emanation

Data emanation is the transmission of data across electromagnetic signals. Almost all activities within a computer or across a network are performed using some form of data emanation. However, this term is often used to focus on emanations that are unwanted or on data that is at risk due to the emanations.

Emanations occur whenever electrons move. Movement of electrons creates a magnetic field. If you can read that magnetic field, it could be recreated elsewhere in order to reproduce the electron stream. If the original electron stream was used to communicate data, then the recreated electron stream is also a recreation of the original data. This form of electronic eavesdropping sounds like science fiction, but it is science fact. The U.S. government has been researching emanation security since the 1950s under the TEMPEST project.

To protect against eavesdropping and data theft requires a multipronged effort. First, maintain physical access control over all electronic equipment. Second, where physical access or proximity is still possible for unauthorized personnel, use shielded devices and media. Third, always transmit any sensitive data using secure encryption protocols.

War driving

War driving is the act of using a detection tool to look for wireless networking signals. Often, war driving is used to describe someone looking for a wireless network they are not authorized to access. In a way, war driving is performing a site survey for possibly malicious or at least unauthorized purposes. War driving derives its name from the legacy attack concept of war dialing, which was used to discover active computer modems by dialing all numbers in a prefix or area code.

War driving can be performed with a dedicated handheld detector, with a PDA with WiFi capabilities, or a notebook with a wireless network card. War driving can be performed using native features of the OS, or specialized scanning and detecting tools can be used.

Once a wireless network is detected, the next step is to determine if the network is open or closed. An open network has no technical limitations as to what devices can connect to it, while a closed network has technical limitations to prevent unauthorized connections. If the network is closed, an attacker may try to guess or crack the technologies preventing the connection. Often, the closed feature is just disabling SSID broadcasting. This restriction is easily overcome with a wireless SSID scanner (see the next section for more information). Following this, the next step for a hacker is to determine if encryption is in use, what type is in use, and if it is possible to overcome that protection.

SSID broadcast

Wireless networks traditionally announce their SSID on a regular basis within a special packet known as the beacon frame. When the SSID is broadcast, any device with an automatic detect and connect feature is not only able to see the network, they can initiate a connection with the network. Network administrators may choose to disable SSID broadcast to hide their network from unauthorized personnel. However, the SSID is still needed to direct packets to and from the base station, so it is still a discoverable value with a wireless packet sniffer. Thus, the SSID should be disabled if the network is not for public use, but realize that hiding the SSID is not true security as any hacker with basic wireless knowledge can easily discover the SSID.

Blue jacking

Blue jacking is the sending of messages to Bluetooth-capable devices without the permission of the owner/user. Just about any Bluetooth-enabled device, such as a PDA, cell phone, and even notebook computers, can receive a blue jacked message. Most blue jacking is the sending of a vCard (a virtual business card) to a target device over the OBEX protocol (which

is also used by infrared communications). Bluetooth on most PDA and cell phone devices is only accessible from 10 meters away or less, while on a notebook Bluetooth may be accessible from up to 100 meters away.

A blue jack message is often positioned in the name field of the vCard, with little to nothing else. This limits the messages to short strings of text. But still, this stunt can be used to pull off various pranks, teasing, and even advertisements. Some multimedia message–capable phones are also able to receive images and sound. Blue jacking is mostly harmless as it does not contain any malicious code, or at least has not so far.

Bluesnarfing

Bluesnarfing is the unauthorized accessing of data via a Bluetooth connection. Often the term *blue jacking* is mistakenly used to describe or label the activity of bluesnarfing. Successful bluesnarfing attacks against PDAs, cell phones, and notebooks have been able to extract calendars, contact lists, text messages, e-mails, pictures, videos, and more. Because bluesnarfing is the stealing of data, it is illegal in most countries.

Bluesnarfing typically occurs over a paired link between the hacker's system and the target device. If the device is not enabled to be seen by the public (i.e., discoverable) or to allow pairing, bluesnarfing is usually not possible. There was a Bluetooth flaw that could be exploited to perform bluesnarfing against phones that were set up as private, but this has long since been patched. It is true that bluesnarfing is also possible against non-discoverable devices if you know their Bluetooth MAC address, but this is usually not a practical attack as the 48-bit address must be guessed.

Rogue access points

One vulnerability commonly discovered during a site survey is the presence of rogue wireless access points. A wireless access point can be connected to any open network port or cable. Such unauthorized access points usually aren't configured for security or, if they are, aren't configured properly or in line with the organization's approved access points. Rogue wireless access points should be discovered and removed in order to eliminate an unregulated access path into your otherwise secured network.

It is not an uncommon tactic for an attacker to find a way to visit your company (via a friend who is an employee or by going on a company tour, posing as a repair man or breakfast taco seller, or even breaking in at night) in order to plant a rogue access point. After a rogue access point is positioned, an attacker can gain entry to the network easily from a modest distance away from your front door.

Weak encryption

Weak keys and weak encryption are not attacks but rather are vulnerabilities in how a cryptography system is used that make various types of attacks possible. The term *weak keys* implies that the cryptographic key selected to encrypt a file or a communication

session is either too short or too easily guessed. Weak keys are generally anything less than 64 bits in length. As a result of weak keys, attackers have an easier time cracking encrypted communications because they have to try fewer possible permutations during a full brute-force attack than they would for strong keys (those at least 128 bits long). In general, you should avoid using weak keys by only using cryptography solutions that use longer, stronger keys.

Mathematical attacks are a specific type of attacks against cryptography. They're directed against the algorithm in an attempt to exploit the arithmetic it employs. The goal of a mathematical attack is to either decrypt an encrypted message or to discover the key used for encryption.

Weak encryption can also describe any cryptography system that either has a design or implementation flaw or is being asked to provide security beyond its capabilities. This is unfortunately a recurring event across the globe as organizations use poor cryptography or use good cryptography poorly. One example of this is the WEP system from 802.11. WEP is based on RC4, but due to flaws in design and implementation, WEP is weak in several areas, two of which are the use of a static common key and poor implementation of IVs (initiation vectors). Due to these weaknesses, a WEP crack can reveal the WEP key after it finds enough poorly used IVs. When the WEP key is known, the attacker can join the network, then listen in on all other wireless client communications.

Exam Essentials

Data emanation Data emanation is the transmission of data across electromagnetic signals. Almost all activities within a computer or across a network are performed using some form of data emanation.

War driving War driving is the act of using a detection tool to look for wireless networking signals. Often, war driving is used to describe someone looking for a wireless network they are not authorized to access.

SSID broadcast Wireless networks traditionally announce their SSID on a regular basis within a special packet known as the beacon frame. When the SSID is broadcast, any device with an automatic detect and connect feature is not only able to see the network, they can initiate a connection with the network.

Blue jacking Blue jacking is the sending of messages to Bluetooth-capable devices without the permission of the owner/user, usually as a prank.

Bluesnarfing Bluesnarfing is the unauthorized accessing of data via a Bluetooth connection. Bluesnarfing is data theft and therefore a crime.

Rogue access points A rogue wireless access point can be connected to any open network port or cable. Such unauthorized access points usually aren't configured for security or, if they are, aren't configured properly or in line with the organization's approved access points. Rogue wireless access points should be discovered and removed in order to eliminate an unregulated access path into your otherwise secured network.

Weak encryption Weak encryption is any cryptography system that either has a design or implementation flaw or is being asked to provide security beyond its capabilities.

802.11 and 802.11x 802.11 is the IEEE standard for wireless network communications. Versions include 802.11a (2 MB), 802.11b (11 MB), and 802.11g (54 MB). The 802.11 standard also defines Wired Equivalent Privacy (WEP).

WEP Wired Equivalent Privacy (WEP) is defined by the IEEE 802.11 standard. It was designed to provide the same level of security and encryption on wireless networks as is found on wired or cabled networks. WEP provides protection from packet sniffing and eavesdropping against wireless transmissions. A secondary benefit of WEP is that it can be configured to prevent unauthorized access to the wireless network. WEP uses a predefined shared secret key.

Site surveys A site survey is the process of investigating the presence, strength, and reach of wireless access points deployed in an environment. Site surveys should be conducted to ensure that sufficient signal strength is available at all locations that are likely locations for wireless device usage, while at the same time minimizing or eliminating the wireless signal from locations where wireless access shouldn't be permitted.

Review Questions

1. Firewalls provide security through what mechanism?

 A. Watching for intrusions

 B. Controlling traffic entering and leaving a network

 C. Requiring strong passwords

 D. Preventing misuse of company resources

2. A switch can be used to prevent broadcast storms between connected systems through the use of what?

 A. SSL

 B. S/MIME

 C. VLANs

 D. LDAP

3. Which form of cable media is least vulnerable to eavesdropping?

 A. Fiber optic

 B. STP

 C. Coax

 D. Wireless

4. What is a blind FTP site?

 A. A site where users don't authenticate

 B. A site where all traffic is encrypted

 C. A site where only anonymous access is allowed

 D. A site where users can upload but not download

5. Which of the following allows the deployment of a publicly accessible web server without compromising the security of the private network?

 A. Intranet

 B. DMZ

 C. Extranet

 D. Switch

6. Which of the following is *not* one of the IP address ranges reserved for private use by RFC 1918?

 A. 10.0.0.0–10.255.255.255

 B. 192.168.0.0–192.168.255.255

 C. 169.254.0.0–169.254.255.255

 D. 172.16.0.0–172.31.255.255

7. A network-based IDS is *not* suitable for detecting or protecting against which of the following?

 A. E-mail spoofing

 B. Denial-of-service attacks

 C. Attacks against the network

 D. Attacks against an environment that produce significant traffic

8. What tool is used to lure or retain intruders in order to gather sufficient evidence without compromising the security of the private network?

 A. Firewall

 B. IDS

 C. Router

 D. Honeypot

9. Which of the following is a denial-of-service attack that uses network packets that have been spoofed so that the source and destination address are that of the victim?

 A. Land

 B. Teardrop

 C. Smurf

 D. Fraggle

10. What is the purpose of a site survey?

 A. Improve wireless signal strength

 B. Eliminate unwanted access locations

 C. Distribute WEP keys

 D. Plan the design of a wired network

Answers to Review Questions

1. B. Firewalls provide protection by controlling traffic entering and leaving a network.

2. C. Switches can create VLANs. Broadcast storms aren't transmitted between one VLAN and another.

3. A. Fiber optic cable is nearly invulnerable to eavesdropping.

4. D. At a blind FTP site, users can upload but not download. An anonymous FTP site is one where users don't authenticate and possibly where only anonymous access is allowed. Only through S/FTP or by using FTP inside SSL or a VPN link is all traffic encrypted.

5. B. A DMZ provides a network segment where publicly accessible servers can be deployed without compromising the security of the private network.

6. C. The 169.254.0.0–169.254.255.255 range is the Automatic Private IP Addresses (APIPA) range of addresses that are automatically assigned to Windows clients when a DHCP server isn't reachable.

7. A. Network-based IDSs aren't suitable for protecting against e-mail spoofing.

8. D. A honeypot is used to lure or retain intruders in order to gather sufficient evidence without compromising the security of the private network.

9. A. A land DoS attack uses network packets that have been spoofed so that the source and destination address are that of the victim. A teardrop attack uses fragmented IP packets. Smurf and fraggle attacks use spoofed ICMP and UDP packets, respectively, against an amplification network.

10. B. The purpose of a site survey is to eliminate unwanted access locations. Site surveys aren't used to improve wireless signal strength, distribute WEP keys, or plan the design of a wired network.

Chapter

3

Access Control

COMPTIA SECURITY+ EXAM OBJECTIVES COVERED IN THIS CHAPTER INCLUDE THE FOLLOWING:

✓ **3.1 Identify and apply industry best practices for access control methods.**

- Implicit deny
- Least privilege
- Separation of duties
- Job rotation

✓ **3.2 Explain common access control models and the differences between each.**

- MAC
- DAC
- Role & Rule based access control

✓ **3.3 Organize users and computers into appropriate security groups and roles while distinguishing between appropriate rights and privileges.**

✓ **3.4 Apply appropriate security controls to file and print resources.**

✓ **3.5 Compare and implement logical access control methods.**

- ACL
- Group policies
- Password policy
- Domain password policy
- User names and passwords
- Time of day restrictions
- Account expiration
- Logical tokens

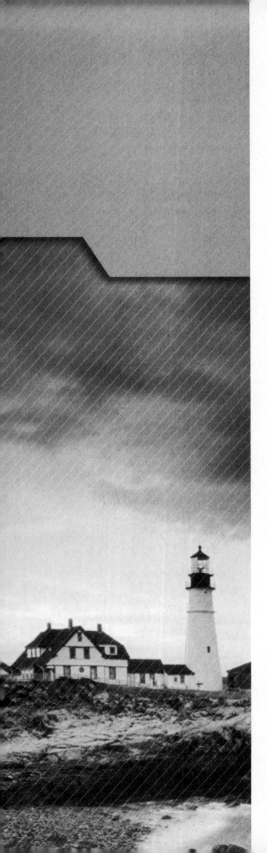

✓ **3.6 Summarize the various authentication models and identify the components of each.**

- One, two and three-factor authentication
- Single sign-on

✓ **3.7 Deploy various authentication models and identify the components of each.**

- Biometric reader
- RADIUS
- RAS
- LDAP
- Remote access policies
- Remote authentication
- VPN
- Kerberos
- CHAP
- PAP
- Mutual
- 802.1x
- TACACS

✓ **3.8 Explain the difference between identification and authentication (identity proofing).**

✓ **3.9 Explain and apply physical access security methods.**

- Physical access logs/lists
- Hardware locks
- Physical access control – ID badges
- Door access systems
- Man-trap
- Physical tokens
- Video surveillance – camera types and positioning

The Security+ exam will test your basic IT security skills—those skills needed to effectively secure stand-alone and networked systems in a corporate environment. To pass the test and be effective in implementing security, you need to understand the basic concepts and terminology related to access control as detailed in this chapter.

3.1 Identify and apply industry best practices for access control methods.

Access control or privilege management refers to controlling and managing users and their privileges and activities within a secured environment. Managing user privileges is a key element in maintaining security. About 80 percent of the security violations that companies experience originate from within their secured facility. This means an organization is more at risk from its own users than from external intruders and hackers. Thus, privilege management is necessary to sustain a secure and productive network. Issues of privilege management are discussed in the following sections.

For more information on privilege management, see Chapter 3 of the *CompTIA Security+ Study Guide, 4th Edition* (Sybex, November 2008).

Privilege management is often addressed using one of three primary schemes: user, group, or role. These schemes correspond directly to the access control methodologies of *Discretionary Access Control (DAC)*, *Mandatory Access Control (MAC)*, and *Role-Based Access Control (RBAC)*. These access control models are discussed in section 3.2.

Implicit deny

Implicit deny is the default security stance that if you are not specifically granted access or privileges over a resource, you are denied access by default. This default deny statement is implicit in the permission management system and does not need to be specifically defined. This is usually different on firewall and router access rule sets, where a default deny all rule must be included as the last rule. Implicit deny is the default response when an implicit allow or deny is not present.

Least privilege

Least privilege (a.k.a. the principle of least privilege) is the security stance that users are granted only the minimum necessary access, permissions, and privileges that are required for them to accomplish their work tasks. This ensures that users are unable to perform any task beyond the scope of their assigned responsibilities.

Separation of duties

Separation of duties is the division of administrator or privileged tasks into distinct groupings; in turn, each grouping is individually assigned to unique administrators. The application of separation of duties results in no one user having complete access or power over an entire network, server, or system. Each administrator has his or her own uniquely defined area of responsibility and privileges only within that specifically assigned area. If an administrator goes rogue or his or her account is compromised, the entire network is not automatically compromised.

Separation of duties is the application of the principle of least privilege to administrative users. However, it also requires that several administrators work together to perform high-risk, sweeping tasks in an organization. This helps prevent fraud, reduce errors, and prevent conflicts of interest. For example, those who configure security should not be the same people who test security; those who are in accounts receivable should not be performing accounts payable; and those who are programmers should not be the same people who test code and approve applications for deployment.

Job rotation

Job rotation, cross-training, and rotation of duties are counterbalances to the application of separation of duties. If all high-level tasks are performed by individual administrators, what happens if one person leaves the organization? If no one else has the knowledge to perform the tasks, the organization suffers. By implementing job rotation, multiple people have the knowledge to perform each task. Those people do not always have the permissions to perform those tasks, but they can be called upon if needed to perform them once the privileges are granted. This reduces the risk of a person leaving the organization who happens to be the only individual with the proprietary knowledge or know-how of a mission-critical function. The implementation of job rotation reduces the administrative impact to the organization by employing multiple administrators who are cross-trained in their respective job roles. This helps guarantee continued administrative support for a specific role or job function in the event of a loss in administrative personnel.

Exam Essentials

Principle of least privilege The principle of least privilege is a security rule of thumb that states that users should be granted only the level of access needed for them to accomplish

assigned work tasks, and no more. Furthermore, those privileges should be assigned for the shortest time period possible.

Privileges A privilege is an ability or activity that a user account is granted permission to perform. User accounts are often assigned privileges based upon their work tasks and their normal usage.

Implicit deny Implicit deny is the default security stance that if you are not specifically granted access or privileges over a resource, you are denied access by default.

Separation of duties Separation of duties is the division of administrator or privileged tasks into distinct groupings, with each group in turn assigned to unique administrators. The application of separation of duties results in no single user having complete access or power over an entire network, server, or system.

Job rotation Job rotation means there are multiple people who have the knowledge to perform each highly privileged task. Those people do not always have the permissions to perform those tasks, but they can be called upon if needed to perform them once the privileges are granted. This reduces the risk of a person leaving the organization who happens to be the only individual who has the proprietary knowledge or know-how of a mission-critical function.

3.2 Explain common access control models and the differences between each.

The mechanism by which users are granted or denied the ability to interact with and use resources is known as *access control*. Access control is often referred to using the term *authorization*. Authorization defines the type of access to resources users are granted—in other words, what users are authorized to do. Authorization is often considered the next logical step immediately after authentication. *Authentication* is proving your identity to a system or the act of logging on. With proper authorization or access control, a system will properly control access to resources in order to prevent unauthorized access.

 For more information on this topic, refer to Chapter 3 of the *CompTIA* Security+ Study Guide, 4th Edition (Sybex, November 2008).

There are three common access control methods:

- Mandatory Access Control *(MAC)*
- Discretionary Access Control *(DAC)*
- Role-Based Access Control *(RBAC)*

These three models are widely used in today's IT environments. Familiarity with these three models is essential to the Security+ exam.

 These three access control models aren't mutually exclusive. Two or more of them can be deployed simultaneously in a single environment.

MAC

MAC (Mandatory Access Control) is a form of access control commonly employed by government and military environments. MAC specifies that access is granted based on a set of rules rather than at the discretion of a user. The rules that govern MAC are hierarchical in nature and are often called *sensitivity labels, security domains,* or *classifications.* MAC environments define a few specific security domains or sensitivity levels, and then use the associated labels from those domains to impose access control on objects and subjects.

A government or military implementation of MAC typically includes the following five levels (in order from least sensitive to most sensitive):

- Unclassified
- Sensitive but unclassified
- Confidential
- Secret
- Top secret

Objects or resources are assigned sensitivity labels corresponding to one of these security domains. Each specific security domain or level defines the security mechanisms and restrictions that must be imposed in order to provide protection for objects within that domain.

MAC can also be deployed in private sector or corporate business environments. Such cases typically involve the following four security domain levels (in order from least sensitive to most sensitive):

- Public
- Sensitive
- Private
- Confidential

The primary purpose of a MAC environment is to prevent *disclosure*: the violation of the security principle of *confidentiality*. When an unauthorized user gains access to a secured resource, this is a security violation. Objects are assigned a specific sensitivity label based on the damage that would be caused if disclosure occurred. For example, if a top secret resource was disclosed, it could cause grave damage to national security.

A MAC environment works by assigning subjects a *clearance level* and assigning objects a *sensitivity label*—in other words, everything is assigned a classification marker. *Subjects* or users are assigned clearance levels. The name of the clearance level is the same as the name of the sensitivity label assigned to *objects* or resources. A person (or other subject, such as a program or a computer system) must have the same or greater assigned clearance level as the resources they wish to access. In this manner, access is granted or restricted based on the rules of classification (that is, sensitivity labels and clearance levels).

MAC is named as it is because the access control it imposes on an environment is mandatory. Its assigned classifications and the resulting granting and restriction of access can't be altered by users. Instead, the rules that define the environment and judge the assignment of sensitivity labels and clearance levels control authorization.

MAC isn't a very granularly controlled security environment. An improvement to MAC includes the use of *need to know*: a security restriction where some objects (resources or data) are restricted unless the subject has a need to know them. The objects that require a specific need to know are assigned a sensitivity label, but they're compartmentalized from the rest of the objects with the same sensitivity label (within the same security domain). The need to know is a rule in and of itself, which states that access is granted only to users who have been assigned work tasks that require access to the cordoned-off object. Even if a user has the proper level of clearance, without need to know he or she is denied access. Need to know is the MAC equivalent of the principle of least privilege from DAC (described in the following section).

DAC

DAC (Discretionary Access Control) is the form of access control or authorization that is used in most commercial and home environments. DAC is user directed or, more specifically, controlled by the owner and creators of the objects (resources) in the environment. DAC is identity based: Access is granted or restricted by an object's owner based on user identity and on the discretion of the object owner. Thus, the owner or creator of an object can decide which users will be granted or denied access to their object.

DAC uses *access control lists (ACLs)*. An ACL is a security logical device attached to every object and resource in the environment. It defines which users are granted or denied the various types of access available based on the object type. Individual user accounts or user groups can be added to an object's ACL and granted or denied access.

If your user account isn't granted access through an object's ACL, then you're denied access by default. If your user account is specifically granted access through an object's ACL, then you're granted the specific level or type of access defined. If your user account is specifically denied access through an object's ACL, then you're denied the specific level or type of access defined. In some cases (such as with Microsoft Windows OSes), a Denied setting in an ACL overrides all other settings. Table 3.1 shows an access matrix for a user who is a member of three groups, and the resulting access to a folder on a network server. As you can see, the presence of the Denied setting overrides any other access granted from another group. Thus, if your membership in one user group grants you write access over an object, but another group specifically denies you write access to the same object, then you're denied write access to the object.

TABLE 3.1 Cumulative Access Based on Group Memberships

Sales Group	User Group	Research Group	Resulting Access
Change	Read	None specified	Change
Read	Read	Change	Change
None specified	Read	Denied	Denied
Full Control	Denied	None specified	Denied

The security concept of the *principle of least privilege* is connected to DAC. The principle of least privilege states that users should be granted only the minimum level of access that is necessary for them to perform their work tasks, and no more.

Role & Rule Based Access Control

Role Based Access Control (RBAC) is another form of rules based access control. It may be grouped with the nondiscretionary access control methods along with MAC. The rules used for RBAC are basically job descriptions: Users are assigned a specific role in an environment, and access to objects is granted based on the necessary work tasks of that role. For example, the role of backup operator may be granted the ability to back up every file on a system to a tape drive. The user given the backup operator role would then be able to perform that function.

RBAC is most suitable for environments with a high rate of employee turnover. It allows the job descriptions or roles to remain static even when the user performing that role changes often.

The acronym RBAC has a second definition: *Rule* Based Access Control. This form of access control is typically used in relation to network devices that filter traffic based on filtering rules. Be sure you understand the context of the Security+ exam question before assuming *Role* or *Rule* when you see RBAC.

Exam Essentials

User, group, and role management Privilege management can be addressed using one of three primary schemes: user, group, or role. These schemes correspond directly to the access control methodologies of DAC, MAC, and RBAC.

MAC Mandatory Access Control (MAC) is based on classification rules. Objects are assigned sensitivity labels. Subjects are assigned clearance labels. Users obtain access by having the proper clearance for the specific resource. Classifications are hierarchical.

Common MAC hierarchies Government or military MAC uses the following levels: unclassified, sensitive but unclassified, confidential, secret, and top secret. Private sector or corporate business environment MAC uses these: public, sensitive, private, and confidential.

DAC Discretionary Access Control (DAC) is based on user identity. Users are granted access through ACLs on objects, at the discretion of the object's owner or creator.

RBAC Role-Based Access Control (RBAC) is based on job description. Users are granted access based on their assigned work tasks. RBAC is most suitable for environments with a high rate of employee turnover.

3.3 Organize users and computers into appropriate security groups and roles while distinguishing between appropriate rights and privileges.

Being able to organize users and computers into appropriate security groups and roles is an important part of establishing and maintaining the security of an organization. Often, this sorting process is dependent upon the mission and goals of the organization, the collection of job tasks, and the classification of both subjects (users) and objects (resources). Once this organizational scheme is defined and applied, distinguishing and determining appropriate rights and permissions is often a function of the application of the principle of least privilege and separation of duties.

There are two overarching approaches to privilege management: centralized and decentralized. In centralized privilege management, a single server (or set of servers) is responsible for managing, controlling, and implementing all security controls, access rights, and privileges. A domain network and a RADIUS authentication server are great examples of centralized privilege management solutions. In decentralized privilege management, each system is responsible for managing, controlling, and implementing security controls, access rights, and privileges. A workgroup network is a perfect example of a decentralized privilege management solution.

Exam Essentials

Centralized privilege management In centralized privilege management, a single server (or set of servers) is responsible for managing, controlling, and implementing all security

controls, access rights, and privileges. A domain network and a RADIUS authentication server are great examples of centralized privilege management solutions.

Decentralized privilege management In decentralized privilege management, each system is responsible for managing, controlling, and implementing security controls, access rights, and privileges. A workgroup network is an example of a decentralized privilege management solution.

3.4 Apply appropriate security controls to file and print resources.

The application of appropriate security controls to file and print resources is dependent upon the mission and goals of the organization, the collection of job tasks, and the classification of both subjects (users) and objects (resources). Once the organizational scheme is defined and applied, distinguishing and determining appropriate security controls for file and print resources is often a function of the application of the principle of least privilege and separation of duties.

3.5 Compare and implement logical access control methods.

In addition to the foundational access control methodologies of MAC, DAC, and RBAC, other logical methods of access or privilege management can be applied. These include applications specific to an access control model as well as those completely independent of such models.

ACL

An access control list (ACL) is a collection of usernames and group names with specific permission allow/deny assignments embedded onto a resource object. An ACL contains individual access control entries (ACEs) that each focus on a single user or group.

Group policies

A group policy is a tool of Windows environments (typically Microsoft Active Directory networks) that allows centralized control and management over Windows client and server

systems with a network (a.k.a. domain). A group policy is basically a text file of Registry settings that are applied to a system during startup or bootup as the system rejoins the domain and/or as users log on. Group policies or group policy objects (GPOs) can be applied to computer containers of local, site, domain, or organizational units. GPOs are used to define settings such as password policies, auditing policies, and various security configurations.

Password policy

A password policy is both a set of rules written out as part of the organizational security policy that dictates the requirements of user and device passwords as well as a technical enforcement tool (typically a native part of an operating system) that enforces the password rules. The password policy typically comprises the requirements for minimum password length, maximum password age, minimum password age, password history retention, and some sort of complexity requirement. This latter setting often enforces a minimum of three out of four standard character types (uppercase and lowercase letters, numbers, and symbols) to be represented within the password, along with disallowing the username, real name, and e-mail address from appearing within the password.

Generally, passwords over 12 characters are considered fairly secure, and those over 15 characters are considered very secure. Usually, the more characters in a password, along with some character type complexity, the more resistant it is to password-cracking techniques, specifically brute force attacks. Requiring regular password changes, such as every 90 days, and forbidding the reuse of previous passwords (password history) will improve the security of a system that uses passwords as the primary means of authentication.

Domain password policy

A domain password policy is the password policy within a GPO that is applied throughout a Microsoft Active Directory domain to all Windows domain members. Within an Active Directory domain, password policy can be set only at the domain level. Thus, it is not possible to set or modify the domain password policy at the local, site, or organizational unit (OU) levels.

User names and passwords

The combination of a username and a *password* is the most common form of authentication (see Figure 3.1). If the provided password matches the password stored in a system's accounts database for the specified user, then that user is authenticated to the system. However, just because using a username and password is the most common form of authentication, that doesn't mean it's the most secure. On the contrary, it's generally considered to be the least secure form of authentication.

FIGURE 3.1 A basic logon process employing a username and password

Logon or Security Server

Numerous means to improve the basic username/password combination have been developed. First is the storage of passwords in an accounts database in an encrypted form. Typically that form is the hash value from a one-way hash function. Second is the use of an authentication protocol (or mechanism) that prevents the transmission of passwords in an easily readable form over a network or especially the Internet. Third, strong (complex) passwords are often enforced at a programmatic level. This is used to ensure that only passwords that are difficult for a password-cracking tool to discover are allowed by the system.

The strength of a password is generally measured in the amount of time and effort involved in breaking the password through various forms of cryptographic attacks. These attacks are collectively known as *password cracking* or *password guessing*. A weak password invariably uses only alphanumeric characters; often employs dictionary or other common words; and may include user profile–related information such as birthdates, Social Security numbers, and pet names.

Strong passwords consist of numerous characters (eight or more); include at least three types of characters (uppercase and lowercase letters, numerals, and keyboard symbols); are changed on a regular basis (every 30 days); don't include any dictionary or common words or acronyms; and don't include any part of the subject's real name, username, or e-mail address.

Passwords should be strong enough to resist discovery through attack but easy enough for the person to remember. This can sometimes be a difficult line to walk.

Time of day restrictions

Time of day restrictions are limitations on what time of day, and often what day of the week, a specific user account can log onto the network or a specific system can be accessed by users. This is a tool and technique for limiting access to sensitive environments to normal business hours where oversight and monitoring can be performed to prevent fraud, abuse, or intrusion.

Account expiration

Account expiration is an often unused feature of some operating systems' user accounts that automatically disables or expires a user account at a specific time and on a specific day. Account expiration is a secure feature to employ on user accounts for temporary workers, interns, or consultants. Workers who need valid user accounts but whose employment or access will expire at a specific known date and time can be preconfigured to become disabled. In most cases, such accounts can be reenabled after they expire and new or updated expiration dates established at any time.

Logical tokens

A *token* is a form of authentication factor that is something you have. It's usually a hardware device, but it can be implemented in software as a logical token. A token is used to generate temporary single-use passwords for the purpose of creating stronger authentication. In this way, a user account isn't tied to a single static password. Instead, the user must be in physical possession of the password-generating device. The user enters the currently valid password from the token as his or her password during the logon process.

There are several forms of tokens. Some tokens generate passwords based on time, whereas others generate passwords based on challenges from the authentication server. In either case, the user can use (or attempt to use) the generated password just once before they must either wait for the next time window or request another challenge. Passwords that can only be used once are known as *one-time passwords*. This is the most secure form of password, because regardless of whether its use results in a successful logon, that one-use password is never valid again for reuse. One-time passwords can be employed only when a token device is used, due to the complexity and ever-changing nature of the passwords.

A token may be a device like a small calculator with or without a keypad. It may also be a high-end smartcard (see Figure 3.2). When properly deployed, a token-based authentication system is more secure than a password-only system.

FIGURE 3.2 The smartcard authentication process

Exam Essentials

ACL An access control list (ACL) is the collection of usernames and group names with specific permission allow/deny assignments embedded onto a resource object.

Password policy A password policy is both a set of rules written out as part of the organizational security policy that dictates the requirements of user and device passwords as well as a technical enforcement tool (typically a native part of an operating system) that enforces the password rules.

Domain password policy A domain password policy is the password policy within a GPO that is applied throughout a Microsoft Active Directory domain to all Windows domain members.

3.6 Summarize the various authentication models and identify the components of each.

Authentication is the mechanism by which a person proves their identity to a system. It is little more than the process of proving that a subject is the valid user of an account. Often the authentication process involves a simple username and password. But other more complex authentication factors or credential-protection mechanisms are involved in order to provide strong protection for the logon and account-verification process. The authentication process requires that the subject provide an identity and then proof of that identity. Identity proofing typically takes the form of one or more of the following three authentication factors:

- *Something you know* (such as a password)
- *Something you have* (such as a smartcard)
- *Something you are* (such as a fingerprint)

For more information on this topic, refer to Chapter 3 of the *CompTIA* Security+ Study Guide, 4th Edition (Sybex, November 2008).

This section discusses the specific authentication factors of passwords, tokens, and biometrics. In addition, it addresses the concepts of multi-factor and mutual authentication.

One, two and three-factor authentication

Multi-factor authentication is the requirement that a user must provide two or more authentication factors in order to prove their identity. There are three generally recognized categories of authentication factors:

- Something you know (such as a password)
- Something you have (such as a token)
- Something you are (such as a biometric)

When only one authentication factor is used, this is known as *single factor authentication* (or rarely one factor authentication). When two different authentication factors are used, this is known as *two factor authentication* (see Figure 3.3). If two or more authentication factors are used but some of them are of the same type, then this is known as *strong authentication*. Whenever different factors are used (whether two or three), this is always a more secure solution than any number of the same authentication factors. This is due to the fact that with two or more different factors, two or more different types of attacks must take place in order to steal or capture the authentication factor itself. With strong authentication, even if 10 passwords are required, only a single type of password-stealing attack needs to be waged to break through the authentication security.

FIGURE 3.3 Two factor authentication

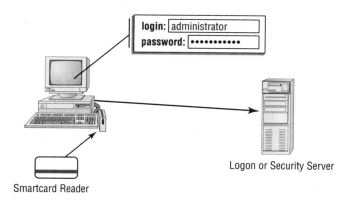

login: administrator
password: ●●●●●●●●●●

Smartcard Reader

Logon or Security Server

Both factors must be valid:
•UserID Password
•Smartcard

Single sign-on

Single sign-on means that once a user (or other subject) is authenticated into the realm, they need not reauthenticate to access resources on any realm entity. (Realm is another term for domain or network.) This allows users to access all the resources, data, applications, and servers they need to perform their work tasks with a single authentication procedure. Single sign-on eliminates the need for users to manage multiple usernames and passwords, since only a single set of logon credentials is required. Some examples of single sign-on include Kerberos, SESAME, NetSP, KryptoKnight, directory services, thin clients, and scripted access. Kerberos is one of the single sign-on solution options you should know about for the Security+ exam; this is discussed in section 3.7 later in this chapter.

Exam Essentials

Single sign-on Single sign-on means that once a user (or other subject) is authenticated into a realm, they need not reauthenticate to access resources on any realm entity.

Multi-factor authentication Multi-factor authentication is the requirement that a user must provide two or more authentication factors in order to prove their identity.

Two-factor authentication Two-factor authentication is when two different authentication factors are used.

Strong authentication Strong authentication is when two or more authentication factors are used but some of them are of the same type.

3.7 Deploy various authentication models and identify the components of each.

The deployment of various authentication models typically involves the implementation of a specific operating system, guidance from a security policy, and numerous specialized technology products, systems, and solutions. The following sections discuss many of these that are relevant for the Security+ exam.

Biometric reader

Biometrics is the term used to describe the collection of physical attributes of the human body that can be used as authentication factors. Biometrics fall into the authentication

factor category of "something you are": You, as a human, have the element of identification as part of your physical body. Biometrics include fingerprints, palm scans (use of the entire palm as if it were a fingerprint), hand geometry (geometric dimensions of the silhouette of a hand), retinal scans (pattern of blood vessels at the back of the eye), iris scans (colored area of the eye around the pupil), facial recognition, voice recognition, signature dynamics, and keyboard dynamics.

Although biometrics are a stronger form of authentication than passwords alone, biometrics in and of themselves aren't the best solution. Even with biometrics, implementing multi-factor authentication is the most secure solution.

The key element in deployment of biometrics as an element of authentication is a biometric device or a biometric reader. This is the hardware designed to read, scan, or view the body part that is to be presented as proof of identification.

As with all forms of hardware, there are potential errors or failures associated with biometric readers. There are two specific error types of concern related to biometric readers, namely false rejection rate (FRR or Type I) errors and false acceptance rate (FAR or Type II) errors. The FRR is the number of failed authentications for valid subjects based on device sensitivity, whereas the FAR is the number of accepted invalid subjects based on device sensitivity. These two error measurements can be mapped on a graph comparing sensitivity level versus rate of errors. The point on this graph where these two rates intersect is known as the crossover error rate (CER). The CER point (as measured against the error scale) is used to determine which biometric device for a specific body part from various vendors or of various models is the most accurate. The comparatively lowest CER point is the more accurate biometric device for the relevant body part.

RADIUS

Remote Authentication Dial-In User Service (RADIUS) is a centralized authentication system. It's often deployed to provide an additional layer of security for a network. By offloading authentication of remote access clients from domain controllers or even the remote access server itself to a dedicated authentication server such as RADIUS, you can provide greater protection against intrusion for the network as a whole. RADIUS can be used with any type of remote access, including dial-up, VPN, and terminal services.

RADIUS is known as an *AAA server*. AAA stands for authentication, authorization (or access control), and auditing. RADIUS provides for distinct AAA functions for remote access clients separate from those of normal local domain clients. RADIUS isn't the only AAA server, but it's the most widely deployed.

When RADIUS is deployed, it's important to understand the terms RADIUS client and RADIUS server, both of which are depicted in Figure 3.4. The RADIUS server is obviously the system hosting the RADIUS service. However, the RADIUS client is the *Remote Access Server (RAS),* not the remote system connecting to RAS. As far as the remote access client is concerned, it only sees the RAS server, not the RADIUS server. Thus, the RAS server is the RADIUS client.

FIGURE 3.4 The RADIUS client manages the local connection and authenticates against a central server.

RAS

A *Remote Access Server (RAS)* is a network server that supports connections from distant users or systems. RAS systems often support modem banks, VPN links, and even terminal services connections.

A *modem* (see Figure 3.5) is a device that creates a network communication link between two computers (or networks) over a telephone line. Modems are one of the slowest remote connection methods still widely supported by operating systems. Most connections are limited to a maximum throughput of 56 Kbps. However, since portable systems can use them to connect to corporate offices using any available telephone line, modems will probably be around for years to come.

FIGURE 3.5 A RAS connection between a remote workstation and a Windows server using modems

A common security protection added to dial-up modems is *callback:* a feature that disconnects the remote user immediately after authentication and then calls the remote user back at a predefined number. Callback ensures that the authenticated user is located at the correct phone number before access to the network is granted.

War dialing a common attack against dial-up modems on a company network. Such an attack dials all the numbers in a prefix range in order to locate modems connected to computer systems. Once attackers locate a modem that answers a computer call, they can focus their efforts on breaking through the logon security barrier.

LDAP

A *directory service* is a managed list of network resources. Through the use of a directory service, large networks are easier to navigate, manage, and secure. Active Directory from Microsoft and eDirectory (or NDS) from Novell are examples of directory services. Both of these products are based on Lightweight Directory Access Protocol (LDAP). Understanding LDAP is an important part of the Security+ exam.

 For more information on this topic, refer to Chapter 3 of the *CompTIA* Security+ Study Guide, 4th Edition (Sybex, November 2008).

LDAP is a standardized protocol that enables clients to access resources within a directory service. A directory service is a network service that provides access to a central database of information, which contains detailed information about the resources available on a network. LDAP follows the *x.500 standard*, which defines what a directory service is and how it is to be constructed (at least from a foundational infrastructure perspective). Clients can interact with directory service resources through LDAP by using authentication that is at least a minimum of a username and password.

LDAP directory structures are hierarchical data models that use branches like a tree and that have a clearly identified and defined root (see Figure 3.6). LDAP operates over TCP ports 389 and 636. It can employ SSL or TLS to provide authentication and data encryption security.

FIGURE 3.6 An example of an LDAP-based directory services structure

mail: John@sybex.com

Remote access policies

As networks grow, it becomes more common for them to support remote connections, whether dial-up, wireless WAN, or virtual private network (VPN); see Figure 3.7. The access control and protection issues involved in managing and administering remote access connections are generally termed communications security.

FIGURE 3.7 A RAS connection between a remote workstation and a Windows server

Workstation or Server
Running Remote Access

Networks exist to share resources. In order to share resources, all entities on a network must share a common protocol. But in order for the protocol to function, a communication medium must be in place to provide support for the transfer of that protocol and its hosted communication data between one system and another. Often that medium is a network cable, such as a 10BaseT (also known as twisted pair cabling). However, the communication medium could be wireless, a VPN link, a dial-up link, a terminal services link, or even a remote control link. In any case, understanding the technology and the security implications of each of these communication media is an essential part of administering an environment.

 For more information on this topic, refer to Chapter 3 of the *CompTIA Security+ Study Guide*, 4th Edition (Sybex, November 2008).

One mechanism often used to help control the complexities of remote connectivity is that of remote access policies. Remote access policies or RAS policies are additional gauntlets of requirements that remote users must be in compliance with to gain access to the internal resources of the LAN. RAS policies can require specific operating systems and patch levels, restrict time and date access, mandate authentication mechanisms, and confirm caller ID and/or MAC address of the remote client. After a connection is established, RAS

policies can be used to enforce idle timeout disconnects, define maximum connect time, mandate minimal encryption levels, enforce IP packet filters, define IP address parameters, and force specific routing paths.

Remote authentication

Remote authentication is a catchphrase that refers to any mechanism used to verify the identity of remote users. Several well known examples of remote authentication include RADIUS, TACACS, 802.1x, and CHAP. Originally, remote authentication referred to solutions that supported authentication mechanisms for dial-up telecommuters. Today, it includes any authentication technology that can be used for remote users, whether connecting over dial-up, VPN, and even wireless.

VPN

A *virtual private network (VPN)* is a communication *tunnel* between two entities across an intermediary network. In most cases, the intermediary network is an untrusted network, such as the Internet, and therefore the communication tunnel is also encrypted. VPNs can be used to connect two networks across the Internet (see Figure 3.8) or to allow distant clients to connect into an office LAN across the Internet (see Figure 3.9). Once a VPN link is established, the network connectivity for the VPN client is exactly the same as a LAN connected by a cable connection. The only difference between a direct LAN cable connection and a VPN link is speed.

FIGURE 3.8 Two LANs being connected using a VPN across the Internet

FIGURE 3.9 A client connecting to a network via a VPN across the Internet

VPNs are often the best solution to allow remote users to access resources on a corporate LAN. They have the following advantages:

- They eliminate the need for expensive dial-up modem banks.

- They do away with long-distance toll charges.

- They allow any user anywhere in the world with an Internet connection to establish a VPN link with the office network.

- They provide security for both authentication and data transmission.

VPN links are established using VPN protocols. There are several VPN protocols, but the three you should recognize are Point-to-Point Tunneling Protocol *(PPTP)*, Layer 2 Tunneling Protocol *(L2TP)*, and Internet Protocol Security *(IPSec)*.

Sometimes VPN protocols are called tunneling protocols. This naming convention is designed to focus attention on the tunneling capabilities of VPNs.

VPNs work through a process called *encapsulation*. As data is transmitted from one system to another across a VPN link, the normal LAN TCP/IP traffic is encapsulated (encased, or enclosed) in the VPN protocol. The VPN protocol acts like a security envelope that provides special delivery capabilities (for example, across the Internet) as well as security mechanisms (such as data encryption).

When firewalls, intrusion detection systems, antivirus scanners, or other packet-filtering and -monitoring security mechanisms are used, you must realize that the data payload of VPN traffic won't be viewable, accessible, scannable, and so on, because it's encrypted. Thus, in order for these security mechanisms to function against VPN transported data, they must be placed outside of the VPN tunnel to act on the data after it has been decrypted and returned back to normal LAN traffic.

VPNs provide the following four critical functions:

- **Access control**—Restricts users from accessing resources on a network.

- **Authentication**—Proves the identity of communication partners.

- **Confidentiality**—Prevents unauthorized disclosure of secured data.

- **Data integrity**—Prevents unwanted changes of data while in transit.

As with any type of remote access connection, VPN clients can be authenticated through RADIUS.

Kerberos

Early authentication transmission mechanisms sent logon credentials from the client to the authentication server in clear text. Unfortunately, this solution is vulnerable to eavesdropping and interception, thus making the security of the system suspect (if not decimating it). What was needed was a solution that didn't transmit the logon credentials in a form that could be easily captured, extracted, and reused.

One such method for providing protection for logon credentials is *Kerberos*: a trusted third-party authentication protocol that was originally developed at MIT under Project Athena. The current version of Kerberos in widespread use is version 5. Kerberos is used to authenticate network principles (subjects) to other entities on the network (objects, resources, and servers). Kerberos is platform independent; however, some operating systems require special configuration adjustments to support true interoperability (for example, Windows Server 2003 or Windows 2000 Server with Unix).

Kerberos is a centralized authentication solution. The core element of a Kerberos solution is the Key Distribution Center (KDC), which is responsible for verifying the identity of principles and granting and controlling access within a network environment through the use of secure cryptographic keys and tickets.

Kerberos is a trusted third-party authentication solution because the KDC acts as a third party in the communications between a client and a server. Thus, if the client trusts the KDC and the server trusts the KDC, then the client and server can trust each other.

Kerberos is also a single sign-on solution. Single sign-on means that once a user (or other subject) is authenticated into the realm, they need not reauthenticate to access resources on any realm entity. (A *realm* is the network protected under a single Kerberos implementation.)

The basic process of Kerberos authentication is as follows:

1. The subject provides logon credentials.

2. The Kerberos client system encrypts the password with the Data Encryption Standard (DES) and transmits the protected credentials to the KDC.

3. The KDC verifies the credentials and then creates a ticket granting ticket (TGT—a hashed form of the subject's password with the addition of a time stamp that indicates a valid lifetime). The TGT is encrypted and sent to the client.

4. The client receives the TGT. At this point, the subject is an authenticated principle in the Kerberos realm.

5. The subject requests access to resources on a network server. This causes the client to request a service ticket (ST) from the KDC.

6. The KDC verifies that the client has a valid TGT and then issues an ST to the client. The ST includes a time stamp that indicates its valid lifetime.

7. The client receives the ST.

8. The client sends the ST to the network server that hosts the desired resource.

9. The network server verifies the ST. If it's verified, it initiates a communication session with the client. From this point forward, Kerberos is no longer involved.

Figure 3.10 shows the Kerberos authentication process.

FIGURE 3.10 The Kerberos authentication process

The Kerberos authentication method helps to ensure that logon credentials aren't compromised while in transit from the client to the server. The inclusion of a time stamp in the tickets ensures that expired tickets can't be reused. This prevents replay and spoofing attacks against Kerberos.

Kerberos supports mutual authentication (client and server identities are proven to each other). It's scalable and thus able to manage authentication for large networks. Being centralized, Kerberos helps reduce the overall time involved in accessing resources within a network.

 Kerberos is used to provide security and protection for authentication credentials alone. It isn't used in any way to provide encryption or security for other types of data transfer.

CHAP

CHAP (Challenge-Handshake Authentication Protocol) is an authentication protocol used primarily over dial-up connections (usually Point-to-Point Protocol [PPP]) as a means to provide a secure transport mechanism for logon credentials. It was developed as a secure

alternative and replacement to Password Authentication Protocol (PAP), which transmitted authentication credentials in clear text.

CHAP uses an initial authentication protection process to support logon and an ongoing verification process to ensure the subject/client is still who they claim to be. The process is as follows.

1. The initial authentication process performs a one-way hash function (specifically, MD5) on the subject's password and then passes the username and hash value to the authentication server.

2. The authentication server compares the username to its accounts database and the hash value to that stored for the identified user in its database.

3. If there is a match, the server transmits a challenge to the client.

4. The client produces the correct response and transmits it back to the server.

5. The server computes the response.

6. The server compares the response to that received by the client.

7. If everything matches, the subject is authenticated and allowed to communicate over the link.

Figure 3.11 shows the CHAP authentication process.

FIGURE 3.11 CHAP authentication

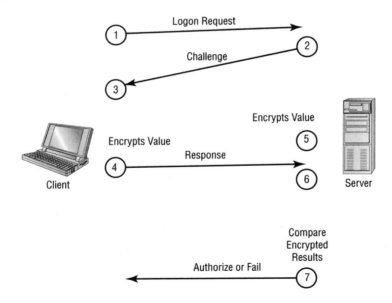

Once the client is authenticated, CHAP periodically sends a challenge to the client at random intervals. The client must compute the correct response to the issued challenge; otherwise the connection is automatically severed. This post-authentication verification process ensures that the authenticated session hasn't been hijacked.

PAP

Password Authentication Protocol (PAP) was an early POTS authentication mechanism that transmitted authentication credentials in clear text. PAP is mostly unused today, as it was superseded by CHAP and numerous EAP add-ons.

Mutual

Mutual authentication is two-way authentication. The subject (user) authenticates to the object (server), and the object (server) authenticates back to the subject (user). In this way, both ends of the communication have proof of the identity of the other partner.

802.1x

802.1x is a port-based authentication mechanism. 802.1x is based on EAP and is commonly used in closed environment wireless networks. When 802.1x is in use, it makes a port-based decision on whether to allow or deny a connection based on the authentication of a user or service. 802.1x was initially used to compensate for the weaknesses of WEP, but today it is often used as a component in more complex authentication and connection management systems, including RADIUS and NAC (Network Access Control).

Like many technologies, 802.1x is vulnerable to man-in-the-middle and hijacking attacks due to the authentication mechanism occurring only at the establishment of the connection.

TACACS

Terminal Access Controller Access Control System (TACACS) is another example of an AAA server. TACACS is an Internet standard (RFC 1492); however, Cisco's proprietary implementations of *XTACACS* and *TACACS+* have quickly gained in popularity. TACACS is a centralized remote access authentication solution (see Figure 3.12) similar to RADIUS; it uses ports TCP 49 and UDP 49.

FIGURE 3.12 Centrally managed remote access authentication with TACACS

Exam Essentials

LDAP Lightweight Directory Access Protocol (LDAP) is used to allow clients to interact with directory service resources. LDAP is based on x.500 and uses TCP ports 389 and 636. It uses a tree structure with a district root.

Kerberos Kerberos is a trusted third-party authentication protocol. It uses encryption keys as tickets with time stamps to prove identity and grant access to resources. Kerberos is a single sign-on solution employing a Key Distribution Center (KDC) to manage its centralized authentication mechanism.

CHAP The Challenge-Handshake Authentication Protocol (CHAP) is an authentication protocol used primarily over dial-up connections (usually PPP) as a means to provide a secure transport mechanism for logon credentials. CHAP uses a one-way hash to protect passwords and periodically reauthenticates clients.

Passwords Passwords are the most common form of authentication, but they're also the weakest. Passwords can be improved through the use of strong password policies enforced by software.

Tokens Tokens are a "something you have" type of authentication factor. They support one-time passwords, which are the most secure form of passwords.

Multi-factor authentication Multi-factor authentication is the requirement that a user must provide two or more authentication factors in order to prove their identity.

Mutual authentication Mutual authentication is two-way authentication. The subject (user) authenticates to the object (server), and the object (server) authenticates back to the subject (user).

Biometrics Biometrics is the collection of physical attributes of the human body that can be used as authentication factors ("something you are"). Biometrics include fingerprints, palm scans (use of the entire palm as if it were a fingerprint), hand geometry (geometric dimensions of the silhouette of a hand), retinal scans (pattern of blood vessels at the back of the eye), iris scans (colored area of the eye around the pupil), facial recognition, voice recognition, signature dynamics, and keyboard dynamics.

3.8 Explain the difference between identification and authentication (identity proofing).

Identification and authentication are commonly used as a two-step process, but they are distinct activities. Identification is the claiming of an identity. This only needs to occur once per authentication or access process. Any one of the three common authentication factors can be employed for identification. Once identification has been performed, the authentication process must take place. Authentication is the act of verifying or proving the claimed identity. The issue is both checking that such identity actually exists within the known accounts of the secured environment and also ensuring that the human claiming the identity is the correct, valid, and authorized human to use that specific identity.

Authentication can take many forms, most commonly of one-, two-, or three-factor configurations. The more unique factors used in an authentication process, the more resilient and reliable the authentication itself becomes. If all of the proffered authentication factors are valid and correct for the claimed identity, it is then assumed that the accessing person is who they claim to be. Then the permission and action restriction mechanisms of authorization take over to control the activities of the user/human from that point forward.

Exam Essentials

Identification Identification is the act of claiming an identity using just one authentication factor.

Authentication Authentication is the act of proving a claimed identity using one or more authentication factors.

3.9 Explain and apply physical access security methods.

Physical security is an area that is often overlooked when designing security for an environment. However, without physical security, there is no security. As you prepare for the Security+ exam, don't overlook the aspects and elements of physical security. As a security professional, you need to reduce the overall opportunities for intrusions or physical security violations to occur. This can be accomplished using various mechanisms, including prevention, deterrence, and detection.

For more information on this topic, refer to Chapter 3 of the *CompTIA Security+ Study Guide*, 4th Edition (Sybex, November 2008).

To ensure proper physical security, you should design the layout of your physical environment with security in mind. This means all equipment is placed in locations that can be secured, and access or entrance into those locations is controlled and monitored. Good physical security access control also recognizes that some computers and network devices are more important or mission critical than others and therefore require greater physical security protection.

Mission-critical servers and devices should be placed in dedicated equipment rooms that are secured from all possible entrance and intrusion (see Figure 3.13). These rooms shouldn't have windows and should have floor-to-roof walls (rather than short walls that end at a drop ceiling). Equipment rooms should be locked at all times, and only authorized personal should ever be granted entrance. The rooms should be monitored, and all access should be logged and audited.

FIGURE 3.13 An example of a multilayered physical security environment

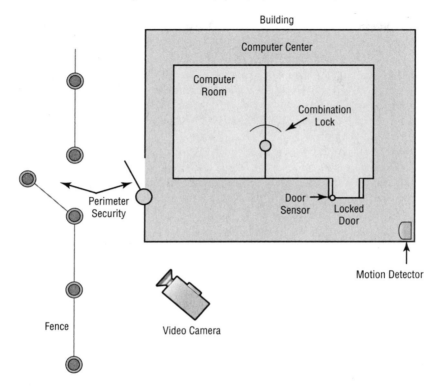

Physical barriers are erected to control access to a location. Some of the most basic forms of physical barriers are walls and fences. Fences are used to designate the borders of a geographic area where entrance is restricted; a high fence, the presence of barbed wire, or electrified fencing all provide greater boundary protection. Walls provide protection as well, preventing entry except at designated points such as doors and windows. The stronger the wall, the more security it provides. And the greater the number of walls between the untrusted outside and the valuable assets located inside, the greater the level of physical security.

Physical access logs/lists

The presence of security guards at an entrance or around the perimeter of a security boundary serves as a deterrent to intruders and provides a form of physical barrier. Guard dogs can also protect against intrusion by detecting the presence of unauthorized visitors.

A security guard can check each person's credentials before granting entry. You can also use a biometrically controlled door. In either entrance control system, a log or list of entries and exits, along with visitors and escorts, can be maintained. Such a log will assist

in tracking down suspects or verifying all personnel are accounted for in the event of an emergency.

Hardware locks

Although you need walls and fences to protect boundaries, there must be a means for authorized personnel to cross these barriers into the secured environment. Doors and gates can be locked and controlled in such a way that only authorized people can unlock and/or enter through them. Such control can take the form of a lock with a key that only authorized people possess.

Hardware locks, conventional locks, and even electronic or smart locks are used to keep specific doors or other access portals closed and prevent entry or access to all but authorized individuals. With the risks of lock picking and bumping, locks resistant to such attacks must be used whenever valuable assets are to be protected from tampering or theft.

Physical access control – ID badges

In the realm of physical security, access controls are mechanisms designed to manage and control entrance into a location such as a building, a parking lot, a room, or even a specific box or server rack. Being able to control who can gain physical proximity to your environment (especially your computers and networking equipment) lets you provide true security for your data, assets, and other resources.

One method to control access is to issue each valid worker an ID badge that can serve as either a simple photo ID or an electronic smartcard. A photo ID requires a security guard to view, discriminate, and then grant or deny access. In this process, the security guard can also add the name and action to an access roster. A smartcard can be used with an automated system that can electronically unlock and even open doors when a valid smartcard is swiped. Smartcard use is also easy to log and monitor. Additionally, the same smartcard used for facility access can also serve as a photo ID as well as an authentication factor for accessing the company network.

Door access systems

Doors used to control entrance into secured areas can be protected by locks that are keyed to biometrics. A biometric lock requires that the person present a biometric factor, such as a fingerprint, hand scan, retinal scan, and so on, to the validation mechanism. Only after the biometric is verified is the door unlocked and the person allowed entry. When biometrics are used to control entrance into secured areas, they serve as a mechanism of identity proofing as well as authentication.

However, door access systems need not be exclusively biometric. Smartcards and even traditional metal keys can function as authentication factors for physical entry points.

Many door access systems, whether supporting biometrics, smartcards, or even PINs, are often designed around the electronic access control (EAC) concept. An EAC system is a door-locking and access mechanism that uses an electromagnet to keep a door closed, a reader to accept access credentials, and a door-close spring and sensor to ensure the door recloses within a reasonable time frame.

Mantrap

Some high value or high security environments may also employ mantraps as a means to control access to the most secured, dangerous, or valuable areas of a facility. A *mantrap* is a form of high-security barrier entrance device (see Figure 3.14). It's a small room with two doors: one in the trusted environment and one opening to the outside. The mantrap works like this:

1. A person enters the mantrap.
2. Both doors are locked.
3. The person must properly authenticate to unlock the inner door again entry. If the authentication fails, security personnel are notified and the intruder is detained inside the mantrap.

FIGURE 3.14 A mantrap

Mantraps often contain scales and cameras in order to prevent *piggybacking*. Piggybacking occurs when one person authenticates, opens a door, and lets another person enter without that second person authenticating to the system.

Physical tokens

A physical token is any item that can be carried for use as an authentication factor. This includes metal keys, smart cards, photo IDs, synchronous tokens, asynchronous tokens, and biometrics. A physical token is the expression of the Type II authentication factor of something you have.

Video surveillance – camera types and positioning

Video surveillance, close circuit television (CCTV), and security cameras are all means to provide a deterrent to unwanted activity and also to record the occurrence of events. Cameras should be positioned to watch exit and entry points along any change in authorization level—for example, doors allowing entry into a facility from outside, doors allowing entry into work areas from common areas, and doors allowing entry into high security areas from work areas. Cameras should also be used to monitor activities around valuable assets and resources, such as server rooms, safes, vaults, or component closets, as well as to provide additional protection in public areas such as parking structures and walkways.

Cameras should be configured to record to storage media. This has traditionally been some sort of tape, such as VCR tape. However, modern systems may record to DVD, NVRAM, or hard drives.

Cameras vary in their type. Typical security cameras operate by recording visible light images but often require additional lighting in low-light areas. Alternative camera types include those that only record when motion is detected, those that are able to record in infrared, and those that can automatically track movement.

Exam Essentials

Physical access control Physical access control refers to mechanisms designed to manage and control entrance into a location. Being able to control who can gain physical proximity to your environment (especially your computers and networking equipment) allows you to provide true security for your data, assets, and other resources. Without physical access control, you have no security.

Physical barriers Physical barriers are erected to control access into a location. Some of the most basic forms of physical barriers are walls and fences.

Boundary-crossing devices Doors and gates can be locked and controlled in such a way that only authorized personnel can unlock and enter through them. This control can take the form of a lock with a key that only authorized people possess. A security guard can check a person's credentials before granting entry. You can also use a biometrically controlled door.

Security guards The presence of security guards at an entrance or around the perimeter of a security boundary serves as a deterrent to intruders and provides a form of physical barrier. Guard dogs can also perform a basic function to protect against intrusion by detecting the presence of unauthorized visitors.

Mantraps A mantrap is a form of high-security barrier entrance device. It's a small room with two doors: one in the trusted environment and one opening to the outside. A person must properly authenticate to unlock the inner door and gain entry.

Biometrics used for physical security Locked doors that are used to control entrance into secured areas can be protected by locks that are keyed to biometrics.

Review Questions

1. What method of access control is best suited for environments with a high rate of employee turnover?

 A. MAC

 B. DAC

 C. RBAC

 D. ACL

2. Which of the following is the strongest form of authentication?

 A. Biometric

 B. Two-factor

 C. Something you have

 D. Username and password

3. Kerberos is used to perform what security service?

 A. Authentication protection

 B. File encryption

 C. Secure communications

 D. Protected data transfer

4. What form of authentication periodically reauthenticates the client during a logon session?

 A. Kerberos

 B. Certificates

 C. Multi-factor

 D. CHAP

5. Which is the strongest form of password?

 A. More than eight characters

 B. One-time use

 C. Static

 D. Uses different types of keyboard characters

6. Which of the following technologies can be used to add an additional layer of protection between a directory services–based network and remote clients?

 A. SMTP

 B. RADIUS

 C. PGP

 D. VLAN

7. LDAP operates over what TCP ports?

 A. 636 and 389

 B. 110 and 25

 C. 443 and 80

 D. 20 and 21

8. Which of the following can be considered a physical barrier?

 A. Strong passwords

 B. Firewalls

 C. Security guard

 D. AES

9. In a MAC environment, when a user has clearance for assets but is still unable to access those assets, what other security feature is in force?

 A. Principle of least privilege

 B. Need to know

 C. Privacy

 D. Service level agreement

10. Which of the following is not a benefit of single sign-on?

 A. Browsing multiple systems

 B. Fewer usernames and passwords to memorize

 C. More granular access control

 D. Stronger passwords

Answers to Review Questions

1. C. RBAC is best suited for environments with a high rate of employee turnover because access is defined against static job descriptions rather than transitive user accounts (DAC and ACL) or assigned clearances (MAC).

2. B. Two-factor is always more secure than any single factor of authentication.

3. A. Kerberos is a third-party authentication service; thus it provides authentication protection. Kerberos can't be used to encrypt files, secure nonauthentication communications, or protect data transfer.

4. D. CHAP periodically reauthenticates the client during a logon session. Kerberos, certificates, and multi-factor authentication mechanisms don't perform reauthentication.

5. B. A one-time password is always the strongest form of password. A static password is always the weakest form of password. A password with more than eight characters and using different types of keyboard characters is usually strong, but these factors alone are unable to indicate their strength.

6. B. RADIUS is a centralized authentication solution that adds an additional layer of security between a network and remote clients. SMTP is the e-mail forwarding protocol used on the Internet and intranets. PGP is a security solution for e-mail. VLANs are created by switches to logically divide a network into subnets.

7. A. LDAP operates over TCP ports 636 and 389. POP3 and SMTP operate over TCP ports 110 and 25, respectively. TLS operates over TCP ports 443 and 80 (SSL operates only over TCP port 443; HTTP operates over TCP port 80). FTP operates over TCP ports 20 and 21.

8. C. A security guard can be considered a physical barrier. Strong passwords, firewalls, and AES are all technology barriers.

9. B. Need to know is the MAC environment's granular access control method. The principle of least privilege is the DAC environment's concept of granular access control. Privacy and SLAs aren't forms of access control.

10. C. Single sign-on doesn't address access control and therefore doesn't provide granular or nongranular access control. Single sign-on provides the benefits of browsing multiple systems, fewer credentials to memorize, and the use of stronger passwords.

Chapter

4

Assessments and Audits

COMPTIA SECURITY+ EXAM OBJECTIVES COVERED IN THIS CHAPTER INCLUDE THE FOLLOWING:

✓ **4.1 Conduct risk assessments and implement risk mitigation.**

✓ **4.2 Carry out vulnerability assessments using common tools.**

- Port scanners
- Vulnerability scanners
- Protocol analyzers
- OVAL
- Password crackers
- Network mappers

✓ **4.3 Within the realm of vulnerability assessments, explain the proper use of penetration testing versus vulnerability scanning.**

✓ **4.4 Use monitoring tools on systems and networks and detect security-related anomalies.**

- Performance monitor
- Systems monitor
- Performance baseline
- Protocol analyzers

✓ **4.5 Compare and contrast various types of monitoring methodologies.**

- Behavior-based
- Signature-based
- Anomaly-based

✓ **4.6 Execute proper logging procedures and evaluate the results.**

- Security application

- DNS

- System

- Performance

- Access

- Firewall

- Antivirus

✓ **4.7 Conduct periodic audits of system security settings.**

- User access and rights review

- Storage and retention policies

- Group policies

The Security+ exam will test your basic IT security skills—those skills needed to effectively secure stand-alone and networked systems in a corporate environment. To pass the test and be effective in implementing security, you need to understand the basic concepts and terminology related to assessments and audits as detailed in this chapter.

4.1 Conduct risk assessments and implement risk mitigation.

Risk identification is an essential part of an organization's security endeavor. Without performing a risk assessment and analysis, you won't know what problems your security policy needs to address. Computer systems and networks can never be completely secure. However, that fact shouldn't prevent you from securing your environment as much as possible. Using asset identification, risk assessment, threat identification, and vulnerability management focuses your security endeavors on those areas that pose the greatest threat to your assets.

For more information on this topic, see Chapter 3 of the *CompTIA Security+ Study Guide, 4th Edition* (Sybex, November 2008).

Asset identification

You don't know what to protect if you don't know what you have. A thorough asset inventory must be performed to identify mission-critical systems as well as everyday items (such as paperclips and sticky notes) that your organization needs to perform its services and produce its products. Once you have a master inventory, you can prioritize your assets. You can then perform risk assessment for the most important items first; after you provide additional protection for them, you move on to less important items.

Risk assessment

The goal of risk assessment, risk management, and risk analysis is to minimize the impact of risks on an organization. This is done through *mitigation* (applying safeguards or countermeasures), *transfer* or *assignment* (outsourcing or obtaining insurance), or *acceptance* (accepting the potential losses). This process identifies potential threats, evaluates the potential impact

of those threats, and weighs the cost in terms of protection mechanisms needed and the potential loss or interruption of business continuity.

Four common formulas are associated with risk assessment and risk analysis:

Exposure factor (EF) This is the percentage of asset value loss that would occur if a risk was realized (for example, if an attack took place).

Single loss expectancy (SLE) This is the potential dollar-value loss from a single risk realization incident. It's calculated by multiplying the EF by the asset value.

Annualized rate of occurrence (ARO) This number is the statistical probability that a specific risk may be realized a certain number of times in a year. It's obtained from a risk assessment company or an insurance company.

Annual loss expectancy (ALE) This is the potential dollar value loss per year per risk. It's calculation by multiplying the SLE by the ARO.

Threat identification

A *threat* is any person or tool that can take advantage of a vulnerability. Threat identification is a formal process of outlining the potential threats to a system.

Vulnerabilities

A *vulnerability* is a weakness, error, or hole in the security protection of a system, network, computer, software, and so on. When a vulnerability exists, threats may exist to exploit it. You can use countermeasures and safeguards to patch vulnerabilities. Once a vulnerability is patched, threats no longer impose a danger to your systems.

Exam Essentials

Asset identification A thorough asset inventory must be performed to identify mission-critical systems as well as everyday items (such as paperclips and sticky notes) that your organization needs to perform its services and produce its products. Once you have a master inventory, you can prioritize your assets.

Risk assessment The goal of risk assessment is to minimize the impact of risks on an organization. This is done through mitigation, assignment, or acceptance. This process identifies potential threats, evaluates the potential impact of those threats, and weighs the cost in terms of protection mechanisms needed and the potential loss or interruption of business continuity.

Risk assessment formulas The different risk assessment formulas are exposure factor (EF), single loss expectancy (SLE), annualized rate of occurrence (ARO), and annual loss expectancy (ALE).

Threats A threat is any person or tool that can take advantage of a vulnerability. Threat identification is a formal process of outlining the potential threats to a system.

Vulnerabilities A vulnerability is a weakness, error, or hole in the security protection of a system, network, computer, software, and so on. When a vulnerability exists, threats may exist to exploit it. You can use countermeasures and safeguards to patch vulnerabilities.

4.2 Carry out vulnerability assessments using common tools.

Vulnerability assessments are used to discover weaknesses in deployed security systems in order to improve or repair them before a breach occurs. By using a wide variety of assessment tools, security administrators can learn of deficiencies quickly. Only through vigilance and constant monitoring and assessment can a security endeavor prove successful.

 For more information on this topic, see Chapter 3 of the *CompTIA Security+ Study Guide, 4th Edition* (Sybex, November 2008).

Port scanners

A *port scanner* is a vulnerability assessment tool that sends probe or test packets to a target system's ports in order to learn about the status of those ports. A port can be in one of two states: open and closed. If a valid request for connection is sent to an open TCP port (a SYN flagged packet), a normal response can be expected (a SYN/ACK flagged packet). If the TCP port is closed, the response is a RST packet. However, if a firewall is present, the firewall can filter out the responses of closed ports, resulting in no packet being received by the probing system. This is known as filtering. Thus, a port scanner will have direct proof that a port is open or closed but can assume a filtered port if no response is received.

While this form of probing works effectively, it also produces traffic that is likely recorded or logged by the target system or the firewall protecting it. Thus, many other forms of port scanning have been developed. Some scanning techniques use standard packets but in an unexpected context, such as FIN or ACK flagged packets. These packets have no valid meaning outside of a valid TCP setup or teardown handshake, thus when used out of context they may illicit a response that is meaningful to the probing entity. Even a normal data packet, which does not have any header flags enabled, can be used in a scan called a NULL scan. There are even some methods of scanning that use invalid packet constructions, such as the XMAS scan, which has numerous header flags enabled (like the lights on a Christmas tree).

The actual details of how these scans operate are a bit beyond the Security+ content. However, it is important to understand that port scans allow security testers and hackers to discover what ports are open on a system. Once the open ports are known on a target, this information can lead to other important details, such as the identity of the host operating

system and what types of services are hosted on the target. Many port scanning tools, such as nmap, can not only detect open, closed, and stealthed ports, they can also determine the OS and identify active services on a port. Sometimes these actions are performed using a database of characteristics and sometimes they are performed using banner grabbing queries. A banner grab occurs when a request for data or identity is sent to a service on an open port and that service responds with information that may directly or indirectly reveal its identity.

Vulnerability scanners

A *vulnerability scanner* is a tool used to scan a target system for known holes, weaknesses, or vulnerabilities. These automated tools have a database of attacks, probes, scripts, and so on that are run against one or more systems in a controlled manner. Vulnerability scanners are designed to probe targets and produce a report of the findings. They can be used from within a private network to test internal systems directly or from outside the network to test border devices against breaching attacks.

Vulnerability scanners are designed not to cause damage while they probe for weaknesses, but they can still inadvertently cause errors, slower network performance, and actual downtime. Thus, it is important to plan out their use and prepare for potential recovery actions.

Vulnerability scanners can be commercial products, such as Retina, or open source, such as Nessus. Most organizations take advantage of several vulnerability scanners in order to gain the most complete perspective on their security status. Each time a vulnerability scanner is to be used, it should be updated from the vendor.

Protocol analyzers

A *protocol analyzer* is a tool used to examine the contents of network traffic. A protocol analyzer can be a physical tool, such as a NetScout Sniffer appliance, or a software product, such as Wireshark. In either case, a protocol analyzer is first a packet-capturing tool that can collect network traffic and store it in memory or onto a storage device. Once a packet is captured, it can be analyzed either with complex automated tools and scripts or manually.

Protocol analyzers can be used to discover communication problems caused by hardware and software issues. Protocol analyzers can detect protocol anomalies that may be due to misconfiguration, malfunction, or malicious intent. Often, when security administrators attempt to track down a network communication problem or discover the source of an attack, they will use a protocol analyzer.

OVAL

OVAL (Open Vulnerability and Assessment Language) is a international security community standard designed to promote the exchange of standardized security content across all platforms and for all tool sets and services. OVAL is based on XML. Tools that support OVAL have access to all of the documentation and security information of the OVAL worldwide community.

Password crackers

A *password cracker* is a tool used to reverse-engineer the secured storage of passwords in order to gain (or regain) access to an unknown or forgotten password. Password crackers are used to attack the hashed password storage systems used on secure operating systems and services. Most passwords are stored in hash form rather than their original characters. This prevents an attacker from easily gaining direct access to password characters. However, even with secure environments only storing and transmitting password hashes, the hashing process can be attacked.

In a process of reverse hash matching, a hacker or security administrator can obtain password hashes from network traffic, directly from the authentication system, from backup tapes, etc. Once a password hash (or an entire database of hashes) is on hand, a password cracking tool can reverse-engineer the hash to discover the original password characters. While hashing itself is a one-way process that cannot be reversed in the same way that encryption can be decrypted, it is possible to reverse-engineer hashes. This process involves hashing a potential password and comparing the result to the stolen or target hashes. This process is repeated until all potential passwords have been exhausted or successful matches are found.

This process is found in all four of the well-known forms of offline password cracking techniques: dictionary, brute force, hybrid, and precomputed hash. A dictionary attack uses a text file of potential passwords. The dictionary attack is often completed quickly, but has the lowest chance of success. A brute force attack tries all valid combinations of characters and lengths until a match is found. A brute force attack is always successful if given enough time to run. However, with a sufficiently long target password (15 or more characters), brute force attacks are rendered impractical. A hybrid attack uses a dictionary list as its password source but uses brute force techniques to make modifications on a progressively increasing level. For example, the first round would take each source password and make all possible one-character modifications, and then the second round would make all possible two-character modifications. The hybrid method has the benefit of focusing on words the target users may have used due to their interests and background while not having to try all possible combinations.

The precomputed hash mechanism takes a different approach to the same problem of reverse-engineering password hashes. Instead of hashing potential passwords as part of the attack itself, a database of potential password hashes is produced beforehand. Then when a password hash is obtained, the precomputed hash attack simply compares the stolen hash with the database to see if there is a match. If the database was built using the same hashing algorithm, a wide enough character set, and at least as many characters as the original target password, this tactic is very fast and effective.

To defend against password crackers, users should select passwords that are long (15+ characters), not based on a single word, and changed on a regular basis. In fact, users should no longer think of passwords as single words but instead think of passwords as passphrases, which are comprised of numerous words, often forming complete sentences with capitalization and punctuation.

Network mappers

A *network mapper* is a specialized tool that borrows features from port scanners and protocol analyzers in order to actively or passively build a logical infrastructure map of a network. A network mapper can probe all addresses in the network range and elicit responses that reveal OS type and possibly services hosted. However, hackers also have network mappers that only passively listen to existing traffic in order to extract the details to build a network infrastructure map.

Network mappers are useful for checking inventory and verifying online systems as well as network functionality. They can also be used to discover rogue systems that appear on the map that are not authorized or approved. However, in the wrong hands a network mapper can give hackers information about the network that could lead to more damaging intrusions or compromises.

Exam Essentials

Port scanner A port scanner is a vulnerability assessment tool that sends probe or test packets to a target system's ports in order to learn about the status of those ports.

Vulnerability scanner A vulnerability scanner is a tool used to scan a target system for known holes, weaknesses, or vulnerabilities. These automated tools have a database of attacks, probes, scripts, and so on that are run against one or more systems in a controlled manner.

Protocol analyzer A protocol analyzer is a tool used to examine the contents of network traffic.

OVAL OVAL (Open Vulnerability and Assessment Language) is an international security community standard designed to promote the exchange of standardized security content across all platforms and for all tool sets and services.

Password crackers A password cracker is a tool used to reverse-engineer the secured storage of passwords in order to gain (or regain) access to an unknown or forgotten password. There are four well-known types of password cracking techniques: dictionary, brute force, hybrid, and precomputed hash.

Network mapper A network mapper is a specialized tool that borrows features from port scanners and protocol analyzers in order to actively or passively build a logical infrastructure map of a network.

4.3 Within the realm of vulnerability assessments, explain the proper use of penetration testing versus vulnerability scanning.

A *penetration test* is a form of vulnerability scan that is performed by a special team of trained white hat security specialists rather than by an internal security administrator using an automated tool. Penetration testing (a.k.a. ethical hacking) uses the same tools, techniques, and skills of real-world criminal hackers as a methodology to test the deployed security infrastructure of an organization. Penetration testing is usually performed without the IT or security staff being aware of it, as senior management often schedules ethical hacking events. This allows the penetration test to assess the performance of the infrastructure and the response personnel.

Penetration tests can take many forms, including hacking in from the outside, simulating a disgruntled employee, social engineering attacks, physical attacks, as well as remote connectivity and VPN attacks. The goal of penetration testing is to discover weaknesses before real criminals do. Most penetration testing requires high levels of knowledge and skill on the part of the testers. Few automated tools are employed as real hackers often write their own surgically precise attack tools and scripts based on their target. Security administrators do use automated tools for vulnerability scanning to check for policy compliance and for known issues. Penetration testing is used to discover new weaknesses that these automated tools are not able to discover. Vulnerability scanning only gives you the security perspective of the scanner's vendor whereas penetration testing gives you the perspective of real-world criminal hackers.

 For more information on this topic, see Chapter 3 of the *CompTIA Security+ Study Guide, 4th Edition* (Sybex, November 2008).

Exam Essentials

Penetration testing A penetration test is a form of vulnerability scan that is performed by a special team of trained white hat security specialists rather than by an internal security administrator using an automated tool. Penetration testing (a.k.a. ethical hacking) uses the same tools, techniques, and skills of real-world criminal hackers as a methodology to test the deployed security infrastructure of an organization.

4.4 Use monitoring tools on systems and networks and detect security-related anomalies.

Vulnerability scanning and penetration testing are important aspects of detecting and responding to new vulnerabilities and weaknesses. In addition to these important tools, ongoing monitoring of performance, throughput, and protocol use can reveal trends toward downtime, change in job focus, and the need for infrastructure upgrades.

 For more information on this topic, see Chapter 3 of the *CompTIA Security+ Study Guide, 4th Edition* (Sybex, November 2008).

Performance monitor

A *performance monitor* is used to watch the relative activity of system metrics and compare them to known baselines, problem trends, or malicious anomalies. Performance monitoring is an essential tool for a network manager and security administrator, as it can be used to predict changes based on trending data, detect deviations from security policy and required/expected baselines, and watch the effect of malicious events across a wide number of system components. Performance monitoring can be performed live while a person watches the activity or it can record the metrics to a file for historical archiving.

Systems monitor

A systems monitor is used to watch over system metrics, such as CPU usage, active processes, memory consumption, free drive space, system temperatures, etc. Performance monitoring and system monitoring are quite similar—in fact, they are often either the same or have significant overlap in what is viewed or monitored through their respective interfaces. However, in general, performance monitoring watches over real-time activities of users, processes, and resources, while system monitoring watches over more physical elements or environmental issues.

Performance baseline

A performance baseline is an expected level of system performance as measured through a performance monitoring tool. A *baseline* can be defined in a policy, extracted from real activity levels, or determined by general consensus (defining what is wanted). Once a baseline is established, comparison to the baseline determines when a system needs adjustment,

improvement, or repair to return performance levels to baseline levels. Deviations from baselines can be symptoms of an overtaxed infrastructure, misconfigurations, malfunctions, or malicious activity.

Protocol analyzers

Protocol analyzers were discussed earlier in this chapter; please see section 4.2.

Exam Essentials

Performance monitor A performance monitor is used to watch the relative activity of system metrics and compare them to known baselines, problem trends, or malicious anomalies.

Systems monitor A systems monitor is used to watch over system metrics, such as CPU usage, active processes, memory consumption, free drive space, system temperatures, etc.

Performance baseline A performance baseline is an expected level of system performance as measured through a performance monitoring tool. A baseline can be defined in a policy, extracted from real activity levels, or determined by general consensus (defining what is wanted).

4.5 Compare and contrast various types of monitoring methodologies.

There are many tools used for monitoring or overseeing the activities within the complex infrastructures of networks and systems, such as performance monitors, system monitors, IDS, protocol analyzers, etc. Many of these tools also support one or more methodologies of monitoring. These methodologies determine how a tool knows when a measurement or event is normal, abnormal, benign, malicious, etc.

 For more information on this topic, see Chapter 3 of the *CompTIA Security+ Study Guide, 4th Edition* (Sybex, November 2008).

Behavior-based

A behavior-based monitoring or detection method relies upon the establishment of a baseline or a definition of normal and benign. Once this baseline is established, the monitoring tool is able to detect activities that vary from that standard of normal. The strength of a

behavior-based system is that it can detect any type of change or difference, including new heretofore unseen and unknown issues, such as zero-day intrusion attacks. However, the weaknesses of behavior-based attacks include the fact that defining what is normal is a very difficult challenge. Determining what is benign or malicious when nonstandard activity occurs is also not easy nor often possible with an automated behavior-based tool.

Signature-based

A signature-based monitoring or detection method relies on a database of signatures or patterns or known malicious or unwanted activity. The strength of a signature-based system is that it can quickly and accurately detect any event from its database of signatures. However, the primary weakness of a signature-based system is that it is unable to detect new and unknown activities or events. Thus, new zero-day attacks are unseen by a signature-based system. As new attacks are discovered and the pattern database improved, the deployed signature-based tools need to have their local databases updated.

Anomaly-based

An anomaly-based monitoring or detection method relies on definitions of all valid forms of activity. This database of known valid activity allows the tool to detect any and all anomalies. Anomaly-based detection is commonly used for protocols. Because all the valid and legal forms of a protocol are known and can be defined, any variations from those known valid constructions are seen as anomalies. Anomaly detection is very effective at stopping abnormal events. However, just because traffic or events are within normal values does not necessarily mean the contents of that event or traffic are not malicious in nature.

Exam Essentials

Behavior-based detection A behavior-based monitoring or detection method relies upon the establishment of a baseline or a definition of normal and benign. Once this baseline is established, the monitoring tool is able to detect activities that vary from that standard of normal.

Signature-based detection A signature-based monitoring or detection method relies on a database of signatures or patterns or known malicious or unwanted activity. The strength of a signature-based system is that it can quickly and accurately detect any event from its database of signatures.

Anomaly-based detection An anomaly-based monitoring or detection method relies on definitions of all valid forms of activity. This database of known valid activity allows the tool to detect any and all anomalies.

4.6 Execute proper logging procedures and evaluate the results.

The key aspect of this issue is understanding that auditing is the primary means by which security violations are discovered. Through the use of a system's auditing capabilities, audit trails or logs are created. Audit trails enable auditors or administrators to detect when security violating activities have occurred and may assist in understanding how such a violation was allowed to occur.

 For more information on this topic, see Chapter 3 of the *CompTIA Security+ Study Guide, 4th Edition* (Sybex, November 2008).

Auditing is the process of recording information about various online, electronic, digital events between subjects and objects. It's often synonymous with *logging* and *monitoring*. The goal of auditing is to check compliance with security policy and to discover security violations or system errors. Some common activities that are audited include logging on, logging off, reading files, deleting files, using remote access services, and using applications.

Effective auditing starts with detailed planning. You must know what you want to audit for in order to properly configure a system (if not an entire network) to record the desired information. Auditing everything will result in too much audit output, whereas auditing too little won't gather sufficient information for detection or event reconstruction.

The recorded results of auditing are called *audit trails* or *logs*. Logs are reviewed in order to discover abnormalities, discrepancies, or outright security violations. With sufficiently extensive logging, it's possible to reconstruct events leading up to a security violation. Auditing often enables system administrators to discover the perpetrator of the violation as well as pinpoint the systems and resources involved.

A closely related issue is *system scanning*. System scanning, penetration testing, and vulnerability scanning are all similar concepts. The point is to test the configuration of a system or network to determine if all known security weaknesses have been patched or addressed correctly. System scanning produces an audit report listing all of the weaknesses and vulnerabilities of the scanned system. Often the report includes suggestions or recommendations on how to resolve the discovered problems.

Security application

The proper logging procedures for a security application often depend upon exactly what type of security application it is. However, common logging procedures can be applied universally. First, all logged events should include as much detail as possible. The more detail is available, the more valuable the log becomes when tracking down a violation. Second, all logged items should be secured against tampering and locked down against access by

unauthorized users. Third, a backup or secondary log should be created in tandem to the primary log, preferably on a different system. This is commonly known as centralized logging. Finally, every activity performed by this application, every action performed by a user controlling this application, and every event seen by this application should be recorded into a log. This level and breadth of logging is necessary to fully establish a chain of custody, confirm proper use, and validate all findings. Additionally, you should work from copies of logs instead of the originals when performing in-house reviews or investigations in order to absolutely preserve their integrity for potential legal action.

DNS

DNS server logging should mainly be concerned with two primary activities: changes to the zone data and queries for zone transfers. By logging all changes, it becomes possible to track down when and how invalid or incorrect information appeared in the zone file. Logging zone transfers requests and not just actual valid zone transfers helps determine if reconnaissance attacks against the DNS are being attempted and if they are successful.

System

System logging is as varied as the security policies and functions of an organization. Most of the details of what to log, how long to keep logs, and who is allowed to access those logs is determined by the organization, its policies, and the sensitivity or value of its resources. However, rules of thumb for proper logging procedures include logging all attempts to access all resources that are of a sensitive nature, duplicating all logs on centralized logging servers, and protecting all logs from unauthorized access and modification.

Performance

Performance logging is usually not as sensitive as security logging, but it is still important information that should be protected against modification or unauthorized access. For each watched system or performance metric, a threshold should be defined. Whenever the measurement of the metric exceeds that threshold, the details of event should be logged.

Access

Access logs are an important part of security monitoring. As with all sensitive logs, proper logging procedures include logging all attempts to access any resources that are of a sensitive nature. All logs should be duplicated on centralized logging servers and should be protected from unauthorized access and modification. Additionally, pay attention to success and failure events, especially when they're related to logon and resource access. Repeated failures often indicate intrusion attempts or users attempting to exceed their privileges. However, success events can also be indications of intrusion when the valid user of an account is on vacation or unable to log on, but his or her account is in use.

Firewall

Firewall logs are important when seeking information about attempted and successful intrusion attempts. Whether your firewall logs record all events or just denied events is an organizational decision. As with all sensitive logs, rules of thumb for proper logging procedures include logging all attempts to access any resources that are of a sensitive nature, duplicating all logs on centralized logging servers, and protecting all logs from unauthorized access and modification.

Antivirus

Most antivirus logging is the recording of discovery of malicious software. Items that are scanned that are not seen as malicious do not typically mandate that a log entry be created. As with all sensitive logs, proper logging procedures include logging all attempts to access resources that are of a sensitive nature. All logs should be duplicated on centralized logging servers and should be protected from unauthorized access and modification.

Exam Essentials

Auditing Auditing is the process of recording information about various online, electronic, digital events between subjects and objects. The goal of auditing is to check compliance with security policy and to discover security violations or system errors. Some common activities that are audited include logging on, logging off, reading files, deleting files, using remote access services, and using applications.

Proper logging procedures As with all sensitive logs, rules of thumb for proper logging procedures include logging all attempts to access for all resources that are of a sensitive nature. All logs should be duplicated on centralized logging servers, and all logs should be protected from unauthorized access and modification.

4.7 Conduct periodic audits of system security settings.

Auditing or reviewing system security settings is a standard element of security management. This is a task that should be performed on a regular basis across the entire organization on both logical infrastructure components as well as physical facility elements.

For more information on this topic, see Chapter 3 of the *CompTIA Security+ Study Guide, 4th Edition* (Sybex, November 2008).

User access and rights review

User access and rights reviews often are based on a review of assigned resources privileges. A *privilege* is an ability or activity that a user account is granted permission to perform. User accounts are often assigned privileges based on their work tasks and their normal activities. The *principle of least privilege* is a security rule of thumb that states that users should be granted only the level of access needed for them to accomplish their assigned work tasks, and no more. Furthermore, those privileges should be assigned for the shortest time period possible.

Exploitation of privileges is known as *privilege abuse* or *privilege escalation*. Privilege escalation occurs when a user account is able to obtain unauthorized access to higher levels of privileges, such as a normal user account that can perform administrative functions. Privilege escalation can occur through the use of a hacker tool or an incorrectly configured environment. It can also occur when lazy administrators fail to remove older privileges as a user is granted new privileges based on new job descriptions. An accumulation of privileges can be considered a form of privilege escalation.

Auditing and review of access and privilege should be used to monitor and track not just the assignment of privilege and the unauthorized escalation of privilege but also privilege usage. Knowing what users are doing and how often they do it may assist administrators in assigning and managing privileges.

Storage and retention policies

Storage and retention policies often revolve around collections of logs and audit trails, security monitoring reports, and backups. These types of policies define what types of data sets are to be protected, how they are to be stored, how they are to be secured, how long they will be retained, who will be allowed to access the data, for what purposes the data can be put to use, and how the data will be destroyed at the end of its retention lifetime. The answers to these items are fully dependent upon the organization and their internal and external requirements to best business practice, industry standards, rules of law, and protection against lawsuits.

Periodic audits of the storage and retention policies as well as the procedures followed to implement the policy will reveal deficiencies or oversights.

Group policies

Group policies (as discussed in Chapter 1) are used to implement controls on domain members. As with any element of security, group policies should be inspected and reviewed on a regular basis. The primary reason to audit group policies is to ensure that the deployed group policies are in compliance with the written baselines and security policies. If there is any deviation, either the group policy needs to be adjusted or the written policy changed. Group policies are used to define and control a wide variety of function, capability, and security elements of domain members, including auditing, passwords, and user rights.

Exam Essentials

Periodic audits Periodic audits are used to ensure that deployed elements of infrastructure and procedures are in compliance with standards and security policy.

Review Questions

1. What is the primary goal of auditing?
 A. Detect virus infections
 B. Look for rogue services
 C. Scan for open ports
 D. Check compliance with security policy

2. Which of the following risk assessment formulas represents the total potential loss a company may experience within a single year due to a specific risk to an asset?
 A. EF
 B. SLE
 C. ARO
 D. ALE

3. What is an asset?
 A. An item costing more than $10,000
 B. Anything used in a work task
 C. A threat to the security of an organization
 D. An intangible resource

4. Which of the following is not a feature or capability of a port scanner?
 A. Determine open ports
 B. Determine active services
 C. Determine target OS
 D. Determine weakness of OS

5. What is a significant difference between vulnerability scanners and penetration testing?
 A. One tests both the infrastructure and personnel
 B. One only tests internal weaknesses
 C. One only tests for configuration errors
 D. One is used to find problems before hackers do

6. A password cracker is needed to quickly rediscover a password. It is believed the password is only seven characters long, but was computer generated. Which of the following techniques would be the best method to use?
 A. Online guessing
 B. Dictionary
 C. Brute force
 D. Hybrid

7. Which of the following is the least valid approach or method used in penetration testing?

 A. Use automated tool attacks

 B. Perform attacks from the Internet

 C. Social engineer attacks

 D. Attack remote connectivity portals

8. What detection technique is best suited for detecting zero-day malicious content within valid transmissions?

 A. Performance monitoring

 B. Behavior-based

 C. Signature-based

 D. Anomaly-based

9. Which of the following is the least important aspect of proper logging procedures?

 A. Perform centralized logging

 B. Deter unauthorized access

 C. Use high-speed data links

 D. Prevent modification

10. What is the purpose of regular audits of system security settings?

 A. Check for intrusions and breaches

 B. Check that implementation matches policy

 C. Check for performance improvements

 D. Check the inventory for insurance purposes

Answers to Review Questions

1. D. The primary goal of auditing is to check compliance with security policy. Virus infection detection is handed by a virus scanner. Rogue service detection is performed manually or with a sniffer. Port scanning is performed with a port-scanning tool.

2. D. The annual loss expectancy (ALE) represents the total potential loss a company may experience within a single year due to a specific risk to an asset. EF is the percentage of asset value loss that would occur if a risk was realized. SLE is the potential dollar value loss from a single risk realization incident. ARO is the statistical probability that a specific risk may be realized a certain number of times in a year.

3. B. An asset is anything used in a work task.

4. D. A port scanner can determine open ports, OS type, and active services. It cannot determine whether an OS is vulnerable or has a weakness.

5. A. The primary difference between vulnerability assessment and penetration testing is that penetration testing tests both the infrastructure and the personnel. Vulnerability assessment is performed by a security administrator using an automated tool that is designed solely to test the configuration of target systems.

6. C. The method of brute force password cracking is best suited for situations where the complexity of the password is unknown, it is likely not based on a single word, and it has a reasonable character length.

7. A. Penetration testing is used to perform security testing with the tools and techniques of real criminal hackers. Using an automated tool is the purview of security assessment and probably not used by most criminal hackers due to its lack of zero-day attacks and minimal customization of exploits.

8. B. Behavior-based detection is best suited to detect zero-day malicious content in valid traffic.

9. C. The use of high-speed data links is the least important requirement (if a requirement at all) for proper logging procedures. Centralized logging, access control, and integrity management are much more important.

10. B. The purpose of regular audits of system security settings is to check that implementation matches policy.

Chapter

5

Cryptography

COMPTIA SECURITY+ EXAM OBJECTIVES COVERED IN THIS CHAPTER INCLUDE THE FOLLOWING:

✓ **5.1 Explain general cryptography concepts.**

- Key management
- Steganography
- Symmetric key
- Asymmetric key
- Confidentiality
- Integrity and availability
- Non-repudiation
- Comparative strength of algorithms
- Digital signatures
- Whole disk encryption
- Trusted Platform Module (TPM)
- Single vs. Dual sided certificates
- Use of proven technologies

✓ **5.2 Explain basic hashing concepts and map various algorithms to appropriate applications.**

- SHA
- MD5
- LANMAN
- NTLM

✓ **5.3 Explain basic encryption concepts and map various algorithms to appropriate applications.**

- DES
- 3DES
- RSA
- PGP
- Elliptic curve

- AES
- AES256
- One time pad
- Transmission encryption (WEP, TKIP, etc)

✓ **5.4 Explain and implement protocols.**

- SSL/TLS
- S/MIME
- PPTP
- HTTP vs. HTTPS vs. SHTTP
- L2TP
- IPSEC
- SSH

✓ **5.5 Explain core concepts of public key cryptography.**

- Public Key Infrastructure (PKI)
- Recovery agent
- Public key
- Private keys
- Certificate Authority (CA)
- Registration
- Key escrow
- Certificate Revocation List (CRL)
- Trust models

✓ **5.6 Implement PKI and certificate management.**

- Public Key Infrastructure (PKI)
- Recovery agent
- Public key
- Private keys
- Certificate Authority (CA)
- Registration
- Key escrow
- Certificate Revocation List (CRL)

The Security+ exam will test your knowledge of cryptography. You will need to be familiar with both symmetric and asymmetric cryptography as well as hashing, certificates, and digital signatures. Make the effort to memorize the various examples of cryptography discussed in this chapter.

5.1 Explain general cryptography concepts.

There is a wide breadth of topics related to cryptography. Some of these are foundational issues, some are security services, and others are solutions or implementations. This section discusses many important general cryptography concepts that are addressed on the Security+ exam.

Key management

Key management is the term used to describe the various mechanisms, techniques, and processes used to protect, use, distribute, store, and control cryptographic keys. A key management solution should follow these basic rules:

- The key should be long enough to provide the necessary level of protection.
- Keys should be stored and transmitted securely.
- Keys should be truly random, should use the full spectrum of the keyspace (the range of valid values that can be used as a key for a specific algorithm), and should never repeat.
- The lifetime of a key should correspond to the sensitivity of the data it's protecting.
- The more a key is used, the shorter its lifetime should be.
- The shorter the key length or bit length of the algorithm, the shorter the lifetime of the key.
- Keys should be backed up or escrowed in case of emergency.
- Keys should be properly destroyed at the end of their lifetime.

Centralized key management gives complete control of cryptographic keys to the organization and takes control away from the end users. A centralized key management solution requires a significant investment in infrastructure, processing capabilities, administrative oversight, and communication bandwidth.

In a centralized management solution, copies of all or most cryptographic keys are often stored in escrow. This allows administrators to recover keys in the event that a user loses their key, but it also allows management to access encrypted data whenever it chooses.

Other important aspects of centralized key management are that keys must be created only on secured, dedicated servers; keys can be distributed only to authorized users and only in a secure fashion; keys can be modified only by administrators; and revocation of keys and corresponding digital certificates is at the discretion of the organization. Figure 5.1 shows an example of a centralized key management solution.

FIGURE 5.1 A centralized key-generating facility

Key
transmittal
process

Key generator

Centralized key management is often unacceptable to a public or open user community because it does not provide any control over privacy, confidentiality, or integrity. In fact, every key generated by the centralized system is usually stored in escrow. Therefore, nothing encrypted by an end user is completely private, because an administrator could extract the key from escrow and use it to decrypt a message or file.

An alternate scheme is known as decentralized key management. In this type of environment, end users generate their keys (whether symmetric or asymmetric) and submit keys only as needed to centralized authorities (see Figure 5.2). For example, to request a digital certificate, an end user would transmit only their public key to the CA. The end user's private key is always kept private so they're the only entity in possession of it. Plus, because the public key is already public, its compromise won't result in a complete compromise of the end user's secured solution.

In a decentralized key management system, end users are ultimately responsible for managing their own keys and using escrow to provide fault tolerance. If an end user fails to take the necessary precautions, a lost or corrupted key could mean the loss of all data encrypted with that key.

Cryptographic keys and digital certificates should be stored securely. If a private key (asymmetric) or a secret key (symmetric) is ever compromised, then the security of all data encrypted with those keys is lost. Reliable storage mechanisms must be used to protect cryptographic keys. There are two methods or mechanisms for storing keys: hardware based or software based.

FIGURE 5.2 A decentralized key generating system

Keys can be stored in either software solutions or hardware solutions. Both offer unique benefits and shortcomings. A software solution offers flexible storage mechanisms and often, customizable options. However, such a solution is vulnerable to electronic attacks (viruses or intrusions), may not properly control access (privilege-elevation attacks), and may be deleted or destroyed. Most software solutions rely on the security of the host operating system, which may not be sufficient.

Hardware solutions aren't as flexible. However, they're more reliable and more secure than software solutions. Hardware solutions may be expensive and are subject to physical theft. If a user isn't in physical possession of the hardware storage solution, they can't gain access to the secured or encrypted resources. Some common examples of hardware key storage solutions include smartcards and flash memory drives.

In some situations, you may use multiple key pairs. One key set might be used for authentication and encryption and the other for digital signatures. This allows the first key pair to be escrowed and included on data backups of a centralized key management scheme. The second key set is then protected from compromise, and the privacy of the owner's digital signature is protected, preventing misuse and forgery.

Steganography

Steganography is a process by which one communication is hidden inside another communication. This can be as simple as hiding a code within a sentence that can be extracted by reading only every fifth word or as complex as embedding a text document inside a movie or audio file. One of the most common forms of steganography is to hide text inside graphics. Steganography often uses passwords as secrets to prevent third parties from extracting the

stored communication and may also employ encryption to prevent or hinder brute force attempts at extraction. Steganography can be used to detect theft, fraud, or modification when the hidden communication is a watermark.

Symmetric key

Symmetric cryptography is also called private key cryptography or secret key cryptography. It uses a single shared encryption key to encrypt and decrypt data (see Figure 5.3). When symmetric cryptography is used to encrypt files on a hard drive, the user is the only person in possession of the single secret key. When symmetric cryptography is used to encrypt communications traffic, the two communication partners each have a copy of the one shared secret key. For example, the secure communication session protocol of Secure Socket Layer (SSL) uses symmetric cryptography. In either use, symmetric cryptography protects confidentiality.

FIGURE 5.3 A symmetric encryption system

Symmetric cryptography is very fast in comparison to asymmetric cryptography (discussed next). Its speed is due to the way its algorithms are designed and the fact that a single key is used to encrypt and decrypt data.

Symmetric cryptography provides for strong encryption protection when larger keys are used. However, the protection is secure only as long as the keys are kept private. If a symmetric key is compromised or stolen, it no longer offers true protection (just as your door lock no longer provides security if someone gets a copy of your house key).

Key exchange or distribution under symmetric cryptography is a common problem. To use symmetric cryptography to encrypt communications traffic between you and someone else over the Internet (or some other untrusted network), you must have a means to securely exchange the secret keys. If you already have a means to exchange the secret keys securely, why aren't you using that mechanism to communicate? Thus, some out-of-band communication solution must be implemented to securely exchange keys. Mechanisms include shipping a floppy with a key, reading it over the phone, or using a different network to transmit the key. However, the preferred method is to deploy a complete *Public Key Infrastructure* (PKI) solution that employs asymmetric cryptography to exchange symmetric cryptographic keys. The exchanged secret keys are used to encrypt the traffic for a single communication

session, then they're discarded. PKI is simply a concept of how to deploy different aspects of various cryptography mechanisms into a single, complete, real-world solution.

Because each member of a network in a symmetric cryptography solution needs to have a shared secret key with every other member in order to support secure communications, $n(n − 1)/2$ keys are needed. Thus, symmetric cryptography isn't scalable when used alone.

Symmetric cryptography is divided into two forms:

Block cipher A block cipher is a solution that works against a complete static data set. That data set is broken into fixed-length segments called blocks, and each block is encrypted separately.

Stream cipher A stream cipher is a solution that works against data that is constantly being produced on the fly. Stream ciphers can operate on a bit, character, or buffer basis of encrypting data in real-time. A buffer, much like a block, waits to be filled by data as it's produced. When the buffer block is full, that block is encrypted and then transmitted to the receiver.

Other than the basic difference in whether the original data is preexisting and static or produced on the fly, both ciphers function in much the same manner. Unless the symmetric cryptography solution is based around a one time pad (meaning every key is used only once), the same encryption key is used on each block or buffer block for a given data set or communication session.

The most widely used symmetric cryptography solutions are listed in Table 5.1.

TABLE 5.1 Common Symmetric Cryptography Solutions

Name	Block Size	Key Size (in bits)
Advanced Encryption Standard (AES; uses the Rijndael block cipher algorithm)	128	128, 192, and 256
Triple Data Encryption Standard (3DES)	64	168
Data Encryption Standard (DES)	64	56
International Data Encryption Algorithm (IDEA)	64	128
Blowfish	64	32 to 448
Twofish	128	128, 192, or 256
Rivest Cipher 5 (RC5)	32, 64, 128	0–2040
Carlisle Adams/Stafford Tavares (CAST-128)	64	40 to 128 in increments of 8

Asymmetric key

Asymmetric cryptography is also called public key cryptography. It uses key pairs consisting of a public key and a private key (see Figure 5.4). Each communication partner in an asymmetric cryptography solution needs its own unique key pair set (a private key and a public key); this makes asymmetric cryptography much more scalable than symmetric. The private key of the key pair must be kept private and secure. The public key of the key pair is distributed freely and openly.

FIGURE 5.4 An asymmetric encryption system

Encrypts using recipient's public key Decrypts using recipient's private key

Message Message

The public and private keys are related mathematically, but possession of the public key doesn't allow someone to generate the private key. Thus, the integrity of the private key is protected. In addition, the keys always work in unison: If the public key is used to encrypt data, only the private key can decrypt it. Likewise, if the private key is used to encrypt data, only the public key can decrypt it.

Asymmetric cryptography functions as follows:

1. The sender writes a message.

2. The sender encrypts the message with the sender's private key to produce the interim message package.

3. The sender encrypts the interim message package with the recipient's public key to produce the message package.

4. The sender transmits the message package to the recipient.

5. The recipient decrypts the message package using the recipient's private key to produce the interim message package.

6. The recipient decrypts the interim message package using the sender's public key to extract the original message.

Asymmetric cryptography is much slower than symmetric cryptography, so it isn't generally suited for encrypting a large amount of data. It's often used as the secure exchange mechanism for symmetric cryptographic keys. It provides several security services: authentication, integrity protection, and non-repudiation.

The most widely used asymmetric cryptography solutions are as follows:

- Rivest-Shamir-Adleman (RSA)
- Diffie-Hellman

- Elliptic Curve Cryptography (ECC)
- El Gamal

Confidentiality

Confidentiality protects the secrecy of data, information, or resources. It prevents or minimizes unauthorized access to data (see Figure 5.5). It ensures that no one other than the intended recipient of a message receives it or is able to read it. Confidentiality protection provides a means for authorized users to access and interact with resources, but it actively prevents unauthorized users from doing so.

FIGURE 5.5 Cryptographic systems protect data from internal and external disclosure.

Cryptography protects information from being disclosed during external attacks.

Cryptography protects private records from attack.

Integrity and availability

Integrity is the security service that protects the reliability and correctness of data. Integrity protection prevents unauthorized alterations of data (see Figure 5.6). It ensures that data remains correct, unaltered, and preserved. Integrity protection provides a means for authorized changes to be implemented, but it actively prevents unauthorized changes to protected data. Integrity protection resists changes by unauthorized activities (such as viruses or intrusions) and accidents by authorized users (such as mistakes or oversights). Often an integrity check uses a hashing function to verify that data remains unchanged in storage or after transit.

FIGURE 5.6 A simple integrity-checking process for an encrypted message

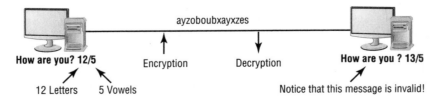

Availability is the security service that provides protection for the use of a resource in a timely and effective manner. Often availability protection controls support sufficient bandwidth and timeliness of processing as deemed necessary by the organization or situation. When availability is protected, users can perform their work tasks in an efficient and timely manner. When availability is violated, workers cannot accomplish their assigned tasks. Availability can be violated through the destruction or modification of a resource, overloading of a resource host, interference with communications to a resource host, or compromise on an access client from being able to communicate with a resource host.

Non-repudiation

Non-repudiation prevents the sender of a message or the perpetrator of an activity from being able to deny that they sent the message or performed the activity. In asymmetric cryptography, non-repudiation is supported when a sender's private key is used to successfully decrypt a message. This proves that the sender's private key was used to encrypt the data. Because the sender is the only user who has possession of the sender's private key, no one else could have encrypted and sent the message. Often the security service of non-repudiation is dependent upon authentication and authorization (access control) mechanisms.

Authentication verifies the identity of the sender or recipient of a message. In cryptography terms, authentication occurs differently in symmetric cryptography than it does in asymmetric cryptography. In symmetric cryptography, a single shared secret key is held only by the two communication partners. Thus, when an encrypted message is received and is properly decrypted by the recipient's copy of the shared secret key, authentication occurs. The recipient is authenticated because possession of the correct key proves that this is the correct recipient of the encrypted message. Likewise, the sender is authenticated because the recipient's ability to extract an intelligible message from the received encrypted material using the secret key proves that the sender, the only other user with possession of the same secret key, encrypted and sent the message.

In asymmetric cryptography, a sender uses the recipient's public key to encrypt data. This forces authentication of the recipient because the recipient is the only user in possession of the corresponding private key. Likewise, when the sender's private key is used to encrypt data, then any recipient can verify the sender's identity by decrypting that data with the sender's public key.

Access control restricts access to secured data to authorized users. Cryptographic access control is enforced through the concept of possession of encryption keys. In a symmetric cryptography solution, a maximum of two people have valid possession of the shared secret key. Thus possession of the shared secret key is proof of authorization: The holder of the shared secret key is authorized to access anything encrypted with that key. In asymmetric cryptography, only one person is in valid possession of the private key. Thus, possession of the private key is proof of authorization: The holder of the private key is authorized to access anything encrypted with the corresponding public key.

Comparative strength of algorithms

The comparative strengths of algorithms are based on numerous factors. The two most common are key length and work factor. Key length was addressed in the "Key management" section earlier in this chapter. Work factor is a judgment or measurement of the amount of time and effort involved in performing a complete brute force attack on a specific algorithm. Algorithms with larger work factors are considered stronger than those with smaller work factors. While there really isn't a hard measurement guideline, it is used as a relative measurement between compared algorithms and is based around the keyspace, the speed and number of computers used, as well as the philosophy or approach of the attack itself.

Digital signatures

A *digital signature* is an electronic mechanism to prove that a message was sent from a specific user (that is, it provides for non-repudiation) and that the message wasn't changed while in transit (it also provides integrity). Digital signatures operate using a hashing algorithm and either a symmetric or an asymmetric encryption solution.

Digital signatures using asymmetric encryption solutions operate as follows:

1. The sender writes a message.
2. The sender computes a hash of the message.
3. The sender uses the sender's private key to encrypt the hash.
4. The sender attaches the encrypted hash to the message.
5. The complete message package is sent to the receiver.
6. The receiver strips off the encrypted hash (the digital signature).
7. The receiver uses the sender's public key to decrypt the sender's private key and thus extract the hash from the digital signature.
8. The receiver computes a hash of the message.
9. The receiver compares the two hash values.

Digital signatures using symmetric encryption solutions (see Figure 5.7) operate as follows:

1. The sender writes a message.
2. The sender computes a hash of the message.
3. The sender uses the shared secret key to encrypt the hash.
4. The sender attaches the encrypted hash to the message.
5. The complete message package is sent to the receiver.
6. The receiver strips off the encrypted hash.
7. The receiver uses the shared secret key to decrypt the hash.

8. The receiver computes a hash of the message.

9. The receiver compares the two hash values.

FIGURE 5.7 A digital signature process using symmetric encryption

In either case, if the hash values match, the recipient gets verification that integrity was maintained and that the sender did send the message (non-repudiation). If the hash values don't match, the recipient doesn't have verification of either integrity protection or non-repudiation.

Whole disk encryption

Whole disk encryption is often used to provide protection for an operating system, its installed applications, and all locally stored data. However, whole disk encryption only provides reasonable protection when the system is fully powered off. If a system is accessed by a hacker while it is active, there are several ways around hard drive encryption. These include a firewall DMA attack or slowing down memory decay rates with liquid nitrogen. The details of these attacks are not important for this exam. However, knowledge that whole disk encryption is only a partial security control *is* important.

In order to maximize the defensive strength of whole disk encryption, a long and complex passphrase should be used to unlock the system upon bootup. This passphrase should not be written down or used on any other system or for any other purpose. Any time the system is not actively in use, it should be powered down and physically locked against unauthorized access or theft. Hard drive encryption should be viewed as a delaying tactic, rather than a true prevention of access to hard drive stored data.

Trusted Platform Module (TPM)

The Trusted Platform Module (TPM) is both a specification for a cryptoprocessor as well as the chip in a mainboard supporting this function. A TPM chip is used to store and process cryptographic keys for the purposes of a hardware supported/implemented hard drive encryption system. Generally, a hardware implementation rather than a software-only implementation of hard drive encryption is considered to be more secure.

When TPM-based whole disk encryption is in use, the user/operator must supply a password or physical USB token device to the computer to authenticate and allow the TPM chip to release the hard drive encryption keys into memory. While this seems similar to a software implementation, the key difference is that if the hard drive is removed from its original system, it cannot be decrypted. Only with the original TPM chip can an encrypted hard drive be decrypted and accessed. With software-only hard drive encryption, the hard drive can be moved to a different computer without any access or use limitations.

Single vs. Dual sided certificates

The intended topic was the single sided versus mutual exchange of certificates during session establishment. A single sided or one-way certificate exchange occurs whenever only one party in a communication provides their certificate or proof of identity. This commonly occurs on the Internet when using SSL to craft a secure communication link with an e-commerce website. In this situation, only the web server's certificate is sent to the visiting client. Such a session configuration is fine unless a sophisticated man-in-the-middle attack is performed where the client communicates with a false front site that is masquerading as the legitimate web server.

Mutual or two-way certificate exchange eliminates this weakness and assures both parties that the opposing entity is valid. This method of dual certificate exchange is more common within private enterprise networks.

Use of proven technologies

In general, when deploying security it is in an organization's interest to use proven and tested technologies. Relying upon new technologies, experimental products, or untested implementations is often a recipe for security disaster. Your organization should select proven security technologies products with a reasonable track record of success. Doing otherwise greatly increases the risks and likelihood of security compromise.

Exam Essentials

Key management basics Keys should be long enough to provide the necessary level of protection, should be stored and transmitted securely, should be random, and should use the full spectrum of the keyspace. In addition, they should be escrowed, properly destroyed at

the end of their lifetime, used in correspondence with the sensitivity of the protected data, and have a shortened use lifespan if they're used repeatedly.

Centralized key management Centralized key management gives complete control of cryptographic keys to the organization and takes control away from the end users. In a centralized management solution, copies of all cryptographic keys are stored in escrow.

Decentralized key management In decentralized key management, end users generate their keys (whether symmetric or asymmetric) and submit keys only as needed to centralized authorities. The end user's private key is always kept private so they are the only entity in possession of it.

Symmetric cryptography Symmetric cryptography is also called private key cryptography or secret key cryptography. Symmetric cryptography uses a single shared encryption key to encrypt and decrypt data. It provides the security service of confidentiality protection.

Strengths and weaknesses of symmetric cryptography Symmetric cryptography is very fast in comparison to asymmetric cryptography. It provides for strong encryption protection when larger keys are used. However, the protection is secure only as long as the keys are kept private. Key exchange under symmetric cryptography is a common problem. Symmetric cryptography isn't scalable when used alone.

Block ciphers A block cipher is a solution that works against a complete static data set. That data set is broken into fixed-length segments called blocks, and each block is encrypted separately.

Stream ciphers A stream cipher is a solution that works against data that is constantly being produced on the fly. Stream ciphers can operate on a bit, character, or buffer basis of encrypting data in real-time. A buffer, much like a block, waits to be filled by data as it's produced. When the buffer block is full, that block is encrypted and then transmitted to the receiver.

Common symmetric cryptography solutions The common symmetric solutions are Advanced Encryption Standard (AES), Triple Data Encryption Standard (3DES), Data Encryption Standard (DES), International Data Encryption Algorithm (IDEA), Blowfish, Twofish, Rivest Cipher 5 (RC5), and Carlisle Adams/Stafford Tavares (CAST-128).

Asymmetric cryptography Asymmetric cryptography is also called public key cryptography. It uses key pairs consisting of a public key and a private key. Each communication partner in an asymmetric cryptography solution needs only a key pair.

Strengths and weaknesses of asymmetric cryptography Asymmetric cryptography is scalable. The private key of the key pair must be kept private and secure. The public key of the key pair is distributed freely and openly. Possession of the public key doesn't allow someone to generate the private key. Asymmetric cryptography is much slower than symmetric cryptography. It provides three security services: authentication, integrity protection, and non-repudiation.

Common asymmetric cryptography solutions The common asymmetric solutions are Rivest-Shamir-Adleman (RSA), Diffie-Hellman, Elliptic Curve Cryptography (ECC), and El Gamal.

Confidentiality Confidentiality prevents or minimizes unauthorized access to data. It ensures that no one other than the intended recipient of a message receives it or is able to read it.

Integrity Integrity protection prevents unauthorized alterations of data. It ensures that data remains correct, unaltered, and preserved. Integrity protection provides a means for authorized changes to be implemented, but it actively prevents unauthorized changes to protected data.

Digital signatures A digital signature is an electronic mechanism to prove that a message was sent from a specific user and that the message wasn't changed while in transit. Digital signatures operate using a hashing algorithm and either a symmetric or an asymmetric encryption solution.

Authentication The security service that verifies the identity of the sender or receiver of a message is authentication.

Non-repudiation Non-repudiation prevents the sender of a message or the perpetrator of an activity from being able to deny that they sent the message or performed the activity.

Access control Access control restricts access to secured data to authorized users. Cryptographic access control is enforced through the possession of encryption keys.

Key storage Cryptographic keys and digital certificates should be stored securely. If a private key (asymmetric) or a secret key (symmetric) is ever compromised, then the security of all data encrypted with the key is lost.

Software key storage A software solution offers flexible storage mechanisms and often, customizable options. However, a software solution is vulnerable to electronic attacks (viruses or intrusions), may not properly control access (privilege-elevation attacks), and may be deleted or destroyed. Most software solutions rely on the security of the host OS, which may not be sufficient.

Hardware key storage Hardware solutions aren't as flexible. However, they're more reliable and more secure than software solutions. Hardware solutions may be expensive and are subject to physical theft. If a user isn't in physical possession of the hardware storage solution, they can't gain access to the secured or encrypted resources. Some common examples of hardware key storage solutions include smartcards and flash memory drives.

Private key protection In a symmetric system, all entities in possession of the shared secret key must protect the privacy and secrecy of that key. If the key is compromised anywhere or by anyone, the entire solution (all entities using the same key) is compromised (everything protected by that key).

Use of multiple key pairs In some situations, you may use multiple key pairs. One key set might be used for authentication and encryption and the other for digital signatures. This allows the first key pair to be escrowed and included on data backups of a centralized key management scheme. The second key set is then protected from compromise, and the privacy of the owner's digital signature is protected, preventing misuse and forgery.

5.2 Explain basic hashing concepts and map various algorithms to appropriate applications.

Hashing is a type of cryptography that isn't an encryption algorithm. Instead, hashing is used to produce a unique identifier—known as a hash value, hash, checksum, message authentication code (MAC), fingerprint, or message digest—of data. The data could be a file, a hard drive, a network traffic packet, or an e-mail message. The hash value is used to detect when changes have been made to a resource. In other words, hashing is used to detect violations of data integrity.

For example, a hash value computed now may be compared with a hash value created last week. If the two values are the same, the data hasn't been changed. If the two values are different, the data has been modified. Figure 5.8 shows the basic functionality of a hash or MAC value.

FIGURE 5.8 The MAC value is calculated by the sender and the receiver using the same algorithm.

Message

MAC Value: A

| Message | MAC Value: A |

MAC value is calculated independently by the user.

Message

MAC Value: A

If the MAC values are equal, the message is valid.

Unlike traditional cryptography, which transforms data into ciphertext, hashing produces a hash value without modifying the original data. Because of this special feature, hashing can be used to protect or verify data integrity. It can also be used to verify whether a copy procedure produced an exact duplicate of a data set. For example, when a hard drive is being imaged to create an exact duplicate (as is done in forensic investigations), a hash is produced of the original drive before the duplication process. Then a hash is produced of

the original drive and the duplicate drive after the duplication process. If the two hashes of the original drive are the same, no modifications have occurred to the original drive. If the duplicate drive's hash value is the same as the original drive's hash value, that proves the duplicate is an exact copy of the original.

Hashing takes a variable-length input and produces a fixed-length output. For example, Message Digest 5 (MD5) is a 128-bit hash algorithm. This means that no matter what the size of the input data, the output hash will always be 128 bits long.

The strength of hashing is the fact that it can be performed in only one direction. It isn't mathematically possible to convert a hash value back to its original data. Thus, if someone obtains your hash value, they won't be able to re-create the original data that produced the hash.

However, that isn't to say that hashing is totally attack proof. Hashing can be attacked using reverse engineering, reverse hash matching, or a birthday attack. These attack methods are commonly used by password-cracking tools. Most secure systems store passwords in their accounts database in hashed form. Hashes can't be performed in reverse, so this is generally a secure solution. However, because the hash algorithm used by commercial software is known (or can be easily discovered), password crackers can be written to exploit the stored password hashes. Attack tools compare hashes from potential passwords with the hashes stored in the accounts database. Potential passwords are either generated on the fly using all possible combinations of characters or pulled from a precompiled list of passwords (known as dictionary lists). Each potential password is hashed, and that hash value is compared with the accounts database. If a match is found, the password cracker tool has discovered a password for a user account.

This form of hashing attack exploits the mathematical characteristic that if two messages are hashed and their hashes are the same, the messages must be the same. This can be written $H(M)=H(M')$ then $M=M'$.

The most common or widely used hashing algorithms are as follows:

- **Secure Hash Algorithm (SHA-1)**—160-bit hash value
- **Message Digest 5 (MD5)**—128-bit hash value
- **Message Digest 4 (MD4)**—128-bit hash value
- **Message Digest 2 (MD2)**—128-bit hash value

SHA

As discussed in the previous section, the SHA or SHA-1 hashing algorithm produces a hash value output of 160 bits.

MD5

As discussed in the previous section, the MD5 hashing algorithm produces a hash value output of 128 bits.

LANMAN

LANMAN, or what is typically referred to as LM or LAN Manager, is a legacy storage mechanism developed by Microsoft to store passwords. LM was replaced by NTLM on Windows NT 4.0 and should be disabled and avoided on all current versions of Windows.

One of the most significant issues with LM is that it limited passwords to a maximum of 14 characters. Shorter passwords were padded out to 14 characters using null characters. The 14 characters of the password were converted to uppercase and then divided into two 7-character sections. Each 7-character section was then used as a DES encryption key to encrypt the static ASCII string of "KGS!@#$%". The two results were recombined to form the LM hash. Obviously, this system is fraught with problems. Specifically, the process is reversible and not truly a one-way hash, and all passwords were ultimately no stronger than 7 characters.

As a user, you can completely avoid LM by using passwords of at least 15 characters.

NTLM

NTLM exists in two versions. NTLM v1 is a challenge-response protocol system which, using a server-issued random challenge along with the user's password (in both LM hash and MD4 hash), produces two responses that are sent back to the server (assuming a 14-character or less password, otherwise only an MD4 hash based response is generated). NTLM v2 is also a challenge-response protocol system but uses a much more complex process which is based on MD5. Both versions of NTLM produce a hash-like result which is nonreversible and thus much more secure than LM hashing. However, reverse-engineering password-cracking mechanisms can ultimately reveal NTLM v1 or v2 stored passwords if the passwords are relatively short (under 15 characters) and given enough processing power and time on the part of the hacker.

Exam Essentials

Hashing Hashing is used to produce a unique data identifier. Hashing takes a variable-length input and produces a fixed-length output. It can be performed in only one direction. The hash value is used to detect violations of data integrity.

Hashing attacks Hashing can be attacked using reverse engineering, reverse hash matching, or a birthday attack. These attack methods are commonly used by password-cracking tools.

Common hash algorithms The common hash algorithms are Secure Hash Algorithm (SHA-1), which is a 160-bit hash value; Message Digest 5 (MD5), which is a 128-bit hash value; Message Digest 4 (MD4), which is a 128-bit hash value; and Message Digest 2 (MD2), which is a 128-bit hash value.

5.3 Explain basic encryption concepts and map various algorithms to appropriate applications.

The Security+ exam assumes you'll be able to differentiate between symmetric and asymmetric cryptography systems as well as hashing algorithms. You should be able to recognize specific examples of all three forms of cryptography.

DES

DES was addressed in the "Symmetric key" section earlier in this chapter.

3DES

3DES was addressed in the "Symmetric key" section earlier in this chapter.

RSA

RSA was addressed in the "Asymmetric key" section earlier in this chapter.

PGP

Pretty Good Privacy (PGP) is another e-mail security and encryption product that functions in much the same way as S/MIME (see discussion of S/MIME later in this chapter). PGP was developed by Phillip R. Zimmerman in 1991. It has widespread popularity with the general public as well as corporations that wish to use secured private e-mail. PGP uses RSA or Diffie-Hellman asymmetric cryptography solutions. It's similar to S/MIME, but it's a proposed e-mail security standard of its own known as PGP/MIME.

Another popular feature of PGP is digital signatures. A digital signature is a means by which PGP users can sign their e-mails so that both PGP- and non-PGP-using recipients can see the text or body of the message. However, a PGP recipient can then verify or authenticate the message by testing the signature. Digital signatures provide a means to verify the source of a message; this is known as non-repudiation. The digital signature also includes a hash value of the message and allows the recipient to verify that the integrity of the message hasn't been violated while in transit.

The process of using a digital signature is more complex than encrypting a message. It requires not only a shared asymmetric cryptography solution between the communication

partners, but also that both parties use the same hashing algorithm. The procedure for employing a digital signature is as follows (see Figure 5.9):

1. The sender creates a hash of the original message.

2. The sender encrypts the hash with the sender's private key.

3. The sender attaches the encrypted hash to the original message and sends it to the recipient. (Note: the original message is in clear text form.)

4. The recipient strips off the encrypted hash (the digital signature).

5. The receiver uses the sender's public key to decrypt the sender's private key and thus extract the hash from the digital signature.

6. The recipient generates a hash of the received original message (without the attached encrypted hash).

7. The recipient compares the generated hash to the extracted hash from the sender. If they match, the recipient knows the message hasn't changed and the message is from the identified sender.

FIGURE 5.9 The asymmetric-based e-mail digital signature process

Elliptic curve

Elliptic curve cryptography (ECC) is basically cryptographic mathematical magic—or at least that's the way it seems to most mortals who don't have a Ph.D. in mathematics. Basically, elliptic curve is a method of applying cryptography in order to obtain stronger encryption from shorter keys. For example, an ECC RSA 160-bit key provides the same protection as an RSA 1024-bit key.

AES

AES was addressed in the "Symmetric key" section earlier in this chapter.

AES256

AES256 was addressed in the "Symmetric key" section earlier in this chapter.

One time pad

One time pad is the basis of many forms of modern cryptography from SSL to IPSec to dynamic one time password tokens. The concept is that a real or virtual paper pad contains codes or keys on each page that are random and do not repeat. Each page of the pad (each key or code) can be used once for a single operation, then it is discarded—never to be reused or be valid again. This concept defines the most secure form of encryption possible. However, because computers cannot create true random numbers, we are using pseudo one time pad systems which are very good, just not perfect.

Transmission encryption (WEP TKIP, etc)

Transmission encryption, specifically related to wireless communications, such as WEP, TKIP (from WPA), and many others, were discussed in Chapter 2.

Exam Essentials

One time pad One time pad is the basis of many forms of modern cryptography from SSL to IPSec to dynamic one time password tokens. The concept is that a real or virtual paper pad contains codes or keys on each page that are random and do not repeat. Each page of the pad (each key or code) can be used once for a single operation, then it is discarded—never to be reused or be valid again.

5.4 Explain and implement protocols.

Cryptographic keys and digital certificates can be used in a wide variety of applications and protocols. Cryptographic keys, both symmetric and asymmetric, are involved in numerous security and protection solutions. These include the following:

- Virtual private network (VPN) protocols such as IPSec
- Communication security protocols such as Secure Sockets Layer (SSL) and Transport Layer Security (TLS)
- The application of SSL to protect web traffic as in HTTP over SSL (HTTPS)
- Proprietary web communication security protocols such as Secure HTTP (SHTTP)
- Secure remote administration solutions, such as Secure Shell (SSH)
- E-mail security solutions, such as Pretty Good Privacy (PGP) and Secure MIME (S/MIME)

SSL/TLS

Secure Sockets Layer (SSL) and *Transport Layer Security (TLS)* are used to encrypt traffic between a web browser and a web server. Through the use of SSL or TLS, web surfers can make online purchases, interact with banks, and access private information without disclosing the contents of their communications. SSL and TLS can make web transactions private and secure. While they aren't true VPN protocols, SSL and TLS operate in much the same manner as VPNs.

SSL was originally developed by Netscape, but it quickly became an Internet standard. Currently SSL version 3.0 is in widespread use across the Internet. TLS is based on SSL, but they aren't interoperable. SSL operates over TCP port 443, whereas TLS can operate over TCP port 443 or 80 (as does HTTP).

SSL can also be used to provide encrypted sessions for other application layer protocols, such as Telnet, FTP, and e-mail. SSL functions at Layer 5 (the Session layer) of the OSI model.

When SSL is to be used to secure the communications between a web browser and web server, a six-step handshake process must be completed to establish the secured session:

1. The client requests a secure connection.

2. The server responds with its certificate, the name of its certificate authority (issuing CA), and its public key.

3. The client verifies the server's certificate, produces a session (symmetric) encryption key, encrypts the key with the server's public key, and sends the encrypted key to the server.

4. The server unpacks the session key and sends a summary of the session details to the client encrypted with the session key.

5. The client reviews the summary and sends its own summary back to the server, likewise encrypted with the session key.

6. After both entities receive a matching session summary, secured SSL communications are initiated.

SSL uses symmetric keys as the session keys. The session keys are available in 40-bit and 128-bit strengths.

S/MIME

Secure Multipurpose Internet Mail Extensions (S/MIME) is an Internet standard for encrypting e-mail. Many e-mail security products are based on the S/MIME standard. S/MIME takes the standard MIME element of e-mail, which enables e-mail to carry attachments and higher-order textual information (fonts, color, size, layout, and so on), and expands this to include message encryption. S/MIME uses RSA (an asymmetric encryption scheme) to encrypt and protect e-mail.

S/MIME works by taking the original message from the server, encrypting it, and then attaching it to a new blank e-mail as an attachment. The new blank e-mail includes the

sender's and receiver's e-mail addresses, to control routing of the message to its destination. The receiver must then strip off the attachment and decrypt it in order to extract the original message. When e-mail encryption is used, confidentiality is protected.

As shown in Figure 5.10, the basic process is as follows:

1. The sender encrypts the message with the recipient's public key.

2. The message is sent to the recipient.

3. The recipient decrypts the message using the recipient's private key.

FIGURE 5.10 The asymmetric-based e-mail encryption process

The process of encrypting e-mail isn't complex; however, it is cumbersome in implementation. Fortunately, an S/MIME add-on package for an e-mail client automates the process. The only restriction to the S/MIME e-mail solutions is that all communication partners must have compatible S/MIME products installed and use a common or compatible source for their asymmetric encryption key pairs.

S/MIME includes the capability to digitally sign e-mails, but this isn't a widely employed feature. Pretty Good Privacy's (PGP) digital signature feature is much more popular.

PPTP

Layer 2 Tunneling Protocol (L2TP) and *Point-to-Point Tunneling Protocol (PPTP)* are widely used VPN protocols. PPTP was originally developed by Microsoft. Cisco and Microsoft worked together in creating L2TP (based on Cisco's L2F and Microsoft's PPTP). Since its development, L2TP has become an Internet standard (RFC 2661) and is quickly becoming widely supported.

Both L2TP and PPTP are based on Point-to-Point Protocol (PPP) and thus work well over various types of remote access connections, including dial-up. L2TP can support just about any networking protocol. PPTP is limited to IP traffic. L2TP uses UDP port 1701, and PPTP uses TCP port 1723.

PPTP can use any of the authentication methods supported by PPP, including the following:

- *Challenge Handshake Authentication Protocol (CHAP)*

- *Extensible Authentication Protocol (EAP)*

- *Microsoft Challenge Handshake Authentication Protocol version 1 (MS-CHAP v.1)*

- *Microsoft Challenge Handshake Authentication Protocol version 2 (MS-CHAP v.2)*

- *Shiva Password Authentication Protocol (SPAP)*

- *Password Authentication Protocol (PAP)*

Note that PPTP can provide data encryption only when MS-CHAP v.2 is employed for authentication.

L2TP can rely on PPP and thus on PPP's supported authentication protocols. But L2TP also supports other authentication and encryption protocols, such as Internet Protocol Security (IPSec). Although it isn't required, L2TP is most often deployed using IPSec.

HTTP vs. HTTPS vs. SHTTP

The World Wide Web is a vast, global, ad hoc collection of online information and storefronts. The primary protocol that supports the Web is *Hypertext Transfer Protocol (HTTP)*. HTTP enables the transmission of *Hypertext Markup Language (HTML)* documents (the base page elements of a website) and embedded multimedia components such as graphics and mobile code (see Figure 5.11). Without HTTP, there would be no Web. However, HTTP is an insecure protocol: it doesn't offer anything in the way of authentication or encryption for web communications. Fortunately, numerous add-on protocols and mechanisms provide these and other security service to the information superhighway.

FIGURE 5.11 A web server providing streaming video, animations, and HTML data to a client

HTTP is the standard foundational protocol used on the Web. It operates over TCP port 80. HTTP is a plain text or clear text communication protocol; thus it offers no security or privacy to transactions. When SSL or TLS is used to secure transactions, this is known as *Hypertext Transfer Protocol over SSL (HTTPS)*. You'll be able to recognize when secure web communications are occurring using SSL or TLS because the URL will begin with HTTPS and a locked padlock icon will appear in the status bar at the bottom of the browser window.

It's important not to confuse HTTPS with a similar protocol, Secure HTTP (S-HTTP). S-HTTP isn't in widespread use. The primary differences are that S-HTTP doesn't use SSL; it encrypts individual web page elements rather than the entire web communication session, and it can only be used to support HTTP. Overall, S-HTTP is less secure than HTTPS.

In addition to web pages, SSL can also be used to secure FTP, Network News Transfer Protocol (NNTP), Telnet, and other Application layer TCP/IP protocols. However, when SSL is used for protecting other application protocols, the destination port is different than that of HTTPS which uses 443; other examples include SMTP over SSL at 465 and POP3 over SSL at 995. S-HTTP is unable to protect anything other than web traffic.

L2TP

L2TP or Layer 2 Tunneling Protocol was developed by combining features of Microsoft proprietary implementation of PPTP and Cisco's L2F VPN protocols. L2TP can be used to tunnel any routable protocol, but contains no native security features. When L2TP is used to encapsulate IPSec, it obtains authentication and data encryption features because IPSec provides them. The only reason to use L2TP encapsulated IPSec instead of naked IPSec is when the secured connection is to cross a PSTN link. Otherwise, IPSec can be used without the extra overhead of L2TP.

IPSEC

Internet Protocol Security (IPSec) is both a stand-alone VPN protocol and a module that can be used with L2TP. You can use IPSec in dial-up or network-to-network connections. When it's employed over dial-up, it usually functions as the encryption protocol in an L2TP link. IPSec by itself is more suitable for network-to-network connections across normal LAN connections, high-speed WAN links, and the Internet.

IPSec isn't a single protocol but rather a collection of protocols. Two of the primary protocols of IPSec are *Authentication Header (AH)* and *Encapsulating Security Payload (ESP)*. AH provides authentication of the sender's data; ESP provides encryption of the transferred data as well as limited authentication.

IPSec can operate in two modes: *tunnel mode* and *transport mode*. In tunnel mode, IPSec provides encryption protection for both the payload and message header by encapsulating the entire original LAN protocol packet and adding its own temporary IPSec header (see Figure 5.12). In transport mode, IPSec provides encryption protection for just the payload and leaves the original message header intact (see Figure 5.13). You should use tunnel mode when you're connecting over an untrusted network.

FIGURE 5.12 IPSec's encryption of a packet in tunnel mode

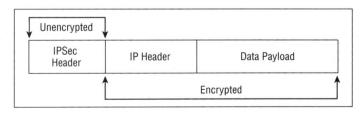

FIGURE 5.13 IPSec's encryption of a packet in transport mode

IPSec provides for encryption security using symmetric cryptography. This means communication partners use shared secret keys to encrypt and decrypt traffic over the IPSec VPN link. One of the mechanisms used by IPSec to manage cryptography is *Internet Key Exchange (IKE)*; it ensures the secure exchange of secret keys between communication partners in order to establish the encrypted VPN tunnel.

IPSec also uses *Internet Security Association and Key Management Protocol (ISAKMP)*, which is known as a *security association manager*. A security association is the agreed-upon method of authentication used by two entities. Without a common method of authentication, a VPN link can't be established. So, ISAKMP is used to negotiate and provide authenticated keying material (a common method of authentication) for security associations in a secured manner. The four major functional components of ISAKMP are

- Authentication of communications peers
- Threat mitigation
- Security association creation and management
- Cryptographic key establishment and management

SSH

Secure Shell (SSH) is a secure replacement for Telnet, rlogon, rsh, and rcp. SSH can be called a remote access or remote terminal solution. It consists of an SSH server component and an SSH client component. SSH offers a means by which a command-line, text-only interface connection with a server can be established over any distance. You can perform any command-line or scriptable activities through the SSH connection, as shown in Figure 5.14.

SSH transmits both authentication traffic and data in a secured encrypted form. Thus, no information is exchanged in clear text. This makes SSH a secure alternative to *Telnet*, which transmits both authentication credentials and data in clear text. SSH operates over TCP port 22.

FIGURE 5.14 A Unix version of SSH, showing a list of available command-line options

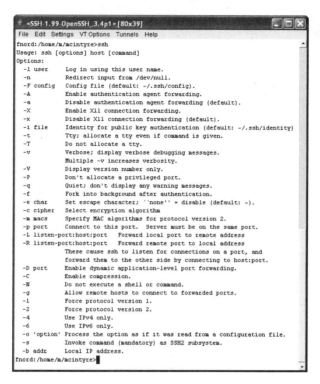

Exam Essentials

VPNs A virtual private network (VPN) is a communication tunnel between two entities across an intermediary network. In most cases, the intermediary network is an untrusted network, such as the Internet, and therefore the communication tunnel is also encrypted.

VPN protocols PPTP, L2TP, and IPSec are VPN protocols.

PPTP Point-to-Point Tunneling Protocol (PPTP) is based on PPP, limited to IP traffic, and uses TCP port 1723. PPTP supports PAP, SPAP, CHAP, EAP, and MS-CHAP v.1 and v.2.

L2TP Layer Two Tunneling Protocol (L2TP) is based on PPTP and L2F, supports any LAN protocol, uses UDP port 1701, and often uses IPSec for encryption.

SSH Secure Shell (SSH) is a secure replacement for Telnet, rlogon, rsh, and rcp. It can be called a remote access or remote terminal solution. SSH encrypts authentication and data traffic, and it operates over TCP port 22.

IPSec Internet Protocol Security (IPSec) is both a stand-alone VPN protocol and a module that can be used with L2TP. IPSec can be used in dial-up or network-to-network connections. It operates at the OSI model Layer 3 (the Network layer).

AH and ESP IPSec isn't a single protocol, but rather a collection of protocols. Two of the primary protocols of IPSec are Authentication Header (AH) and Encapsulating Security Payload (ESP). AH provides authentication of the sender's data; ESP provides encryption of the transferred data as well as limited authentication.

Tunnel mode and transport mode In tunnel mode, IPSec provides encryption protection for both the payload and the message header by encapsulating the entire original LAN protocol packet and adding its own temporary IPSec header. In transport mode, IPSec provides encryption protection for just the payload and leaves the original message header intact.

IKE Internet Key Exchange (IKE) ensures the secure exchange of secret keys between communication partners in order to establish the encrypted VPN tunnel.

ISAKMP Internet Security Association and Key Management Protocol (ISAKMP) is used to negotiate and provide authenticated keying material (a common method of authentication) for security associations in a secured manner. The four major functional components of ISAKMP are authentication of communications peers, threat mitigation, security association creation and management, and cryptographic key establishment and management.

Communication vulnerabilities Every communications technology, mechanism, or solution is vulnerable to one thing or another. With the implementation of cryptography to provide security through encryption, many forms of communication have become more reliable and now offer reliable protection. When encryption is involved, the issue often distills down to the algorithm in use and the length of the key.

Key usage Cryptographic keys and digital certificates can be used in a wide variety of applications. Cryptographic keys, both symmetric and asymmetric, are involved in numerous security and protection solutions. Uses include VPN, IPSec, SSL, TLS, HTTPS, SHTTP, SSH, PGP, and S/MIME.

5.5 Explain core concepts of public key cryptography.

Public key cryptography is technically a subset of asymmetric cryptography. Furthermore, PKI (Public Key Infrastructure) is a framework for deploying asymmetric (or public key) cryptography, along with symmetric cryptography, hashing, and certificates, to obtain a real-world flexible and functional secure communications system. The following sections

discuss various aspects of PKI and its sub-elements (rather than focusing only on public key cryptography).

Public Key Infrastructure (PKI)

Public Key Infrastructure (PKI) isn't a product; rather, it's a blueprint or concept for a solution. It dictates what should happen and which standards to comply with, but it doesn't indicate which technologies or algorithms to use. PKI focuses on proving the identity of communication partners, providing a means to securely exchange session-based symmetric encryption keys through asymmetric cryptographic solutions, and providing a means to protect message integrity through the use of hashing. Most PKI solutions are based around certificates and the use of a certificate authority (CA). The issue of certificates includes concepts of revocation and trust models.

Certificates serve a single purpose: proving the identity of a user or the source of an object. They don't provide proof as to the reliability or quality of the object or service to which they're attached; they only provide proof of where that product or service originated.

Certificates work under a theory known as the trusted third party. This theory states that if user A trusts user C and user B trusts user C, then user A can trust B and vice versa. With certificates, the trusted third party is a certificate authority (CA) (see Figure 5.15). If two users have certificates issued by the CA, then the two users can trust each other's identity. Certificates work this way on the Internet and within private organizations.

FIGURE 5.15 The CA process

Certificate Authority

Message

Certificate Certificate

Mike

Jeff

Jeff can verify that the message with the certificate from Mike is valid if he trusts the CA.

Most certificates used on the Internet and within private networks are based on the X.509 version 3 certificate standard. This standard dictates how certificates are to be constructed and their required components, such as the subject's public key, the CA's distinguishing name, a unique serial number, and the type of symmetric algorithm used for the certificate's encryption (see Figure 5.16).

FIGURE 5.16 A certificate illustrating some of the information it stores

Version	V3
Serial Number	1234 D123 4567 …
Signature Algorithm	Md2RSA
CA's name	Sample Certificate
Valid from:	Sunday, September 8, 2005
Valid to:	Sunday, September 15, 2005
Subject	Mr. Your Name Here, Myco
Public Key	Encrypted Value of Key
Extensions	Subject Type = End Entity
Signature Algorithm Signature	sha1 Encrypted Data

← Digital Signature Area

↑ ↑ Fields of a Simple X.509 Certificate

A user or a subject uses the following procedure to obtain a certificate:

1. The subject requests a certificate from a CA.
2. The request process includes proof of the subject's identity and the subject's public key.
3. The CA verifies the identity of the subject.
4. The CA creates the certificate.
5. The CA validates the certificate by signing it with the CA's private key.
6. The CA issues the certificate to the subject.

Another entity known as a registration authority (RA) may be deployed in a CA solution. The RA can't create new certificates; rather it serves as a distribution point for the certificate revocation list (CRL) and possibly as an Online Certificate Status Protocol (OCSP) host (see the "Revocation" section later in this chapter). CAs must have defined certificate policies and certificate practice statements.

Recovery agent

Recovery agents can also be called key recovery agents or key escrow agents. This topic is discussed in the "Key escrow" section.

Public key

A public key is the key from the public key cryptography key pair set that is designed to be sent out into the public world. Anyone can obtain a person's public key and use it to initiate secure communications with that person. The public key is derived from the private key, but it is not feasible to reverse the process in order to discover the private key.

Private keys

A private key is the key from the public key cryptography key pair set that is designed to be kept secured locally and accessible only to the one individual to whom it belongs. The private key is used to unlock communications sent using the corresponding public key. The private key can also be used in crafting digital signatures.

Certificate Authority (CA)

Certificates are another means of authentication. They typically involve a trusted third-party *certificate authority (CA)*: a private or public entity that issues certificates to entities serving as either clients (subjects) or servers (objects). It's the responsibility of the CA to verify the identity of each entity before issuing a certificate. After a certificate is issued, the entity can use the certificate as proof of their identity.

When you're using certificates in a private network, you are your own trusted third party (that is, you are your own CA). Such a private certificate solution is known as a Public Key Infrastructure (PKI). A PKI is the definition (like a blueprint or schematic) of the mechanisms involved in implementing certificates. For the most part, you must deploy one or more servers with certificate services in order to create your own hierarchy of CAs.

Certificates can be used logically or electronically only (such as by the operating system or web browser directly) or via physical access control devices (such as a smartcard). In a logical deployment, certificates are installed into a client operating system or a specific application. Whenever identity proofing is required, the operating system transmits its certificate to the requesting party. In a physical deployment, the certificate is stored on a smartcard or some form of removable media. When the system needs user authentication, it requests the physical access control device.

When a user requests a certificate, they must usually provide proof of their identity along with their public key. This means they must use the same PKI solution as the CA issuing the certificate. The CA then uses the public key from the subject as the basis to generate the certificate returned to the user (see Figure 5.17). In this fashion, the certificate is tied to the subject's public key–private key pair and provides a mechanism for identity proofing.

FIGURE 5.17 A certificate being issued after identification has been verified

Certificates are commonly used over the Internet as a means of logical or electronic identity proofing. As long as both parties in a communication or transaction trust a specific third-party CA, such as VeriSign, then the two entities can trust that each is who they claim to be. It's very important to understand that a certificate only provides proof of identity, and that proof is based on trusting a third party (the CA that performed testing on the subject's identity). It in no way ensures that the subject or object so identified has benevolent motives or will function, perform, or operate in any specific manner.

A certificate policy is a PKI document that serves as the basis for common interoperability standards and common assurance criteria. Certificate policies are acceptable use policies for certificates: They dictate what is and isn't acceptable with regard to how certificates can be used in an organization. The policies are a set of rules that control how certificates are used, managed, and deployed.

Certificate policies must be all of the following:

- Clear and concise
- Endorsed by senior management
- Restricted to a maximum length of two pages
- Written in bullet-point statements
- Able to provide users (also referred to as subjects) with a clear understanding of the acceptable use policies with regard to certificates

A certificate practice statement (CPS) describes how a CA will manage the certificates it issues. The CPS details how certificate management is performed, how security is maintained, and the procedures the CA must follow to perform any type of certificate management from creation to revocation.

Registration

Registration is the process of obtaining a certificate. While the specifics may vary based on whether the CA is public or private as well as the actual software used for the CA services, the basics of the process are the same throughout. The registration process is as follows:

1. A subject crafts a private key and then generates a public key.
2. The public key is sent to the CA along with proof of subject identity.
3. The CA verifies the subject's identity using whatever level of due diligence is warranted.
4. The CA crafts the certificate by digitally signing the subject's public key with the CA's private key, and then adds a text file containing the details mandated by the x.509 v3 certificate standard.
5. The CA sends the certificate to the subject via a secured pathway.

Some private organizations may generate the initial subject key set on the CA, and then issue them both to the subject.

Key escrow

In a symmetric system, all entities in possession of the shared secret key must protect the privacy and secrecy of that key. If the key is compromised anywhere or by anyone, the entire solution (all entities using the same key) is compromised (everything protected by that key).

In an asymmetric system, each end user must protect their private key. If an end user's private key is ever compromised, then only that one end user's security is lost. All other users in the environment aren't directly affected by the key compromise.

Key escrow is a storage process by which copies of private keys and/or secret keys are retained by a centralized management system (see Figure 5.18). This system securely stores the encryption keys as a means of insurance or recovery in the event of a disaster. In terms of cryptography, a *disaster* is when a key is lost or damaged. If such a key is stored in escrow, it can be recovered by a key escrow agent and used to recover any data encrypted with the damaged or lost key.

FIGURE 5.18 A key archiving or escrow system

CA Key archival system

Key database

However, escrow can be seen in another light if you're an end user who is intent on obtaining complete and total security. If you're assigned your private key or secret key, then the issuing CA (or cryptographic server) probably retains a copy of the key in escrow. This means that at any time a key recovery agent could pull your key out of escrow and use it to decrypt anything you've encrypted with your public key or your secret key without your permission. Obviously, key escrow is great for private corporate environments, but it doesn't apply well to the public Internet.

Recovery is the process of pulling a key or certificate from escrow. Recovery can be used when a user loses their key or their key has been corrupted. This process can also be used to extract a key for the purpose of decrypting data even when the user still has valid possession of their key. The latter option may be necessary in a private corporate environment, but it's unacceptable in a public environment, such as the Internet.

Key recovery can only be performed by a key recovery agent. The key recovery agent is an administrative-level user who has the encryption key to the escrow database. They can decrypt and extract the necessary key from the escrow database and either give a copy to the user or use the key to decrypt all data. If the latter occurs (as is common in most cryptographic

solution implementation), the end user must be issued a new key, which must be used in turn to re-encrypt all the data that should be secured.

A key recovery agent should be a trusted individual. If the environment doesn't warrant the trust of a single key recovery agent, a mechanism known as *M of N control* can be implemented. M of N control indicates that there are multiple key recovery agents (M) and that a specific minimum number of these key recovery agents (N) must be present and working in tandem in order to extract keys from the escrow database. The use of M of N control ensures accountability among the key recovery agents and prevents any one individual from having complete control over or access to a cryptographic solution.

Certificate Revocation List (CRL)

Certificates have a specific expiration date, which is sometimes called the lifetime date. When that date is reached, a certificate is automatically rejected as invalid. However, a CA may have cause to revoke or invalidate a certificate before its predefined expiration date. Revocation is the process by which a CA invalidates a certificate.

Revocation may occur because the subject's identity information has changed, the subject used the certificate to commit a crime, or the subject used the certificate in such a way as to violate the CA's certificate policy.

When a certificate is revoked, it's added to the CA's CRL. When a certificate's expiration date is reached, it's removed from the CRL because the time stamp automatically invalidates the certificate. Thus, the CRL contains only those certificates that have been revoked but have yet to expire. Figure 5.19 shows the certification revocation process.

FIGURE 5.19 Certification revocation process

The CRL is freely distributed to all users and applications. You should always consult it before accepting a certificate. When issued to a requesting user or application, a CRL is assigned a lifetime date as well. When the CRL exceeds this lifetime, it can no longer be relied on, and you should obtain a new, updated version of the CRL.

When a user application, such as a web browser, receives a certificate from a server, such as a web server, the application first verifies that the date on the certificate is still valid.

Next, it checks the local copy of the CA's CRL. If the CRL is no longer valid, an updated copy of the CRL is obtained. The application checks to see whether the certificate appears on the CRL. If it doesn't, the application presents the certificate to the user for a final acceptance choice. The user can elect to accept or reject the certificate as well as indicate whether to make this same acceptance or rejection choice for all future instances of this certificate.

The CRL process is widely used, but it isn't the only mechanism for informing users and applications about the status of certificates. Online Certificate Status Protocol (OCSP) is another solution that functions on a direct query basis. Each time an application receives a new certificate, it sends a query to an OCSP CA server. The CA responds directly to indicate whether the certificate is still valid or has been revoked. By using OCSP, large CRLs aren't transmitted repeatedly to every requesting system, and queries are direct, immediate, and current.

Most cryptographic keys and all certificates have a built-in expiration date. Upon reaching that date, the key or certificate becomes invalid, and no system will accept it. Keys and certificates are assigned a lifetime with control settings known as *valid from* and *valid to* dates. Keys and certificates past their valid to dates should be discarded or destroyed.

If the *valid to* date for a key or certificate is approaching, you should request a renewal. If you fail to renew before the lifetime expires, then you must perform the complete request process from scratch.

Suspension is an alternative to revocation. Suspension can be used when a key or certificate will be temporarily removed from active use but the subject (or the CA) doesn't wish to invalidate it. When a key or certificate is suspended, it can't be used to sign or encrypt any new items, but previously signed or encrypted items can be verified or decrypted. The key or certificate can be reactivated at a later date.

Suspension status checking is an extension of revocation status checking. However, the results indicate whether a certificate or key is currently valid or in suspension (such a status would be labeled *certification hold*).

Renewal is the process by which a key or certificate is reissued with an extended lifetime date before the key or certificate expires. The renewal process doesn't require a complete repeat of the request and identity proofing process; rather, the old key (which is about to expire) is used to sign the request for the new key. This allows the CA to quickly determine whether the end user's key or certificate can be immediately extended (or reissued with a new lifetime date) or rejected and revoked according to its existing lifetime dates. The decision of the CA often depends on the end user's compliance with the organization's certificate policy (the acceptable use policy for the key or certificate).

After a key or certificate is no longer needed, or when it has expired or been revoked, it should be properly disposed of. This process is known as key destruction: the removal of the key or certificate from all software and hardware storage devices. For keys and certificates that are still valid, the CA should be informed about the destruction of the key or certificate. This action allows the CA to update its CRL and OCSP servers.

Reasons to use key destruction include going out of business, changing identity, or having obtained replacement keys or certificates.

Trust models

The term *trust model* refers to the structure of the trust hierarchy used by a certificate authority system. The basic trust model scheme used by CAs is a hierarchical structure with a single top-level root CA. A root CA self-signs its own certificate in order to begin the tree of trust. Below the root CA are one, two, or more subordinate CAs. Below each subordinate CA may be one, two, or more subordinate CAs, and so on. Subordinate CAs can sometimes be called intermediate or leaf CAs. In this model, all CAs have a single parent CA, but they may have multiple child CAs (see Figure 5.20). The root CA is the start of trust; all CAs and participants in a hierarchical trust model ultimately rely on the trustworthiness of the root CA.

FIGURE 5.20 A hierarchical trust structure

Cross-certification occurs when a CA from one organization elects to trust a CA from another organization (see Figure 5.21). This is also called a bridge trust structure. In this way, certificates from either organization are accepted by the other organization. In most cases, the root CA is configured to trust the other root CA.

FIGURE 5.21 A cross or bridge trust structure

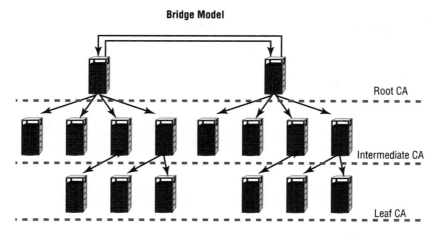

A trust list is a form of trust model where a web browser or similar application is provided a list of root certificates of trusted CAs. The web browser trusts numerous sources of certificates because of the presence of the trusted CA's root certificate on the list of trusted CAs.

Exam Essentials

PKI PKI focuses on proving the identity of communication partners, providing a means to securely exchange session-based symmetric encryption keys through asymmetric cryptographic solutions, and providing a means to protect message integrity through the use of hashing.

Certificates Certificates serve a single purpose: proving the identity of a user or the source of an object. Certificates don't provide any proof as to the reliability or quality of the object or service to which they're attached; they only provide proof of where that product or service originated.

Trusted third parties Certificates work under a theory known as the trusted third party: If user A trusts user C and user B trusts user C, then user A can trust B and vice versa. With certificates, the trusted third party is a certificate authority (CA).

x.509 version 3 certificate standard Most certificates are based on the X.509 version 3 certificate standard. Some of the required components are the subject's public key, the CA's distinguishing name, a unique serial number, and the type of symmetric algorithm used for the certificate's encryption.

Procedure for requesting a certificate To request a certificate, a subject submits a request to a CA with proof of their identity and their public key.

Certificate policies A certificate policy is a PKI document that serves as the basis for common interoperability standards and common assurance criteria. It's a statement that governs the use of digital certificates within an organization. Certificate policies are acceptable use policies for certificates.

Certificate practice statements (CPS) A CPS describes how a CA will manage the certificates it issues. It details how certificate management is performed, how security is maintained, and the procedures the CA must follow to perform any type of certificate management from creation to revocation.

Revocation A CA may have cause to revoke or invalidate a certificate before its predefined expiration date. Revocation may occur because the subject's identity information has changed, the subject used the certificate to commit a crime, or the subject used the certificate in such a way as to violate the CA's certificate policy.

Certificate revocation lists (CRL) When a certificate is revoked, it's added to the CA's CRL. The CRL is freely distributed to all users and applications. It should always be consulted before accepting a certificate.

How a web browser handles new certificates When a web browser receives a certificate from a web server, it verifies that the date on the certificate is still valid. Next, it checks the local copy of the CA's CRL. If the CRL is no longer valid, an updated copy of the CRL is obtained. The application checks to see if the certificate appears on the CRL. If it doesn't, the application presents the certificate to the user for a final acceptance choice.

OCSP Online Certificate Status Protocol (OCSP) is a revocation solution that functions on a direct query basis. Each time an application receives a new certificate, it sends a query to an OCSP CA server. The CA responds directly to indicate whether the certificate is still valid or has been revoked.

Trust models The term *trust model* refers to the structure of the trust hierarchy used by a certificate authority system. The basic trust model scheme used by CAs is a hierarchical structure.

Hierarchical trust models A hierarchical structure has a single top-level root CA. Below the root CA are one, two, or more subordinate CAs. The root CA is the start of trust. All CAs and participants in a hierarchical trust model ultimately rely on the trustworthiness of the root CA.

Cross-certification Cross-certification occurs when a CA from one organization elects to trust a CA from another organization. In this way, certificates from either organization are accepted by the other organization. In most cases, the root CA is configured to trust the other root CA.

Trust lists A trust list is a form of trust model where a web browser or similar application is provided with a list of root certificates of trusted CAs. The web browser trusts numerous sources of certificates because of the presence of the trusted CA's root certificate on the list of trusted CAs.

Key escrow Key escrow is a storage process by which copies of private keys and/or secret keys are retained by a centralized management system. This system securely stores the encryption keys as a means of insurance or recovery in the event of a lost or corrupted key.

Key expiration Most cryptographic keys and all certificates have a built-in expiration date. Upon reaching that date, the key or certificate becomes invalid, and no system will accept it. Keys and certificates are assigned a lifetime with control settings known as *valid from* and *valid to* dates. Keys and certificates past their *valid to* dates should be discarded or destroyed.

Key revocation and status checking Keys and certificates can be revoked before they reach their lifetime expiration date. Status checking is the process of checking the lifetime dates against the current system date, checking the CRL, and/or querying an OCSP server.

Key suspension Suspension is an alternative to revocation. It can be used when a key or certificate will be temporarily removed from active use but the subject (or the CA) doesn't wish to outright invalidate the key or certificate. Suspension allows a key or certificate to be reactivated at a later date.

Key recovery Recovery is the process of pulling a key or certificate from escrow. The recovery process can be used when a user loses their key or their key has been corrupted. Only a key recovery agent can perform key recovery.

M of N control If the environment doesn't warrant the trust of a single key recovery agent, a mechanism known as M of N control can be implemented. M of N control indicates that there are multiple key recovery agents (M) and that a specific minimum number of these key recovery agents (N) must be present and working in tandem in order to extract keys from the escrow database.

Key renewal Renewal is the process by which a key or certificate is reissued with an extended lifetime date before it expires. The renewal process doesn't require a complete repeat of the request and identity proofing process; rather, the old key (which is about to expire) is used to sign the request for the new key.

Key destruction After a key or certificate is no longer needed or it has expired or been revoked, it should be properly disposed of. For keys and certificates that are still valid, the CA should be informed about the destruction of the key or certificate. This action allows the CA to update its CRL and OCSP servers.

5.6 Implement PKI and certificate management.

PKI and certificate management were discussed previously in section 5.5.

Public Key Infrastructure (PKI)

PKI was discussed previously under the "Public Key Infrastructure (PKI)" subhead in section 5.5.

Recovery agent

Recovery agents were discussed previously under the "Key escrow" subhead in section 5.5.

Public key

Public keys were discussed previously under the "Public key" subhead in section 5.5.

Private keys

Private keys were discussed previously under the "Private keys" subhead in section 5.5.

Certificate Authority (CA)

CA was discussed previously under the "Certificate Authority (CA)" subhead in section 5.5.

Registration

Registration was discussed previously under the "Registration" subhead in section 5.5.

Key escrow

Key escrow was discussed previously under the "Key escrow" subhead in section 5.5.

Certificate Revocation List (CRL)

CRL was discussed previously under the "Certificate Revocation List (CRL)" subhead in section 5.5.

Review Questions

1. Hashing is used to test, prove, or verify which security service?

 A. Authentication

 B. Confidentiality

 C. Integrity

 D. Non-repudiation

2. Which of the following symmetric encryption algorithms offers the strength of 168-bit keys?

 A. Data Encryption Standard

 B. Triple DES

 C. Advanced Encryption Standard

 D. IDEA

3. Diffie-Hellman is what type of cryptographic system?

 A. Asymmetric

 B. Symmetric

 C. Hashing

 D. Certificate authority

4. The security service that protects the secrecy of data, information, or resources is known as what?

 A. Integrity

 B. Authentication

 C. Non-repudiation

 D. Confidentiality

5. Digital signatures can be created using all but which of the following?

 A. Asymmetric cryptography

 B. Hashing

 C. Key escrow

 D. Symmetric cryptography

6. Certificates have what single purpose?

 A. Proving identity

 B. Proving quality

 C. Providing encryption security

 D. Exchanging encryption keys

7. When a subject or end user requests a certificate, they must provide which of the following items? (Choose all that apply.)

 A. Proof of identity

 B. Hardware storage device

 C. Public key

 D. Private key

8. From a private corporate perspective, which of the following is most secure?

 A. Decentralized key management

 B. Centralized key management

 C. Individual key management

 D. Distributed key management

9. The mechanism used by a key management system to provide fault tolerance to private keys is called what?

 A. Revocation

 B. Enrollment

 C. Suspension

 D. Escrow

10. When should a key or certificate be renewed?

 A. Every year

 B. Every quarter

 C. Just before it expires

 D. Just after it expires

Answers to Review Questions

1. C. Hashing is used to test whether the integrity of data has been violated. Asymmetric cryptography provides authentication, integrity, and non-repudiation. Symmetric cryptography provides confidentiality.

2. B. Triple DES offers the strength of 168-bit keys. DES offers the strength of 56-bit keys. AES offers the strength of 128-, 192-, or 256-bit keys. IDEA offers the strength of 128-bit keys.

3. A. Diffie-Hellman is an asymmetric cryptographic system. DES and AES are examples of symmetric cryptography. MD5 and SHA-1 are examples of hashing. Certificate authorities issue certificates based on an implemented PKI solution.

4. D. The security service that protects the secrecy of data, information, or resources is known as confidentiality. Integrity protects the reliability and correctness of data. Authentication verifies the identity of the sender or receiver of a message. Non-repudiation prevents the sender of a message or the perpetrator of an activity from being able to deny that they sent the message or performed the activity.

5. C. Key escrow isn't used in digital signatures, but it's a fault-tolerance feature of certificate and key management. Asymmetric and symmetric cryptography along with hashing are used in digital signatures.

6. A. Certificates have the single purpose of proving identity. They don't prove quality or provide encryption security, and they aren't used to exchange encryption keys.

7. A, C. Proof of identity and the subject's public key must be provided to the CA when requesting a certificate. The private key should never be revealed to anyone, not even the CA. A hardware storage device is used after a key or certificate has been issued, not as part of the requesting process.

8. B. Centralized key management is more secure, or at least more desirable, from a private corporate perspective. From a public or individual perspective, decentralized key management is more secure. Individual and distributed key management are nonstandard terms that could be used to refer to decentralized key management.

9. D. Escrow is the mechanism used by a key-management system to provide fault tolerance to private keys. Revocation is the invalidation of keys or certificates before their lifetime dates have expired. Enrollment is when a user requests a new certificate. Suspension is when a key or certificate is temporarily removed from active.

10. C. Keys and certificates should be renewed just before they expire. All the other choices are incorrect.

Chapter 6

Organizational Security

COMPTIA SECURITY+ EXAM OBJECTIVES COVERED IN THIS CHAPTER:

✓ **6.1 Explain redundancy planning and its components.**

- Hot site
- Cold site
- Warm site
- Backup generator
- Single point of failure
- RAID
- Spare parts
- Redundant servers
- Redundant ISP
- UPS
- Redundant connections

✓ **6.2 Implement disaster recovery procedures.**

- Planning
- Disaster recovery exercises
- Backup techniques and practices – storage
- Schemes
- Restoration

✓ **6.3 Differentiate between and execute appropriate incident response procedures.**

- Forensics
- Chain of custody
- First responders
- Damage and loss control
- Reporting – disclosure of

✓ **6.4 Identify and explain applicable legislation and organizational policies.**

- Secure disposal of computers
- Acceptable use policies
- Password complexity
- Change management
- Classification of information
- Mandatory vacations
- Personally Identifiable Information (PII)
- Due care
- Due diligence
- Due process
- SLA
- Security-related HR policy
- User education and awareness training

✓ **6.5 Explain the importance of environmental controls.**

- Fire suppression
- HVAC
- Shielding

✓ **6.6 Explain the concept of and how to reduce the risks of social engineering.**

- Phishing
- Hoaxes
- Shoulder surfing
- Dumpster diving
- User education and awareness training

The Security+ exam will test your basic IT security skills—those skills needed to effectively secure stand-alone and networked systems in a corporate environment. To pass the test and be effective in implementing security, you need to understand the basic concepts and terminology related to organizational security as detailed in this chapter.

6.1 Explain redundancy planning and its components.

Disaster recovery plans (DRPs) should encompass every aspect of an organization. A DRP focuses on restoration of business processes. Additionally, DRP planning encourages the deployment of redundancy in order to prevent downtime. The following sections discuss several redundancy planning options.

For more information on this topic, see Chapter 6 of the *CompTIA Security+ Study Guide, 4th Edition* (Sybex, November 2008).

Hot site

An organization-wide secure recovery procedure involves the use of an alternate site: a secondary location where the business can move to and continue performing mission-critical business operations. There are three levels of alternate sites: hot, warm, and cold.

A *hot site* is a real-time, moment-to-moment mirror image of the original site. It contains a complete network environment that is fully installed and configured with live current business data. The moment the original site becomes inoperable due to a disaster, the hot site can be used to continue business operations without a moment of downtime.

Hot sites are the most expensive, but offer the least amount of downtime. Hot sites have significantly high security risk due to live current business data at both the primary site and at the hot site, plus the real-time communications between them. Additionally, hot sites require dedicated support staff in order to maintain the hot site and keep it consistent with the primary site.

Cold site

A *cold site* is often little more than an empty room. It could be described as a location with no equipment or communications at all, or can be a site with equipment in boxes and essential communications and utilities connected. In either case, it will require weeks of work to set up and configure in order to support the company's processing needs. A cold site is the least expensive option, but does not offer a realistic hope of recovery.

Warm site

A *warm site* is a partially configured alternate site with most of the server and networking infrastructure installed. In the event of a disaster, some final software installation and configuration are needed, and data must be restored from a backup set. A warm site may require hours or a day to get it ready for real-time operation to support the business's mission-critical functions. A warm site is moderately costly, but is a realistic option for recovery if the organization can survive a few days of downtime.

When you return from the alternate site, whether hot, warm, or cold, the disaster could be repeated. The primary site is a new environment, because the original network and computer systems were damaged beyond their ability to support the business; significant changes, repairs, and replacements have occurred to restore the environment. The restored primary site must be stress-tested before the mission-critical operations of the business are transferred back to it. So the least critical functions should be moved back to the primary site first. Then, after the site shows resiliency, you can move more critical functions as the network proves its ability to support the organization once again.

Backup generator

Power is an essential utility for any organization, but especially those dependent upon their IT infrastructure. In addition to basic elements such as power conditioners and UPS devices, many organizations opt for an onsite backup generator to provide power during complete blackouts. A variety of backup generators are available both in terms of size as well as fuel.

Single point of failure

A *single point of failure* is any individual or sole device, connection, or pathway that is moderately to mission-critically important to the organization. If that one item fails, the whole organization will suffer loss. Infrastructures should be designed with redundancies of all moderate or higher important elements in order to avoid single points of failure.

RAID

One example of a high-availability solution is a *Redundant Array of Independent Disks (RAID)*. A RAID solution employs multiple hard drives in a single storage volume, as illustrated in Figure 6.1. RAID 0 provides performance improvement but not fault tolerance. RAID 0, also known as striping, uses multiple drives as a single volume. RAID 1 provides mirroring, meaning that the data written to one drive is exactly duplicated to a second drive in real time. RAID 5 provides striping with parity: three or more drives are used in unison, and one drive's worth of space is consumed with parity information. The parity information is stored across all drives. If any one drive of a RAID 5 volume fails, the parity information is used to rebuild the contents of the lost drive on the fly. A new drive can replace the failed drive, and the RAID 5 system will rebuild the contents of the lost drive onto the replacement drive. RAID 5 can only support the failure of one disk drive.

FIGURE 6.1 Examples of RAID implementations

Spare parts

Maintaining an onsite stash of spare parts can reduce downtime. Having an in-house supply of critical parts, devices, media, and so on enables fast repair and function restore. A

replacement part can then be ordered from the vendor and returned to the onsite spare parts storage. Unexpected downtime due to hardware failure is a common cause of loss of availability. Planning for faster repairs will improve uptime and eliminate lengthy downtimes caused by delayed shipping from a vendor.

Redundant servers

The use of *redundant servers* is another example of avoiding single points of failure. A redundant server is a mirror or duplicate of a primary server that receives all data changes immediately after they are made on the primary server. In the event of a failure of the primary server, the secondary or redundant server can immediately take over and replace the primary server in providing services to the network.

This switchover system can be either hot or cold. A hot switchover or hot failover is an automatic system that can often perform the task nearly instantaneously. A cold switchover or cold failover is a manual system that requires that an administrator perform the manual task of switching from the primary to the secondary system and thus often involves noticeable downtime.

Redundant servers can be located in the same server vault as the primary or can be located offsite. The offsite positioning of the redundant server offers a greater amount of security so that the disaster that damaged the primary server is unlikely to be able to damage the secondary offsite server. However, offsite redundant servers are more expensive due to the cost of housing, as well as real-time communication links needed to support the mirroring operations.

Redundant ISP

In order to fully avoid single points of failure, every communication pathway must be redundant. Thus, every link from the LAN to a carrier network or ISP must be duplicated. This can be accomplished by leasing two lines from the same ISP (which is the most basic form of redundant connection) or from different ISPs. The use of redundant ISPs reduces the likelihood that a failure at a single ISP will cause your organization significant connectivity downtime. However, the best redundant ISP configuration requires that the two (or more) selected ISPs are using distinct Internet or network backbones.

UPS

An *uninterruptible power supply (UPS)* is an essential element of any computing environment. A UPS provides several important services and features. First, a UPS is a power conditioner to ensure that only clean, pure, nonfluctuating power is fed to computer equipment. Second, in the event of a loss of power, the internal battery can provide power for a short period of time. The larger the battery, the longer the UPS can provide power. Third, when the battery reaches the end of its charge, it can signal the computer system to initiate a graceful shutdown in order to prevent data loss.

Redundant connections

This topic was addressed earlier in the "Redundant ISP" subsection.

Exam Essentials

Alternate sites An alternate site is a secondary location where the business can move and continue performing mission-critical business operations. There are three levels of alternate sites: hot, warm, and cold.

6.2 Implement disaster recovery procedures.

Disaster recovery planning and procedures enable an organization to maintain or recover its mission-critical processes in spite of events that threaten its infrastructure. Maintaining business continuity means maintaining the organization's networking and IT infrastructure so that mission-critical functions continue to operate. This must be done in spite of reduced resources and damaged equipment. As long as business operations aren't stopped, business continuity is used to sustain the organization. If business operations are stopped, disaster recovery takes over.

For more information on this topic, see Chapter 6 of the *CompTIA Security+ Study Guide, 4th Edition* (Sybex, November 2008).

Planning

Disaster recovery planning is an essential element of an overall security management plan. Disaster recovery is an expansion of *business continuity planning*. Basically, when business continuity is interrupted, a disaster has occurred. Ultimately, both business continuity and disaster recovery planning rely on proper backup procedures.

A *disaster recovery plan (DRP)* is the collection of detailed procedures used in the event that business functions are interrupted by a significant damaging event. When the primary site is unable to support business functions, the disaster recovery plan is initiated. This plan outlines the procedures for getting the mission-critical functions of the business up and running at an alternate site while the primary site is restored to normal operations.

A disaster recovery plan is developed through critical process inventory and prioritization, a risk analysis and assessment process, and a detailed examination of dependencies of resources.

The overall disaster recovery plan should include plan maintenance and distribution of revisions. Over time, as the environment changes, the disaster recovery plan should be adjusted to comply with those changes. After the plan has been altered to a specified change level (amount of change), it must be redistributed throughout the organization. Only the most current version of the plan should be in existence: All older copies of the plan should be destroyed.

Location refers to selecting the geographic placement of your facility. You should consider the implications of your facility's location: for example, what is the local crime rate? What is the proximity to highways? How close are emergency services? Is the area in a flood zone, subject to earthquakes, or liable to experience excessive rain or snow? Knowing these characteristics will assist in the planning and design of the facility, as well as the selection of the location.

Business continuity and disaster recovery planning consists of the following elements:

Risk analysis and assessment This element includes itemizing the risks to each mission-critical aspect of the organization, and then performing qualitative and quantitative analysis on the risks to determine which risk is the most critical.

Business impact analysis You must determine how much any individual realized risk will negatively affect the business's continuity and also compute the maximum tolerable downtime.

Strategic planning for mitigation of risks You need to determine what countermeasures, safeguards, or responses can be used to minimize the effect of risks.

Integration and validation of the plan This step includes putting the plan into practice in the daily work habits of users, integrating it into the security policy, and validating it through senior management approval and testing.

Training and awareness The organization needs to properly train users on their responses and responsibilities in an emergency and maintain awareness between training periods.

Maintenance and auditing of the plan You must regularly update the plan as the environment changes and constantly monitor the environment, the plan itself, testing, and training of the plan for areas where it can be improved.

Disaster recovery exercises

After a plan has been developed and implemented into an organization, it is important to regularly exercise or drill the plan. Just like a fire drill, drilling and exercising a disaster recovery plan will help train personnel on what to do in an emergency and it will reveal any oversights or omissions. Disaster recovery exercises are important maintenance elements that are essential to the long-term success of an organization.

Backup techniques and practices – storage

Backups are an essential part of business continuity because they provide insurance against damage or loss of data files. The mantra of all security professionals should be: backup,

backup, backup. Backups are the only means of insurance available to your data resources in the event of a loss, disruption, corruption, intrusion, destruction, infection, or disaster.

Backups must be tested in order to prove reliable and usable. Testing a backup means restoring data from the backup media to verify that restoration can be done. If you don't test your restoration process, there is no guarantee that your backup was successful.

There are three primary forms of backup:

Full A *full backup* copies all files to the backup media regardless of the archive bit setting. It clears or resets the archive bit.

Incremental An *incremental backup* copies only those files with a set or flagged archive bit. It clears or resets the archive bit.

Differential A *differential backup* copies only those files with a set or flagged archive bit. It doesn't alter the archive bit.

The archive bit is a file header flag that indicates either a file is new or changed. The archive bit is a common feature on Windows file systems. Other OSes and file systems may rely on timestamps instead of archive bits for backup file selection.

Backup media should be stored securely at an offsite location in order to prevent them from being damaged or destroyed by the same catastrophe that affects the business continuity of the primary site. It should be stored in a fire-protected safe, vault, or safety deposit box. Backup tapes should be moved offsite soon after a backup is complete, and the transportation of the backup tapes should be secured. The tapes should be protected at all times from physical damage, theft, alteration, and destruction.

Schemes

Some of the schemes or elements that should be addressed in a disaster recovery plan include availability and fault tolerance.

Availability is the assurance of sufficient bandwidth and timely access to resources. *High availability* means the availability of a system has been secured to offer very reliable assurance that the system will be online, active, and able to respond to requests in a timely manner, and that there will be sufficient bandwidth to accomplish requested tasks in the time required.

High availability is a form of fault tolerance—or, rather, a benefit of providing reliable fault tolerance. *Fault tolerance* is the ability of a network, system, or computer to withstand a certain level of failures, faults, or problems and continue to provide reliable service. Fault tolerance is also a means of avoiding single points of failure. A single point of failure is any system, software, or device that is mission-critical to the entire environment: If that one element fails, then the entire environment fails. Your environments should be designed with redundancy so that there are no single points of failure. Such a redundant design is fault tolerant.

Another example of a high-availability solution is server clustering (see Figure 6.2). *Server clustering* is a technology that connects several duplicate systems together so they act cooperatively. If one system in a cluster fails, the other systems take over its workload. From a user's perspective, the cluster is a single entity with a single resource access name.

FIGURE 6.2 Server clustering

Restoration

Secure recovery and restoration ensure that mission-critical, sensitive, or secured servers can be restored after a disaster with minimal loss or security violations. Secure recovery ensures that affected systems reboot into a secured state, and that all resources open and active at the time of the fault, failure, or security violation are restored and have their security restrictions reimposed properly. Any damaged files are restored from backup, and their proper security labels are reapplied.

Exam Essentials

Business continuity Maintaining business continuity means maintaining an organization's networking and IT infrastructure so that mission-critical functions continue to operate. This must be done in spite of reduced resources and damaged equipment.

Elements of business continuity planning The elements of business continuity planning include risk analysis and assessment, business impact analysis, strategic planning for mitigation of risks, integration and validation of the plan, training and awareness, and maintenance and auditing of the plan.

Utilities When you're evaluating the mission-critical processes of a business, don't forget that most of those processes depend on utilities, such as electricity and Internet connectivity.

High availability High availability means that the availability of a system has been secured to offer very reliable assurance that the system will be online, active, and able to respond to requests in a timely manner, and that there will be sufficient bandwidth to accomplish requested tasks in the time required. RAID is a high-availability solution.

Fault tolerance Fault tolerance is the ability of a network, system, or computer to withstand a certain level of failures, faults, or problems and continue to provide reliable service. Fault tolerance is also a form of avoiding single points of failure. A single point of failure is any system, software, or device that is mission-critical to the entire environment.

Disaster recovery Disaster recovery is an expansion of business continuity. Basically, when business continuity is interrupted, a disaster has occurred. Ultimately, both business continuity and disaster recovery planning rely upon proper backup procedures.

Backups Backups are the only means of insurance available to your data resources in the event of a loss, disruption, corruption, intrusion, destruction, infection, or disaster. Backups must be tested in order for them to prove reliable and usable.

Common types of backups The three common types of backups are full, incremental, and differential.

Offsite storage Backup media should be stored securely at an offsite location to prevent them from being damaged or destroyed by the same catastrophe that affects the business continuity of the primary site. This location should be a fire-protected safe, vault, or safety deposit box.

Secure recovery Secure recovery ensures that servers can be restored with minimal loss or security violations. It ensures that affected systems reboot into a secured state, and that all resources open and active at the time of the fault, failure, or security violation are restored and have their security restrictions reimposed properly.

Disaster recovery plan A disaster recovery plan is the collection of detailed procedures used in the event that business functions are interrupted by a significant damaging event. When the primary site is unable to support business functions, the disaster recovery plan is initiated. This plan outlines the procedures for getting the mission-critical functions of the business up and running at an alternate site while the primary site is restored to normal operations.

6.3 Differentiate between and execute appropriate incident response procedures.

An *incident response procedure* is to be followed when a security breach or security violation has occurred. One of the most important goals of incident response is *containment*: the protection and preservation of evidence. This may require taking systems offline,

duplicating hard drives using imaging software, making photographs of monitor displays, documenting strange conditions or activities, disconnecting a server from the network, and so on.

 For more information on this topic, see Chapter 6 of the *CompTIA Security+ Study Guide, 4th Edition* (Sybex, November 2008).

For end users, the incident response policy is simple and direct: They should step away from their computer system and contact the incident response team. For the CIRT (Computer Incident Response Team), the incident response policy is more involved. The following sections discuss the responsibilities of a CIRT.

Forensics

Forensics is the collection, protection, and analysis of evidence from a crime in order to present the facts of the incident in court.

One of the most critical aspects of forensics is the initial gathering and protection of evidence. In order for evidence to be presentable in court, you must be able to show that the chain of custody wasn't broken, that the evidence was properly preserved, and that the evidence was collected properly. One aspect of this is to perform analysis on copies of evidence and not the original evidence itself when the evidence is a storage medium.

Evidence should be protected from alteration, damage, and corruption from the moment of its discovery through the rest of its lifetime, which may be concluded after it's presented in court. Evidence preservation includes properly managing the chain-of-custody document, collecting the evidence into transportable containers, clearly labeling those containers, and then providing a secure environment for the evidence. A secure environment prevents damage and theft, but it also maintains the proper temperature and humidity while avoiding dust, smoke, debris, magnetic fields, and vibrations.

Collection of evidence is the procedure of securing evidence by collecting it. This process is often called *bag and tag*. Basically, evidence is gathered, placed in a container, and labeled, and its chain-of-custody document is filled out. It's the responsibility of the crime scene technician to collect evidence.

Chain of custody

The *chain of custody* is a document that indicates various details about evidence across its life cycle. It begins with the time and place of discovery, and identifies who discovered the evidence, who secured it, who collected it, who transported it, who protected it while in storage, and who analyzed it. Ultimately, the chain of custody document details all persons who had controlling authority and access to the evidence. Any gaps in this record casts doubt on the integrity of the evidence as there is a possibility that the evidence was out of authoritative control. The chain of custody must be created and maintained from the moment evidence is discovered through the presentation of the evidence in court.

First responders

When a security breach or perimeter violation is detected, *incident response* must be initiated by the first responders. The goal of a planned and documented incident response is to limit the amount of damage caused by the incident, to recover the environment as quickly as possible, and to gather information about the incident and the perpetrator in order to prevent a recurrence and pursue legal prosecution.

The best way to respond to security violations is to have an incident response plan to follow. This plan defines and describes the procedures to perform in the event of an incident. One of the first steps that should occur when an incident is detected or suspected is to contact the incident response team, which will then follow the procedures in the incident response plan.

Some of the elements commonly found in an incident response plan include the following:

- Documenting everything, include anything seen on screen
- Making backup copies of all affected files, often using a bit-level drive image duplication process
- Collecting all audit logs (often by creating copies) and securing them against alteration

It's important not to log off the system or shut down the computer, because these actions may damage or alter evidence. The CIRT team will guide the first responder as to what action to take. When relevant, one common action is to remove the network cable, but otherwise leave the affected or compromised system untouched. Often, a first responder is an end user, thus it is important that he or she have proper training and awareness of how to handle and report incidents.

Damage and loss control

In the process of responding to an incident, an important goal is to contain the problem. *Containment* means to limit the scope of damage and prevent other systems or resources from being negatively affected. Containment is especially important when the incident includes virus infection, remote control access, a Trojan horse, a logic bomb, or the use of hacker tools. Malicious use of these components may leave residual elements that are activated at a later time.

Depending on the type of incident (for example, an intrusion attack across an Internet link), the incident response team may choose to disconnect or terminate a network segment or ISP connection. After an incident has been contained, the incident response team is responsible for documenting the incident and making recommendations about how to improve the environment to prevent a recurrence. A final step in incident response is to evaluate the response plan and procedures and improve them as necessary.

Reporting – disclosure of

Throughout the implementation of an incident response procedure, you should document every action taken by end users and the incident response team. This documentation will

serve as an audit trail to retrace the actions taken and the events that occurred during the incident. Learning from the incident's documentation includes taking precautions to prevent the recurrence of the incident, updating the security policy and related procedural documents, and assessing the overall impact of asset loss, damage, and risk imposed on the environment by the incident.

After an incident has been resolved, disclosure of the details and the results of the incident should be restricted to authorized parties. Often, the authorized parties are limited to the senior management, the legal team, and some members of the security staff.

Exam Essentials

Chain of custody The chain of custody is a document that indicates various details about evidence across its life cycle. It begins with the time and place of discovery, and identifies who discovered the evidence, who secured it, who collected it, who transported it, who protected it while in storage, and who analyzed it.

Evidence preservation Evidence should be protected from alteration, damage, and corruption from the moment of its discovery through the rest of its lifetime, which may be concluded after it's presented in court.

Collection of evidence Collection of evidence is the procedure of securing evidence by collecting it. This process is often called bag and tag. Basically, evidence is gathered, placed in a container, and labeled, and its chain of custody document is filled out. It's the responsibility of the crime scene technician to collect evidence.

Incident response policy An incident response policy is the procedure to follow when a security breach or security violation has occurred. One of the most important goals of an incident response policy is containment: the protection and preservation of evidence.

Incident response The goal of a planned and documented incident response is to limit the amount of damage caused by an incident, to recover the environment as quickly as possible, and to gather information about the incident and the perpetrator in order to prevent a reoccurrence and pursue legal prosecution.

6.4 Identify and explain applicable legislation and organizational policies.

A security policy is the foundational element of any successful security endeavor. This section provides numerous examples of security policies. These forms of security documentation are designed to guide personnel in working within the desired security boundaries of an organization.

 For more information on this topic, see Chapter 6 of the *CompTIA Security+ Study Guide, 4th Edition* (Sybex, November 2008).

As a standard rule of thumb for security, you should document everything. Documentation is often seen as a keystone of security. Through exhaustive documentation there will always be a detailed record of configurations, actions, procedures, and so on, which will assist in the event of an incident, disaster, or implementation of change.

With complete, detailed, exhaustive documentation, every aspect of your environment and every event in your secured environment are known. Documentation can be reviewed and referenced as new incidents or conditions arise. With proper documentation, the security of an organization is easier to maintain.

Secure disposal of computers

Security policy should dictate how printed material and used storage media are to be handled after their useful lifetime. Secure disposal and destruction of printed material often involves shredding and incineration. Secure disposal and destruction of computers typically focuses on the secure disposal and destruction of storage media. Secure disposal and destruction of storage media may require incineration, physical crushing, magnetic destruction, or the use of an acid bath. After these items have been properly destroyed, they no longer pose a threat to the organization. If a would-be intruder or attacker obtained these items after disposal and destruction, they would be unable to glean any useful information from them. In effect, proper disposal and destruction is a countermeasure to dumpster diving and scavenging.

Acceptable use policies

An *acceptable use policy* defines what is and what is not an acceptable activity, practice, or use for company equipment and resources. Not having an acceptable use policy leads many users into the false assumption that any activity is permitted and that they enjoy privacy even on company equipment. However, there is often no privacy on company equipment: Companies have the right and privilege of auditing, monitoring, and recording all activities that occur using their equipment and access services. An acceptable use policy outlines these monitoring tactics, dictates what users can and can't do, and clearly states that users don't have privacy.

Often, employees must read and sign an acceptable use policy as part of the hiring and training process. This signed policy serves as consent from the user to be watched by the auditing mechanisms employed by the company.

Password complexity

Password management is used to manage passwords across a large network environment. It typically includes the requirement that users create complex passwords. Complex

passwords are long (eight or more characters on the exam; real-world 15 or more characters is preferred), use multiple character types (such as uppercase and lowercase letters, numerals, and symbols), and use no part of the person's e-mail address or user account name. Other password restrictions may be enforced as well, such as a maximum and minimum lifetime, no reuse of old passwords (often called a *password history*), and use of account lockout.

Account lockout automatically disables an account when someone attempts to log on but fails repeatedly because they type in an incorrect password. Account lockout is often configured to lock out an account after three to five failed logon attempts within a short time (such as 15 minutes). Accounts that are locked out may remain permanently disabled until an administrator intervenes or may return to functional status after a specified period of time.

In larger environments, password management also includes a feature for users to change their own passwords as needed or when required. This self-service password reset function eliminates the need for an administrator to be involved in the process of redefining passwords.

Change management

Change is the antithesis of security. In fact, change often results in reduced security. Therefore, security environments often implement a system of change management to minimize the negative impact of change on security. *Change documentation* is one aspect of a change-management system: It's the process of writing out the details of changes to be made to a system, computer, software, network, and so on before they're implemented. Then, the change documentation is transformed into a procedural document that is followed to the letter to implement the desired changes. After the changes are implemented, the system is tested to see whether security was negatively affected. If security has decreased, the change documentation can be used to guide the reversal of the changes to restore the system to a previous state where stronger security was enforced.

Classification of information

Classification is the process of labeling objects (assets, data, information, and so on) with sensitivity labels and subjects (users) with clearance labels. After a resource is classified, the IT infrastructure and all users should read and respect the assigned label. Thus, each object will receive the security it needs.

A *need-to-know* security policy grants and restricts access by compartmentalizing resources, objects, or data within a security domain. To gain access to compartmentalized items, the subjects (users) must obtain or prove the need to know—the necessity to have access to a resource based on assigned work tasks. Without need-to-know policies, such data is restricted from view even for users with sufficient security clearance. This form of access control is used in Mandatory Access Control (MAC) environments, similar to the principle of least privilege that's used in Discretionary Access Control (DAC) environments.

Mandatory vacations

Mandatory vacations is a form of user peer auditing. The process works by requiring each employee to be on vacation for a minimal amount of time each year (typically one to two weeks). While the employee is away, another worker will sit at their desk and perform their work tasks. This process is used to detect fraud, abuse, or incompetence. The technique is often employed in financial environments or where high-value assets are managed.

Personally Identifiable Information (PII)

Personally Identifiable Information (PII) is any data item that is linked back to the human from whom it was gleaned. PII that is medically related is protected under HIPAA laws. However, in the United States, most PII is not generally protected. Companies should clearly disclose what PII is collected and how it will be used in the acceptable use policy (AUP).

Privacy is the level of confidentiality and isolation a user is given in a system. Most users falsely assume that they have privacy on company computers. Privacy assumes that the activities and communications performed are hidden from others or at least protected from being viewed by all but the intended recipients. However, no activity on company property is hidden from view by the auditing and monitoring components of the network.

Due care

Due care is the display of proper security attention in an organization. By designing and implementing an organization-wide security policy, a business shows due care. The organization must put forth the proper and expected level of effort to provide protection from security violations and injury to assets and personnel.

Due diligence

Due diligence is the continuation of the due care process. After a security policy has been designed and deployed, the organization must remain diligent in maintaining the established level of security. By showing due care and due diligence in court, an organization is not held negligent for losses caused by breaches of their security.

Due process

Due process is the concept that the government must respect all of the legal rights of individuals when that person is deprived of their life, liberty, or property due to a court case, legal action, or government/military action. Due process is used to ensure fairness, justice, and liberty in legal proceedings. Due process is guaranteed by the Fifth Amendment to the Constitution of the United States.

SLA

A *service level agreement (SLA)* is a contract with a service company, contract worker, or consultant team that dictates the minimum levels of service or performance demanded by your organization. SLAs can include requirements for uptime, hosting services, response time, downtime reimbursement, failure resolution, and throughput requirements.

Security-related HR policy

HR policies deal with aspects of security that focus directly on personnel. These include termination, hiring, and a code of ethics.

A hiring policy defines the procedures to follow to hire new employees. When you're hiring new employees, it's important to perform background checks, including verifying education, previous work experience, and certifications. Depending on your organization's level of sensitivity, this policy may also require an intense security-focused background check. After you've obtained reasonable assurance as to a new employee's trustworthiness, you can begin to grant that person access privileges to the physical and IT environment. As workers prove their reliability and are able to sustain compliance with security policies, their access may be increased as their assigned work tasks expand.

A termination policy defines the procedures to follow when an employee is fired. When an employee is terminated, their access to the network should be revoked immediately to prevent retaliatory acts and provide security for the company. An employee should return all access tokens, ID badges, and keys to the company as well as any company property such as notebooks, PDAs, cell phones, and so on. After an employee is terminated, they shouldn't be allowed to reenter the work area or access the network—their access should be completely disabled. Otherwise, by distributing their access credentials, the ex-employee may be able to use any remaining level of access privilege to wage retaliatory acts or provide a means for intruders to infiltrate the organization. A similar policy should be designed for employees who quit or leave the organization rather than being terminated.

Not all issues encountered through security incidents or IT operational procedures have a distinct response or procedure. In those situations where no clear policy exists, a solid understanding of a company-wide code of ethics is needed to guide workers through their decision-making processes. Your company needs to establish priority parameters for difficult situations. For example, which is more important: meeting a deadline, following procedures, complying with policy, or remaining within budget? These and many other issues are complex and may involve ethical dilemmas. A company code of ethics provides decision-making guidelines for these situations.

User education and awareness training

Security is useless if users aren't properly trained to perform their work tasks within the confines of the secured environment. Security training for employees is essential to the success of any security endeavor. It should be part of your security policy and business operations.

This should include communication, awareness training, education, and support through online resources.

As a security professional in any organization, you must keep the lines of communication open. This means you should be up-front about security requirements for all personnel. Clearly train users on how to perform their work tasks while maintaining security.

As a manager, be open to discuss security issues with users from every level and classification. Be ready to discuss good and bad aspects of security. And be willing to assist users in learning to be efficient and productive while sustaining security. By keeping communication open and abundant, you can help prevent users from giving up on security and intentionally bypassing security procedures.

User awareness is an effort to make security a regular thought for all employees. It begins with security training and orientation when a new worker is hired. However, user awareness must continue throughout the life of the organization. It includes regular reminders, refresher seminars, e-mails with security updates, newsletters, intranet websites, posters with security facts or rules, and so on—whatever is necessary to keep users aware of the importance of security.

If an organization fails to maintain user awareness of security, it will experience a slow erosion of security that may ultimately allow a serious intrusion to occur. Unfortunately, user awareness of security is generally the most overlooked element of security management. In fact, the lack of security awareness is the primary reason that social-engineering attacks succeed. With proper information, users can be equipped to recognize social-engineering attacks and avoid being taken in by them.

Education is broad security training, usually focused on teaching a user to perform their work tasks securely. Security education has the ultimate goal of certification. Certification is the act of passing one or more exams in order to earn certification credentials (impressive acronyms to add to your résumé), which verify that you possess certain knowledge, skills, and expertise.

Security documentation, especially work-task-specific instructions, should be posted to an intranet website for easy access. In this way, users can keep themselves current on changing security policies and procedures.

Exam Essentials

Security policy A security policy is the collection of documents that describes the overall purpose and direction of security in an environment, as well as the detailed procedural documents that indicate how various activities are to be performed in compliance with security.

Acceptable use An acceptable use policy defines what is and what is not an acceptable activity, practice, or use for company equipment and resources.

Due care Due care is the display of proper security attention in an organization. By designing and implementing an organization-wide security policy, you show due care.

Privacy Privacy is the level of confidentiality and isolation that a user is given in a system. Most users falsely assume that they have privacy on company computers.

Need to know A need-to-know security policy grants and restricts access by compartmentalizing resources, objects, or data within a security domain. To gain access to those compartmentalized items, the subjects (users) must obtain or prove the need to know: the necessity to have access to a resource based on assigned work tasks.

Password management Password management is the system used to manage passwords across a large network environment. It typically includes a requirement for users to create complex passwords.

SLAs A service level agreement (SLA) is a contract with a service company, contract worker, or consultant team that dictates the minimum levels of service or performance demanded by your organization.

Termination policies A termination policy defines the procedures to follow when an employee is fired. When an employee is terminated, their access to the network should be revoked immediately.

Hiring policies A hiring policy defines the procedures to follow to hire new employees. When you're hiring new employees, it's important to perform background checks. This includes verifying education, previous work experience, and certifications.

Code of ethics Not all issues encountered through security incidents or IT operational procedures have a distinct response or procedure. In those situations where no clear policy exists, a solid understanding of a company-wide code of ethics is needed to guide workers through their decision-making processes. Your company needs to establish priority parameters for difficult situations.

Change documentation Change documentation is the process of writing out the details of changes to be made to a system. After the changes are implemented, the system is tested to see whether security was negatively affected. If security has decreased, the change documentation can be used to guide the reversal of the changes in order to restore the system to a previous state where stronger security was enforced.

Communication As a security professional in any organization, you must keep the lines of communication open. This means you should be up-front about security requirements for all personnel. Clearly train users on how to perform their work tasks while maintaining security.

User awareness User awareness is an effort to make security a common and regular thought for all employees. Unfortunately, user security awareness is generally the most overlooked element of security management. In fact, the lack of security awareness is the primary reason that social-engineering attacks succeed.

Security education Education means broad security training, usually focused on teaching a user to perform their work tasks securely. Security education is broader and has the ultimate goal of certification.

6.5 Explain the importance of environmental controls.

When you're designing a secure facility, it's important to keep various environmental factors in mind. These include the following:

- Controlling the temperature and humidity
- Minimizing smoke and airborne dust and debris
- Minimizing vibrations
- Preventing food and drink from being consumed near sensitive equipment
- Avoiding strong magnetic fields
- Managing electromagnetic and radio frequency interference
- Conditioning the power supply
- Managing static electricity
- Providing proper fire detection and suppression

 For more information on this topic, see Chapter 6 of the *CompTIA Security+ Study Guide, 4th Edition* (Sybex, November 2008).

The following sections highlight some issues from the areas of fire suppression, HVAC, and shielding.

Fire suppression

Fire is a common problem that must be addressed in the design of any facility. Electrical fires are common causes of building fires; they may result from overheated computer or networking equipment, or improperly managed electrical power cables and distribution nodes (power strips).

Early fire detection is important because the earlier the discovery, the less damage will be caused to the facility and equipment. Personnel safety is always of utmost importance. However, in a dedicated, secured, mission-critical server room (often called a *server cage*, *server vault*, or *data center*), the fire-suppression system can be gas-discharge based rather than water based. A gas-discharge system removes oxygen from the air and may even suppress the chemical reaction of combustion, often without damaging computer equipment; however, such systems are harmful to people. If a water based system must be used, employ a preaction system that allows for turning off the release of the water in the event of a false alarm.

HVAC

HVAC management is important on two issues: temperature and humidity. In the mission-critical server vault or room, the temperature should be maintained around 70 degrees Fahrenheit. Throughout the organization, the humidity levels should be managed to keep the relative humidity between 40 percent and 60 percent. Low humidity will allow static electricity buildup with discharges capable of damaging most electronic equipment. High humidity can allow condensation, which leads to corrosion.

Shielding

Shielding is important for network communication cables as well as power distribution cables. Generally, these two types of cables should be run in separate conduits and be isolated and shielded from each other. The strong magnetic fields produced by power distribution cables can interfere with network communication cables. If the environment is electrically noisy, it may be necessary to use STP instead of UTP or run all network communication cables through shielding conduits.

Exam Essentials

Humidity Throughout the organization, the humidity levels should be managed to keep the relative humidity between 40 percent and 60 percent. Low humidity will allow static electricity buildup with discharges capable of damaging most electronic equipment. High humidity can allow condensation, which leads to corrosion.

Shielding Shielding is used to restrict or control interference from electromagnetic or radio frequency disturbances. This can include using shielded cabling or cabling that is resistant to interference, or running cables through shielding conduits.

6.6 Explain the concept of and how to reduce the risks of social engineering.

Social engineering is a form of attack that exploits human nature and human behavior. Social-engineering attacks take two primary forms: convincing someone to perform an unauthorized operation or to reveal confidential information. For example, the victim may be fooled into believing that a received e-mail is authoritative (such as an e-mail hoax), a person on the phone is someone to be respected and obeyed (such as someone claiming to be from tech support or a manager offsite), or a person with them is who they claim to be (such as an A/C repair technician). In just about every case, a social-engineering attack tries

to convince the victim to perform some activity or reveal a piece of information that they shouldn't.

 For more information on this topic, see Chapter 6 of the *CompTIA Security+ Study Guide, 4th Edition* (Sybex, November 2008).

Any form of advertisement could be considered a form of social-engineering attack—ads appeal to you in an attempt to get you to purchase or use a product or service. Although an advertisement's motivation is profit, most social-engineering attacks' motives are more malevolent. Here are some example scenarios of common social-engineering attacks:

- You receive an e-mail warning you about a dangerous new virus spreading across the Internet. The message tells you to look for a specific file on your hard drive and delete it, because it indicates the presence of the virus. Often, however, the identified file is really an essential file needed by your system.

- A website claims to offer free temporary access to its products and services, but it requires that you alter the configuration of your web browser and/or firewall in order to download the access software.

- A secretary receives a phone call from a person claiming to be a client who is running late to meet the CEO. She asks for the CEO's private cell phone numbers so she can call him.

- The helpdesk receives a call from an outside line. The caller claims to be a manager of a department who is currently involved in a sales meeting in another city. He claims he forgot his password and needs it to be reset so that he can log in remotely to download his essential presentation.

- Someone who looks like an A/C repair technician enters the office and claims a service call was received for a malfunctioning unit in the building. He is sure the unit can be accessed from inside your office work area, and he asks to be given free roam to repair the A/C system.

These are just a few examples of possible social-engineering attacks. These may also be legitimate and benign occurrences, but you can see how they could mask the motives and purposes of an intentional attacker.

Methods to protect against social engineering include the following:

- Training personnel about social-engineering attacks and how to recognize common signs

- Requiring authentication when performing activities for personnel over the phone

- Defining restricted information that is never communicated over the phone

- Always verifying the credentials of a repair person and verifying that a real service call was placed by authorized personnel

- Never following the instructions of an e-mail without verifying the information with at least two independent and trusted sources

- Always erring on the side of caution when dealing with anyone you don't know or recognize, whether in person, over the phone, or over the Internet/network

Phishing

Phishing is a form of social-engineering broadcast attack focused on stealing credentials or identity information from any potential target. It is based on the concept of fishing for information. Phishing can be waged in numerous ways using a variety of communication media, including e-mail, the Web, live discussion forums, IM, message boards, and so on.

Hoaxes

A *hoax* is a form of social engineering designed to convince targets to perform some action that will cause problems or reduce their IT security. A hoax is often an e-mail that proclaims some imminent threat is spreading across the Internet and that you must perform certain tasks in order to protect yourself. Victims may be instructed to delete files or change configuration settings, which results in a compromised OS, a nonbooting OS, or a reduction in their security defenses. Additionally, hoax e-mails often encourage the victim to forward the message to all of their contacts in order to "spread the word."

Shoulder surfing

Shoulder surfing occurs when someone is able to watch your keyboard or view your display. This could allow them to learn your password or see information that is confidential, private, or simply not for their eyes. Often, shoulder surfing is stopped by dividing worker groups by sensitivity levels using locked doors.

Dumpster diving

Dumpster diving is the act of digging through trash in order to obtain information about a target organization or individual. Dumpster diving can provide an attacker with information that could make social-engineering attacks easier or more effective. To prevent dumpster diving or at least reduce its value, all documents should be shredded and/or incinerated before being discarded. Additionally, no storage media should ever be discarded in the trash; use a secure disposal technique or service.

User education and awareness training

The only real defense against social-engineering attacks is user education and awareness training. A healthy dose of paranoia and suspicion will benefit users in detecting or noticing

social-engineering attack attempts. Training should include role playing and numerous examples of the various forms of social-engineering attacks.

Exam Essentials

Social-engineering attacks Social engineering is a unique type of attack that attempts to exploit human behavior. Such attacks can take many forms, from skillfully worded websites to clever e-mail messages to personnel impersonations over the phone to face-to-face acting. In just about every case, a social-engineering attack tries to convince the victim to perform some activity or reveal a piece of information that they shouldn't.

Review Questions

1. Which is the best countermeasure to social-engineering attacks?

 A. Preventing the download of mobile code from the Internet

 B. Employee training

 C. Strong password policies

 D. Auditing user activities

2. You run a full backup every Monday. You also run a differential backup every other day of the week. You experience a drive failure on Friday. Which of the following restoration procedures should you use to restore data to the replacement drive?

 A. Restore the full backup and then each differential backup

 B. Restore the full backup and then the last differential backup

 C. Restore the differential backup

 D. Restore the full backup

3. When is business continuity needed?

 A. When new software is distributed

 B. When business processes are interrupted

 C. When a user steals company data

 D. When business processes are threatened

4. When a user signs a(n) _____, it's a form of consent to the monitoring and auditing processes used by the organization.

 A. Acceptable use policy

 B. Privacy policy

 C. Separation of duties policy

 D. Code of ethics policy

5. Evidence is inadmissible in court if which of the following is violated or mismanaged?

 A. Chain of custody

 B. Service level agreement

 C. Privacy policy

 D. Change management

6. If user awareness is overlooked, what attack is more likely to succeed?

 A. Man in the middle

 B. Reverse hash matching

 C. Physical intrusion

 D. Social engineering

7. What form of recovery site requires the least amount of downtime before mission-critical business operations can resume?

 A. Cold

 B. Warm

 C. Hot

 D. Offsite

8. An organization has an OC3 line that it uses for most of its daily operations, as well as its offsite backup operations. This represents what security problem?

 A. Single point of failure

 B. Redundant connections

 C. Backup generator

 D. Offsite backup storage

9. What is the suspected issue when the chain of custody is incomplete?

 A. Lack of a search warrant

 B. Magnetic storage media was erased

 C. Improper evidence collection technique

 D. Integrity violations

10. What is the proper humidity level or range for IT environments?

 A. Below 40%

 B. 40% to 60%

 C. Above 60%

 D. 20% to 80%

Answers to Review Questions

1. **B.** The only real countermeasure to social engineering is employee training. The other three options are good security measures, but they aren't countermeasures to social engineering.

2. **B.** The proper procedure is to restore the full backup and then the last differential backup. The other three options are incorrect or incomplete.

3. **D.** Business continuity is used when business processes are threatened. Security policy is used when new software is distributed. Disaster recovery is used when business processes are interrupted. Incident response is used when a user steals company data.

4. **A.** When a user signs an acceptable use policy, it's a form of consent to the monitoring and auditing processes used by the organization. A privacy policy usually explains that there is no privacy on company systems. A separation of duties policy indicates that administrative functions are divided among several people. The code of ethics policy describes decision-making processes to use when faced with ethical dilemmas.

5. **A.** If the chain of custody is violated or mismanaged, evidence is inadmissible in court. SLAs, privacy policies, and change management aren't associated with evidence gathering or forensics.

6. **D.** Social engineering is more likely to occur if users aren't properly trained to detect and prevent it. The lack of user awareness training won't have as much impact on man-in-the-middle, reverse hash matching, or physical intrusion attacks.

7. **C.** A hot site requires the least amount of downtime before mission-critical business operations can resume because it is a real-time mirror of the primary site.

8. **A.** Having only a single OC3 line (a high speed optical data link) represents the security problem of a single point of failure.

9. **D.** When the chain of custody is incomplete, the suspected issue is that the evidence has had its integrity violated.

10. **B.** The proper humidity level or range for IT environments is 40 percent to 60 percent.

Appendix
A

About the Companion CD

IN THIS APPENDIX:

- What you'll find on the CD
- System requirements
- Using the CD
- Troubleshooting

What You'll Find on the CD

The following sections are arranged by category and summarize the software and other goodies you'll find on the CD. If you need help with installing the items provided on the CD, refer to the installation instructions in the "Using the CD" section of this appendix.

Some programs on the CD might fall into one of these categories:

Shareware programs are fully functional, free, trial versions of copyrighted programs. If you like particular programs, register with their authors for a nominal fee and receive licenses, enhanced versions, and technical support.

Freeware programs are free, copyrighted games, applications, and utilities. You can copy them to as many computers as you like—for free—but they offer no technical support.

GNU software is governed by its own license, which is included inside the folder of the GNU software. There are no restrictions on distribution of GNU software. See the GNU license at the root of the CD for more details.

Trial, demo, or *evaluation* versions of software are usually limited either by time or by functionality (such as not letting you save a project after you create it).

Sybex Test Engine

For Windows

The CD contains the Sybex test engine, which includes two bonus exams located only on the CD.

PDF of Glossary of Terms

For Windows

We have included an electronic version of the Glossary in .pdf format. You can view the electronic version of the Glossary with Adobe Reader.

Adobe Reader

For Windows

We've also included a copy of Adobe Reader so you can view PDF files that accompany the book's content. For more information on Adobe Reader or to check for a newer version, visit Adobe's website at www.adobe.com/products/reader/.

Electronic Flashcards

For PC, Pocket PC, and Palm

These handy electronic flashcards are just what they sound like. One side contains a question or fill-in-the-blank question, and the other side shows the answer.

System Requirements

Make sure your computer meets the minimum system requirements shown in the following list. If your computer doesn't match up to most of these requirements, you may have problems using the software and files on the companion CD. For the latest and greatest information, please refer to the ReadMe file located at the root of the CD-ROM.

- A PC running Microsoft Windows 98, Windows 2000, Windows NT4 (with SP4 or later), Windows Me, Windows XP, or Windows Vista
- An Internet connection
- A CD-ROM drive

Using the CD

To install the items from the CD to your hard drive, follow these steps:

1. Insert the CD into your computer's CD-ROM drive. The license agreement appears.

Windows users: The interface won't launch if you have autorun disabled. In that case, click Start ➤ Run (for Windows Vista, Start ➤ All Programs ➤ Accessories ➤ Run). In the dialog box that appears, type **D:\Start.exe**. (Replace *D* with the proper letter if your CD drive uses a different letter. If you don't know the letter, see how your CD drive is listed under My Computer.) Click OK.

2. Read the license agreement, and then click the Accept button if you want to use the CD.

The CD interface appears. The interface allows you to access the content with just one or two clicks.

Troubleshooting

Wiley has attempted to provide programs that work on most computers with the minimum system requirements. Alas, your computer may differ, and some programs may not work properly for some reason.

The two likeliest problems are that you don't have enough memory (RAM) for the programs you want to use or you have other programs running that are affecting installation or running of a program. If you get an error message such as "Not enough memory" or "Setup cannot continue," try one or more of the following suggestions and then try using the software again:

Turn off any antivirus software running on your computer. Installation programs sometimes mimic virus activity and may make your computer incorrectly believe that it's being infected by a virus.

Close all running programs. The more programs you have running, the less memory is available to other programs. Installation programs typically update files and programs; so if you keep other programs running, installation may not work properly.

Have your local computer store add more RAM to your computer. This is, admittedly, a drastic and somewhat expensive step. However, adding more memory can really help the speed of your computer and allow more programs to run at the same time.

Customer Care

If you have trouble with the book's companion CD-ROM, please call the Wiley Product Technical Support phone number at (800) 762-2974. Outside the United States, call +1 (317) 572-3994. You can also contact Wiley Product Technical Support at http://sybex.custhelp.com. John Wiley & Sons will provide technical support only for installation and other general quality-control items. For technical support on the applications themselves, consult the program's vendor or author.

To place additional orders or to request information about other Wiley products, please call (877) 762-2974.

Index

Note to the reader: Throughout this index **boldfaced** page numbers indicate primary discussions of a topic. *Italicized* page numbers indicate illustrations.

I

T

Wiley Publishing, Inc.
End-User License Agreement

The Best CompTIA Security+ Quick Reference Book/CD Package on the Market!

Brush up on key Security+ topics with hundreds of challenging review questions!

Two bonus exams available only on the CD. Each question includes a detailed explanation.

- Over 200 electronic flashcards.
- Glossary of Key Terms for instant reference.

Reinforce your understanding of key concepts with flashcards for your PC, Pocket PC, or Palm handheld!

- Contains over 200 flashcard questions.
- Runs on multiple platforms for usability and portability.
- Quiz yourself anytime, anywhere.

Use Glossary for instant reference